The RHS Encyclopedia of Practical Gardening

CONTAINER GARDENING

by RAY WAITE

Editor-in-Chief Christopher Brickell

MITCHELL BEAZLEY

The Royal Horticultural Society's Encyclopedia of Practical
Gardening
© Mitchell Beazley Publishers 1979, 1992

The Royal Horticultural Society's Encyclopedia of Practical
Gardening: Container Gardening
© Mitchell Beazley Publishers 1979, 1990

First published 1990
First published in this edition 1992

ISBN 1 85732 900 7

Edited and designed by
Mitchell Beazley Publishers
part of Reed International Books Ltd
Michelin House
81 Fulham Road
London SW3 6RB

Contents

Introduction/glossary 1

Container gardening is an approach ideally suited to patios or paved areas (increasingly popular features in today's smaller gardens). It is also the mainstay of people who have no garden as such but instead use balcony arrangements, hanging baskets and window boxes to create a colourful display. Of course, containers such as urns and terracotta pots have for centuries been a feature of the conventional garden, providing seasonal colour or an eyecatching setting for more permanent planting.

A recent trend is the revival of the conservatory, treated as a luxurious dining or living area, and here too container gardening makes a major contribution. Indeed, any room in a house or apartment, or a workplace, can benefit from a generous display of indoor plants, whether for foliage or flowers.

The aim of this book is to cover the principal aspects of container gardening, both ornamental and useful, in three situations— outdoors, under glass (both greenhouses and conservatories) and in the home. Due emphasis is given to the containers themselves and to aesthetic considerations. Most space, however, is devoted to plant choice, propagation and culture.

Some specific planting suggestions are given. These are not intended to be slavishly copied, but are there to prompt the reader to experiment with his or her own combinations of colour, texture and form.

It is worth underlining here the importance of safety. Containers can be heavy to lift and move and, if they topple, can inflict much damage and injury. Suspended features such as hanging baskets and window boxes must be sensibly proportioned and securely fixed. Stout footwear is advisable when carrying out many gardening operations. Wear rubber gloves when mixing and applying chemicals, and store such substances out of reach of children and animals. Never take risks where electricity is involved.

Success with containers, as with all gardening, has much to do with attention to detail and observation. Bear this in mind as you use this book, and you will be more likely to achieve satisfying results in this highly enjoyable approach to gardening. Patience and a desire to learn will help to ensure success.

Acid A term applied to soil with a pH of below 7.

Alkaline A term applied to soil with a pH over 7.

Annual A plant that completes its life cycle within one growing season.

Axil The upper angle between a leaf, or leaf-stalk, and the stem from which it grows.

Bare-root plant A plant lifted from the open ground with very little soil around the roots.

Bedding plant A plant used for temporary garden display, usually in spring or summer.

Biennial A plant that completes its life cycle within two growing seasons.

Bottom heat The warmth, normally provided artificially, from under the compost in, for example, a propagator, to encourage the initiation and development of roots.

Bract A modified, usually reduced, leaf that grows just below the flowerhead.

Bulb An underground storage organ that consists of layers of swollen fleshy leaves or leaf bases enclosing the following year's bud.

Cheshunt compound A copper-based fungicide used particularly to combat damping-off.

Chlorotic The term given to a plant whose leaves have turned pallid, whitish or yellow, due to lack of vital minerals.

Cold frame A glass-lidded box for increasing soil temperature when propagating hardy plants.

Compost, garden Decayed organic matter used as an addition to, or substitute for, manure.

Compost, seed and potting Mixtures of materials such as peat, sand and loam, plus fertilizer, used for growing seeds, cuttings and plants.

Corm A solid, swollen stem-base, resembling a bulb, that acts as a storage organ.

Cotyledon A seed leaf; usually the first to emerge above ground on germination.

Cultivar A cultivated, as distinct from a botanical, variety.

Current year's growth/wood The shoots grown from buds during the present growing season.

Cutting A separated piece of stem, root or leaf taken in order to propagate a new plant.

Damping-off Diseases which kill seedlings soon after they germinate.

Glossary 2

Dibber A tool that is pushed into the soil to make a hole in which to plant a seedling, cutting or small plant.

Ericaceous Belonging to the rhododendron and heather family; requiring acid conditions.

Fan A tree or shrub with main branches trained like the ribs of a fan against a wall or fence.

Fertilizer Material that provides plant food. It can be organic (made from decayed plant or animal matter), or inorganic (from chemicals).

Forcing The hastening of growth by providing warmth and/or excluding light.

Genus (pl. **genera**) A group (or groups) of allied species in botanical classification.

Germination The development of a seed into a seedling.

Growing bags Commercially prepared sacks containing peat-based compost in which plants can be grown.

Growing point The extreme tip of roots or shoots.

Half-hardy A plant unable to survive the winter without protection but not requiring greenhouse protection all the year round.

Harden off To acclimatize plants raised in warm conditions to colder conditions.

Hardy Describes a plant capable of surviving the winter in the open without protection.

Inflorescence The part of a plant that bears the flower or flowers.

John Innes composts Standard soil mixes that can be easily reproduced to give good results.

Lateral A lateral bud or shoot is on the side of the stem rather than being at the top or the base.

Leader The central, vertical, dominant stem.

Light The glass or plastic cover of a frame.

Node The place where a leaf joins the plant's stem and subtends an axillary bud.

Peat block A block of peat-based compost formed by compression.

Perennial A plant that lives for more than three seasons.

Perlite A neutral, sterile, granular medium for rooting, potting and seed composts.

pH The degree of acidity or alkalinity. Below 7 on the pH scale is acid, above it is alkaline.

Pinching The removal of the growing tip of a shoot, eg to encourage branching.

Plunge To bury plants in containers up to the rims in ash, peat or sand bed.

Pot-bound The conditions reached by a pot plant when its roots have filled the pot and exhausted the available nutrients.

Potting off Taking a small plant that has been pricked off in a box and transplanting into a pot.

Potting on Transplanting a plant from one pot to a larger one.

Pricking off The transplanting of a seedling from a seed tray to a pot or other container or another tray.

Propagator A (usually) heated box in which seeds are germinated and cuttings are rooted.

Repotting Using fresh compost to replace some of the compost around the roots of a pot-grown plant.

Rod The main, woody stem of a vine.

Rose (spray head) The attachment used to direct a fine spray from the spout of a watering can or a hose.

Rosette A small cluster of overlapping leaves.

Seed leaf See Cotyledon.

Semi-ripe cutting Cutting material which is firmer at the base than softwood cuttings; taken from late summer to early autumn.

Sepal A flower's outermost, leaf-like parts.

Softwood cutting Soft cutting material in active growth; taken in spring and early summer.

Space sowing The sowing of seeds individually at a set spacing in the site in which they will grow until pricking out or harvesting.

Spur A slow-growing short branch system that usually carries clusters of flower buds.

Succulent Plant adapted to living in arid conditions by storing water in thick, fleshy leaves or stems.

Syn. Abbreviation for synonym.

Thin To reduce the number of seedlings, buds, flowers, fruitlets or branches.

Top-dressing A material such as organic matter or fertilizer applied to the surface of the soil only, without being dug in.

Truss A cluster of flowers or fruit.

Tuber A swollen underground stem or root that acts as a storage organ and from which new plants or tubers may develop.

Turgid Plant material that contains its full complement of water, so is not under stress.

Vermiculite A lightweight, sterile medium used in seed, cutting and potting composts.

Watering in To water a newly transplanted plant to settle soil around the roots.

Siting and using containers

Choosing containers

The precise choice of container is always very much a matter of personal taste, but the right scale and shape are of the utmost importance for creating a pleasing effect.

Size A container with a sizeable volume of growing medium will dry out less rapidly than a smaller container; it will also be capable of sustaining larger, more vigorous plants. As a general rule, pots with a diameter smaller than 9in/23cm should not be used for hot, dry situations.

Some vases and urns that are very attractively shaped and proportioned have a soil capacity and planting area that are relatively small. Always check that they will give sufficient depth of soil or compost to accommodate plant root systems both in the centre and at the edges of the container—4in/10cm is only just sufficient to ensure adequate root area for small edging plants.

It is best also to consider carefully before choosing containers with narrow mouths, as despite their overall volume these offer only a very confined area for planting. To some extent this difficulty can be overcome by grouping several containers together to create a bolder display.

Stability Always look for containers with large or heavy bases to give stability, especially where there is to be regular traffic of people.

At planting, most plants used will be fairly small. Always allow sufficient space to accommodate the plants when they are fully grown.

Weight Some containers, especially stone ones, can be very heavy to lift and move, although this is a bonus for stability. Such containers are not easily brought home in a car: special delivery may have to be arranged. Some vases are made in sections, but even their individual parts can be weighty and awkward to transport (page 30).

Drainage For drainage, there should always be one large hole or several smaller holes in the base of the container.

Style Modern designs will usually be out of place in old surroundings, but the converse is not necessarily the case.

Materials Containers made in natural materials will usually look best, but will be more expensive to acquire, especially if they have been hand-crafted or sculptured. For more details on materials, see pages 6-9.

Ease of maintenance When siting a container, take into consideration ease of access to facilitate maintenance. For example, it must be possible to reach window boxes for watering, especially if the windows do not open at the bottom. If you plan to site a hanging basket over an entrance, bear in mind the nuisance of dripping water. Situations exposed to unrelieved sunlight can lead to rapid drying out, and wind can cause damage to plants.

Grouping containers

The grouping of containers requires a certain sensitivity. Size and number should be proportionate to the situation. Many small containers scattered about an area do not necessarily make a bold impact and can look fussy. A group of small containers can also be more difficult to maintain. One large container placed to dominate an area can be much more eyecatching and effective, and certainly offers the advantage of easier maintenance.

Tall containers Unless skilfully planted, a single tall, narrow container, such as a chimney pot or drainpipe (pages 16-17), can look insignificant. Such containers tend to look much more imposing when grouped.

Chimney pots of different heights will always create a better effect. If it is only possible to obtain pots of similar height, extra height can be achieved for variation by standing some of the pots on bricks, or by setting the front ones lower by digging a hole in the ground where this is possible. The pots will also look more pleasing if grouped close together. The same principle can be extended to other kinds of containers: as a general rule, a group of pots should present a range of different heights.

Designs If several containers are to be used, the group usually looks better together if they are similar in design, or made from the same material. However, totally different kinds of containers are usually acceptable if they are placed apart and separated by more permanent plantings. There will, of course, be no problem if dissimilar containers are planted with a covering of trailing plants.

Stone, clay & lead containers

Stone

Sculptural stone containers (with ornament-ation sculpted by hand) are extremely effective but can be costly as well as very heavy to move. Some are ornately decorated, but often the simpler shapes and designs suit small to medium-sized gardens best. There is little point in buying a stone container with an elaborate relief design if the carving will be obscured by the plant.

Clay and terracotta

Clay and terracotta pots can be plain or ornamented. An unglazed terracotta pot kept outdoors all year must be frost-proofed. Heavily glazed ones are frost-resistant and more water-retentive. Some smaller pots have deep saucers to act as short-term reservoirs.

Lead

It is still possible to purchase containers in traditional designs made from lead. These are heavy and expensive but extremely long-lasting. They will look well in most settings.

Concrete

Very large containers made from concrete with various finishes of exposed aggregate are suitable for forecourts of large buildings. If they are to be planted for seasonal effect, it is sensible to use separate, smaller containers that fit inside them: these can be made up beforehand (page 36), so that the planting can be removed and replenished easily.

Concrete and reconstituted stone are also used for smaller urns and troughs, and when well crafted can look like sculpted stone.

Plastic and glass fibre

Gardeners should not discount the simulated stone containers made from glass fibre or plastic: well planted, these can be very effective. They are lightweight, and easy to transport when empty; they are also much less expensive. Some can be partially filled with sand for stability: this is best done *in situ*.

Glass fibre is very durable and can simulate a number of natural materials very realistically. This is also true of plastic, but over the years plastic can deteriorate rather badly, faded by sunlight and battered by weather; so check the quality very carefully.

TYPES OF ORNAMENTAL CONTAINER

Fleur-de-lys stone urn

Terracotta square container with lion-head design

African quarter-circle bowl

Large clay pot
on stand

Chinese glazed terracotta octagonal pot

Round terracotta pot

Figurine
clay pot

Ornate round
lead urn

Urn with stone-textured finish

Wood containers

TYPES OF WOODEN CONTAINER

Rustic tub

Oak half-barrel with handles

Half-barrel

Quarter-barrel

Rustic planter

Oak trough

Cedar planter

Containers in natural wood look good in most situations and can be obtained in a variety of styles. Before purchase, inspect tubs for soundness of manufacture. Pay particular attention to the quality of the wood, checking for signs of future splintering or warping and that the metal bands are securely fixed.

Barrels and tubs
Properly coopered barrels are now more difficult to find than they once were, and increasingly expensive. However, garden centres sell wooden tubs that serve well enough as planters. Coopered tubs will last much longer, but with care any container made from wood can give years of service.

The circular form of barrel suits most situations; square or triangular containers fit well into corners. Half-barrels are very popular and of pleasing proportions. Some have integral handles to make lifting and moving easy. Others have ornate tops, largely obscured once planted. Barrels are sometimes cut lengthwise and mounted on wooden feet to form a sort of cradle, providing a long planting area that is ideal for bold, relatively permanent displays.

Painting and varnishing
The wood of a coopered tub should be durable in its natural state, but the external surface of other tubs is best either varnished, or treated with a clear wood preservative, or painted.

There is much to be said for keeping the wood its natural colour. If you paint it, repainting at regular intervals will be necessary. Paint the metal bands also. The colour is a matter of choice but should, of course, tone with its surroundings.

Storing
If unplanted barrels are to be stored for any length of time, it is worth keeping them wet: when the individual slats dry out, they contract and fall apart. Keep empty tubs out of doors in a cool, shady position and regularly and liberally soak or submerge them in water.

Charring and preservative
Although a tub interior can be lined with polythene sheeting before planting, charring is the best way to preserve the internal surface of the wood. Some tubs are purchased ready-charred, otherwise using a blowlamp is the easiest method. Alternatively, give unseasoned wood an application of a good preservative (eg such as used for greenhouses), but avoid creosote, which is injurious to plants.

Preparing a tub

Bore at least three drainage holes (about $\frac{3}{4}$in/20mm) in the base of the tub.

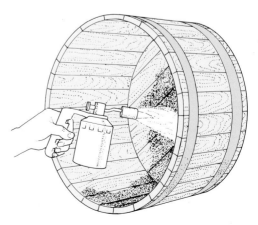

Char the inside of the tub with a blowlamp to help preserve the wood.

9

Window boxes

Window boxes are usually situated on the sunnier elevation of a building and planted for seasonal display. They can, however, be used for more permanent arrangements; and, if suitably planted, they can be deployed in quite shady situations. It is not uncommon in large cities, where the warmth of buildings raises the outside temperature considerably, to use quite tender plants in window boxes.

The size of a box will be dictated by the situation. Generally, a box extending the length of the window will look better than a small box placed centrally.

Fixings

Window boxes can be mounted on wide window sills, and this will give good stability. Make sure, however, that the window(s) can be opened. A fixing below a sill is more common, in which case the back of the box should be screwed securely to the wall and supported underneath by metal or wooden brackets which in turn are screwed into wallplugs. Strong support is vital, as wet compost and plants can become very heavy, and cause considerable damage if the window box falls.

Watering

In a sunny position, window boxes can dry out rapidly. Even if they are in shade, a regular check on watering must be carried out. Be careful about siting anything underneath, as inevitably some water will splash down.

For ideas to make watering of window boxes easier, see pages 40-1.

MAKING A WINDOW BOX

Marine ply, hardwood or lengths of tongued and grooved planking in softwood make a good window box. Use a minimum thickness of $\frac{1}{2}$in/1.25cm. All the materials should be treated with a good wood preservative, but not creosote.

First, cut the timber to the required sizes. Then drill holes $\frac{3}{4}$in/2cm in diameter in the base section. Drill screw holes in the sides. Screw the window box together with galvanized brass or aluminium screws. Decorate the front, if required.

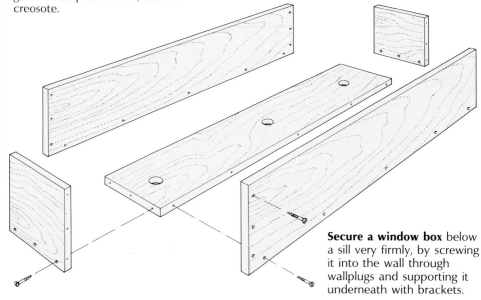

Secure a window box below a sill very firmly, by screwing it into the wall through wallplugs and supporting it underneath with brackets.

Pre-planting

Separate planting units which can be planted up in advance and allowed to establish themselves are ideal for larger window boxes and will form a well-furnished, instant display. If made from wire mesh, they are light and easy to handle. See also page 36.

Making a window box

A window box can be made up to your own design and size, but should be at least 8in/20cm wide and 6in/15cm deep. Marine plywood, hardwood or lengths of softwood are ideal, and a minimum thickness of $\frac{1}{2}$in/1.25cm is adequate for most boxes.

Cut the timber to the required lengths and widths, and apply a good preservative to all surfaces; avoid using creosote as it can damage plants.

Holes in the sides for screwing the pieces together are best drilled beforehand. To prevent rusting, use only galvanized brass or aluminium screws.

Drill the base section of the box to make drainage holes: four holes, each $\frac{3}{4}$in/2cm in diameter, are sufficient in a 6ft 6in/2m base.

The front of the window box can be finished in a variety of ways. A plain wood surface can be painted to match the external décor of the building, or the natural wood grain can be preserved with a good quality varnish, such as the type manufactured for boats. Timber pressure-treated against rotting does not always readily accept paint. However, the greenish tint often left by the impregnation process is not unsightly.

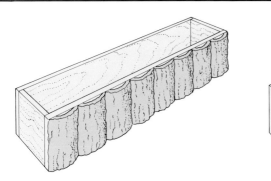

Pieces of cork bark can be used to embellish the front of the window box.

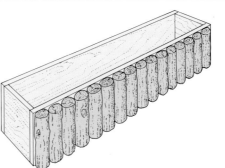

Thin branches of trees or large shrubs, suitably preserved, make a rustic front.

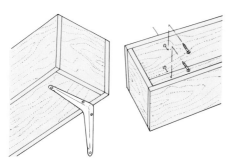

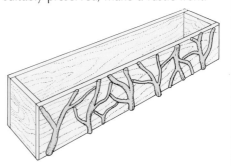

Twiggy branches can be used in a random way to look even more rustic.

Baskets and wall containers

Hanging baskets are the easiest way to brighten up an exterior. They are probably at their best and brightest in summer, but with a careful choice of plants can be of decorative value in winter as well. Their main drawback is that they may need to be watered as often as twice a day.

Wire baskets

There are many types of hanging basket. The most popular are those constructed from galvanized wire. These wire mesh baskets are suspended by three or four wires or chains. Chains are more flexible and therefore much easier to use than wires. Baskets are also available made from green, white or black plastic-coated wire. Black is usually the least obtrusive.

Wooden baskets

Wooden baskets are an alternative to wire ones, and are usually sold in kit form. They can also be made up from scratch (pages 14-15). Wooden baskets can be particularly attractive when well planted and in themselves have a certain decorative value.

Terracotta and plastic bowls

Terracotta bowls suspended on chains can also be decorative in their own right, and are particularly useful indoors or in a doorway, as they do not allow water to drip out onto the floor. This is also true of many of the

plastic bowl types of hanging container with clip-on saucers underneath. To a certain extent, these saucers act as reservoirs, but cannot be totally relied upon to give sufficient water in conditions where the potting medium is likely to dry out.

Other baskets

So-called "baskets" are also available, made in the shape of a bowl from compressed fibre, and suspended in a wire cradle. (This method of suspension is also used with plastic or clay flower pots.)

Wall baskets

It is possible to obtain baskets or similar containers which fix directly onto the wall, so that the display can be seen from one side only. These are best planted in the same way as all-round hanging baskets.

Fixings

Metal brackets can be purchased which make very satisfactory supports for baskets on walls, provided that they are securely screwed into wallplugs. A bracket with a spring-loaded suspension device is obtainable, enabling the basket to be raised and lowered for maintenance purposes (see page 41).

Wall containers can enliven a blank wall, especially when used in groups.

BASKETS AND BOWLS

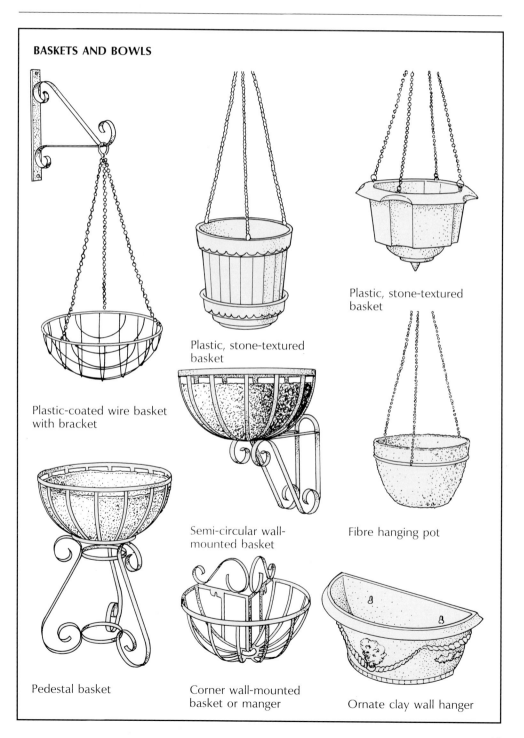

Plastic-coated wire basket with bracket

Plastic, stone-textured basket

Plastic, stone-textured basket

Plastic, stone-textured basket

Semi-circular wall-mounted basket

Fibre hanging pot

Pedestal basket

Corner wall-mounted basket or manger

Ornate clay wall hanger

Hanging baskets

Liners for mesh baskets

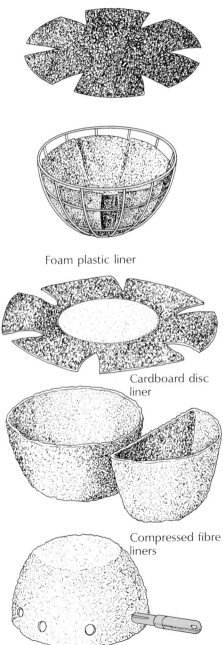

Foam plastic liner

Cardboard disc
liner

Compressed fibre
liners

Planting holes may be made in a fibre bowl
using an old apple corer.

Liners

The bowl types of hanging basket are simply
filled with compost, but mesh baskets need
to be lined in order to retain the compost.

Traditionally, sphagnum moss is used as a
liner but it may be difficult to obtain. However,
baskets ready-lined with moss are sometimes
available. See pages 38-9 for planting details.

Polythene sheeting is a very convenient
liner, but less attractive than moss. However,
once the plants are fully grown, very little of

MAKING A WOODEN HANGING BASKET

A wooden hanging basket can be simply
constructed from several slats of wood, a
few screws and a length of wire. Ideally,
hardwood should be used. However, softwood treated with a preservative is adequate, provided it does not split when
drilled and screwed.

A basket approximately 12in/30cm
square is a convenient size. Use wood at
least $\frac{3}{4}$in/2cm square cut to 12in/30cm
lengths. Make up the base by drilling screw
holes at the ends of the slats of wood used
for the base. The outside base sections
should also be partially drilled to accept
the screws when the middle slats are fixed
to them.

Next, drill holes in the corners to take
galvanized wire of SWG 14 (Standard Wire
Gauge). Cut four pieces of wire into
18in/45cm lengths, pass each one singly
through one of the corner holes and bend
it over neatly underneath the base.

Now build up the sides to a height of
6in/15cm using slats cut to length and
drilled at the ends to accept the corner
wires.

When sufficient height has been built
up, cut the corner wires so that enough
remains to be bent over to make a secure
fixing. Attach the suspension wires to the
basket either by threading them through
the loop formed by bending over the
corner wire on the top slat, or by hammering in staples.

Such a basket will need either a liner or
an inner container.

the lining will be visible. Always use black plastic, as any other colour may look obtrusive. Slits can be made in its sides for plant roots to be inserted.

Polythene sheeting will help to retain moisture but should be punctured at the base to allow surplus water to drain away. Trim sheeting to shape before planting begins.

A good compromise between moss and polythene is first to line the basket with moss and then to place a secondary lining of polythene on top.

Other sorts of liners are available, such as foam plastic or impregnated cardboard discs. When discs are used, slits are cut from the outside edge towards the centre so that the liner takes the shape of the basket when pressed down inside. The ready-made slits in foam plastic or cardboard liners are conveniently placed for planting in the sides.

Another type of liner is a compressed fibre bowl which fits neatly inside a wire basket.

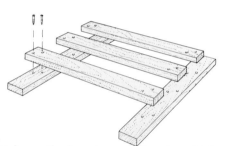

1 Make up the base by screwing the middle slats to the outside ones using brass screws.

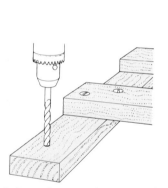

2 Drill a hole in each corner large enough to pass the wires through.

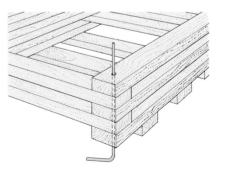

3 Thread a wire through each corner hole. Bend each wire over at top and bottom to fix the slats firmly together.

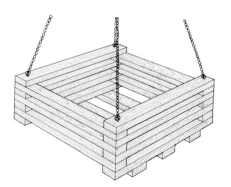

4 Suspend the basket on chains threaded either through a loop of the corner wires or through a staple hammered in each corner.

Improvised containers 1

As well as the purpose-built containers described on the foregoing pages and on pages 22-3, other, perhaps unlikely, items can be adapted for container use.

More obvious examples include chimney pots, tree stumps, hollow logs, wheelbarrows, large shells, bird cages and fish tanks. Alternatively, a more adventurous choice might be a litter basket or car tyres. An old-fashioned stone sink can also make an attractive housing for a miniature alpine garden, especially if treated to give an impression of age (see pages 20-1).

Bear in mind that highly unusual containers will draw attention to themselves, and should be used with restraint, or the resulting effect may be over-elaborate. It is better to have a single eyecatching centrepiece than many such items all of different kinds and all competing for attention.

Chimney pots

Chimney pots come in a variety of sizes, colours and designs and can make an interesting feature on a patio or terrace. A group of at least three pots can give a generous display, but even a single well-placed one can make an impression. The genuine article can be difficult to find, but it is well worth searching demolition sites or making enquiries at local builders.

It is also possible to buy specially made copies of ornate chimney pots whose shapes and sizes have been selected for both decorative impact and stability. As an alternative, large clay or concrete drainpipes can be used. The main problem with this type of container is its relatively small diameter, which limits the choice of plants.

Always place chimney pots or drainpipes in their final positions before planting, because they are difficult to move afterwards. They should be lined with polythene sheeting. This is best done by using several long narrow strips: one single square rolled into a tube is difficult to push down the pot's narrow mouth and achieve a neat finish.

To give extra stability and to help drainage, add pebbles, gravel, sand or builder's ballast, to a depth of about two-thirds of the pot.

IMPROVISED CONTAINERS

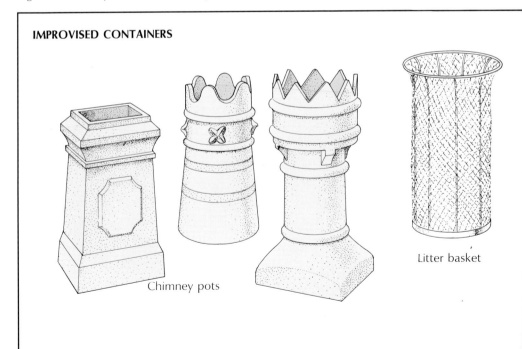

Chimney pots

Litter basket

Tree stumps and hollow logs

A hollow tree stump can be used *in situ*. Any rotten wood in the centre should be cut back to where the wood is solid and the inner surface charred with a blowlamp, as described for preparing a tub (page 9).

A fallen hollow tree can be cut into rounds of about 12in/30cm deep, and these can then be used as individual containers.

Alternatively, rounds of varying depths can be grouped together to create a pleasing feature and a more massed effect.

When hollow rounds are used, a piece of polythene sheeting cut to size should be placed in the bottom, extending up the sides of the round to retain the growing medium. A few slits in the polythene will be sufficient for draining away any excess water.

Wheelbarrows

Wooden wheelbarrows make novel containers and, because they are on wheels, can be moved easily into any position. They are probably best used for seasonal bedding. Those with a spoked wooden or metal wheel are the most attractive, but the wheel of the rubber-tyred type can be disguised with planting. It is possible to obtain smaller, specially made wheelbarrows, but these can look rather out of proportion.

If a natural colour is preferred, treat the wood with a clear preservative. Alternatively, the barrow may be painted to match the décor of adjacent buildings. Paint and preservative must be used inside the barrow as well as on the outside.

Wheelbarrows always tend to look out of place when they are isolated in the midst of a lawn. It is preferable to site them on a patio or other paved surface.

Large shells

Marine items can often look incongruous in a garden setting. Victorian gardeners had a habit of using large clam-like shells in water features. These are still available today, and can also be used to contain small plants situated near water.

It is virtually impossible to bore drainage holes in the hard shell, but if the shell can be

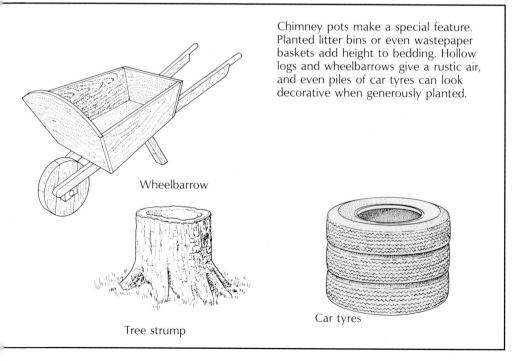

Chimney pots make a special feature. Planted litter bins or even wastepaper baskets add height to bedding. Hollow logs and wheelbarrows give a rustic air, and even piles of car tyres can look decorative when generously planted.

Wheelbarrow

Tree strump

Car tyres

17

Improvised containers 2

tilted slightly forward, some of the water collected can gradually drain away.

Bird cages

Large old bird cages, especially those designed for parrots, make interesting hanging containers, and are really an extension of the hanging basket idea. It is even possible to purchase cages specially made for plants. Although these are primarily made for indoor uses, they can be adapted for an attractive outside display.

A separate inner container will probably be necessary for the actual planting, or plants growing in individual pots can be grouped together in a massed arrangement. A coat of paint will help to preserve the wire of the cage and, if moss is used to retain the potting compost, an inner lining of polythene sheeting will give the wire additional protection.

Car tyres

Perhaps the most unlikely items with which to make improvised containers are old car tyres, but they are very durable and need not

be undecorative. They can be piled one on top of another for extra height (page 17). It is always best to use tyres of the same size, but if this is not possible, place any smaller tyres at the top.

The tyres will look better if painted with P.E.P. (Plastic Emulsion Paint) before use. A stone colour looks quite good.

As the tyres are piled up, fill in the centre with potting compost. It is possible at the same time to insert plants round the edge, between the tyres, so that, in time, much of the outside will be covered with growth. Once the container is completely filled with the growing medium, place more plants in the top.

Another idea is to turn a tyre, complete with its wheel, into a planting vase. Because the tyre has to be cut and manipulated, it is advisable to use only tyres from a car as they are much easier to handle than van tyres.

Make a mark with chalk all the way round the tyre at approximately a quarter of the way across the tread. With a drill, make a hole at a point along the chalk mark large

Making a "vase" from a car tyre and wheel

1 Drill a hole as a starting point for cutting. The hole should be about a quarter of the way up the tread. Then cut through the car tyre with a hacksaw blade.

2 Fold back the larger (three-quarter) part of the tyre to make the bowl of the vase. If the tyre is very firm, you may need to enlist someone to help with this. Paint the finished vase with a coat of P.E.P.

enough to push a hacksaw blade through the tyre; then cut along the mark. For safety when gripping the saw blade, a simple handle can be made by wrapping a strip of cloth around one end of the blade.

The smaller, quarter-section of tyre will form the base of the vase, but it will be necessary to turn the three-quarter section inside out to make the cupped container. If the tyre is very firm, a second pair of hands may be required for this task. The hub forms the pedestal of the vase and, of course, joins both cut sections together. A coat of P.E.P. will complete the job.

Litter baskets

Tall wire baskets of the type seen in parks and town centres have many uses in container gardening. Those that are 3ft/90cm high can be used as free-standing features, while smaller wastepaper types can be made into large hanging baskets, or mounted on short lengths of wooden stakes; plants can then be grown round the sides to achieve a mound of flowers. Placed in a flower bed, a planted bin of this kind will give added height and interest.

Alternatively, make a cylindrical basket by driving thin stakes into the ground or securing them to a wooden base with metal brackets. Then nail chicken netting around the outside. The height and diameter can be adjusted to suit any situation.

To stabilize taller baskets further, an additional stake may need to be driven through the inside, down into the soil.

A liner will be necessary, just as for a hanging basket (see pages 14-15).

Taller baskets, when fully planted, can sometimes be difficult to water thoroughly. Bore a few holes in the bottom half of a length of plastic pipe cut to about two-thirds the depth of the container. While filling the basket with potting compost, set this pipe down through the centre. When water is poured into the top of the pipe, even penetration should take place lower down. Water must, of course, also be applied to the top surface of the compost.

If supplementary feeding is given, the pot-

Wire baskets

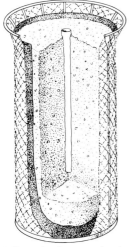 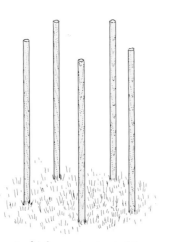 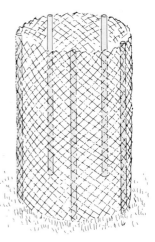

A litter basket can be lined with black polythene punctured with holes for planting. The basket is then filled with compost and a plastic drainage pipe inserted.

A chicken-wire basket is easily made. Drive five thin stakes into open ground, and nail the netting around the outside. Stabilize taller baskets with a stake.

Improvised containers 3

ting compost should last about three years before it needs to be replaced. It can then be used elsewhere in the garden to improve the soil condition of a small area.

Stone sinks
Old-fashioned hewn stone sinks are ideal for growing alpines, miniature bulbs and other small plants.

Several sinks can be grouped together on a paved area, each planted up in a different way, and the effect further enhanced by underplanting. To vary height and interest, the sinks can be raised on bricks or stones at different levels.

The outside of a hewn sink can be roughened and aged to give it a more natural appearance. More modern glazed sinks can also be treated to give the appearance of stone (see below).

Autumn is the ideal time to make up a sink in this way as the cooler weather allows the mixture to remain in a workable condition much longer. Also, as the planting medium dries out less rapidly, ultimately it becomes

much firmer. The work should not, however, be attempted in frosty weather.

Large heavy sinks are best made up *in situ*. For convenience of manipulation they should be mounted on stones or bricks to raise the base about 6-9in/15-25cm from the ground.

Smaller sinks can be prepared elsewhere and moved to their permanent sites when dry. (For tips on moving heavy containers, see page 30.)

Texturing a glazed sink
Remove all the metal fittings: this may mean breaking away completely the old portion of waste pipe. Do not worry if this makes a fairly large hole, as this is necessary for drainage in any case. Clean and wash the sink thoroughly and allow it to become completely dry.

Prepare a mixture comprising:

1 to 2 parts by volume moss peat
1 part by volume sharp sand
1 part by volume cement.

Do not make the mixture too wet. The peat

Texturing a glazed sink

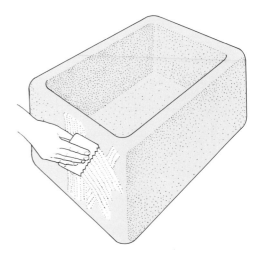

1 Remove all metal fittings, knocking off the remaining part of the waste pipe. Any hole left can be used for drainage. Clean and wash the sink thoroughly and allow it to dry.

2 Cover a quarter of the sink evenly with a bonding agent. Leave to become tacky. Mix peat, sand and cement together with water to form a stiff paste that can be moulded with the hands.

will colour the "stone" and provide interesting textural variation.

Apply a generous coating of a PVA (poly-vinyl acetate) adhesive over approximately a quarter of the glazed outside surface of the sink and allow it to become tacky.

Then apply the peat mixture, kneading it into place to obtain a fairly natural finish. Make sure that the covering extends over the rim and to a depth of 2in/5cm down the inside and 3in/7.5cm under the base.

Continue applying the adhesive and mixture section by section until the whole of the surface has been covered.

To simulate further the appearance of stonework, lightly scar the surface with a stabbing action using an old paint brush or chisel.

After the mixture has dried, paint on a coating of milk, yoghurt or liquid seaweed fertilizer: this will encourage the growth of algae and mosses and rapidly give the sink the appearance of age.

Drying usually takes about three weeks, after which planting can take place.

GROUPING SINKS

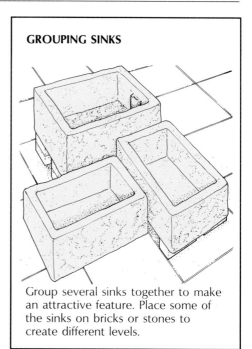

Group several sinks together to make an attractive feature. Place some of the sinks on bricks or stones to create different levels.

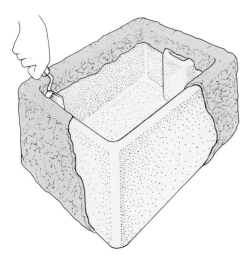

3 Press on the peat mixture firmly about $\frac{1}{4}$in/6mm thick, kneading it to a natural finish. Extend this covering 2in/5cm down the inside and 3in/7.5cm under the base.

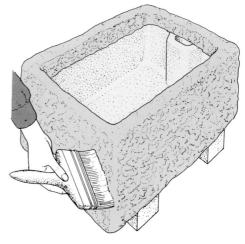

4 Continue applying adhesive, then peat mixture, section by section to the whole surface. Use an old paint brush or chisel to scar lightly. After drying, age by painting with milk and yoghurt.

Specialized containers

Some containers are made specially for growing particular plants such as strawberries, crocus bulbs, or herbs such as parsley.

Strawberry pots

Strawberry pots, and other pots constructed on the same principle, make attractive containers for growing not only strawberries but many other small plants as well. The larger pots can also be used for flowers and give a massed effect when well planted. Some small pots have been specially made for bulbs.

Strawberry pots are made from either clay or plastic. The clay ones are very attractively proportioned, being shaped like large pitchers, with holes in the sides. Each hole is just large enough to take the root of a small plant, and has a lower lip which protrudes sufficiently to retain compost and water.

A clay pot is quite heavy in itself and, once filled with potting compost, becomes quite difficult to move, especially when fully planted (page 30). It is, therefore, best to make the pot up *in situ*.

Plastic strawberry pots are very much smaller in diameter and are built up in sections to form a tower. Like clay pots, they rely on the principle of cupped holes, but are less attractive.

A large plastic dustbin can also be adapted by making holes in the sides.

The lower parts of large containers can be difficult to water thoroughly, but this problem can be overcome if a length of perforated drainpipe or a rolled-up core of chicken netting is inserted down the centre (in the same way as for the litter bin, page 19).

Much smaller versions of strawberry pots are made for growing herbs on a window sill. One type is known as a parsley pot. Generally, these are about 15in/43cm high, with a diameter of 5in/13cm and small but numerous holes into which compost is packed and parsley seeds sown (see page 82).

Types of specialized containers

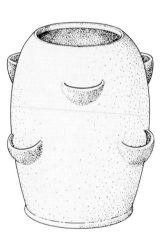

Strawberry pots

Growing bags

Growing bags are specialized forms of container. They are often used in greenhouses, but can be equally useful out of doors. Although they are most often used for vegetable crops, they can be planted with seasonal bedding or permanent decorative plants.

A growing bag is a narrow polythene, bolster-like bag filled with a peat compost. Holes cut out of the topside make it possible to insert two or more plants. The main drawback when growing decorative plants is that the polythene bag is usually highly coloured, with lettering, and tends to be obtrusive; this problem can be largely solved by making a surround of loose bricks or stones, or by constructing a wooden edging. Staking can also be difficult (page 43).

Growing bags have several advantages: they are convenient and easy to handle; they contain a good, consistent, sterile growing medium which is capable of sustaining a primary crop such as tomatoes, followed by another crop such as winter lettuce or early strawberries; and they dispense with the necessity of replacing soil or of sterilizing it at regular intervals. After cropping, the compost can be used elsewhere in the garden for general soil improvement.

A growing bag planted with decorative subjects will successfully grow a summer and, later, a spring display before being discarded. After the summer display, a handful of general fertilizer should be added and thoroughly incorporated before the bag is replanted.

A special growing bag feeder has a tray that fits neatly on top of the bag. It has holes to allow the plants to grow through, and evenly spaced smaller holes so that liquid fertilizer or water can gradually soak down into the compost. This covering also prevents excessive drying out and the exposure of surface roots.

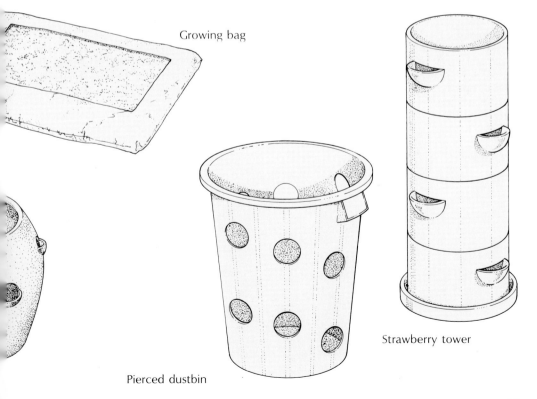

Growing bag

Pierced dustbin

Strawberry tower

Built containers 1

As well as the movable containers described on the previous pages, it is possible to make some more solid structures, from wood, bricks, walling stone and the like.

Wood containers

Thick wooden planking can be made up into containers of various sizes and shapes which can then be grouped together to make a feature in a garden or patio. Care must be taken to apply a good preservative.

The wood should be 1in/2.5cm thick and at least 12in/30cm deep. Softwoods will be less expensive than hardwoods. Both should be treated against rotting, using preservative (not creosote). Hardwoods will last longer.

Railway sleepers

Old railway sleepers are even more suitable, as they are very stable and, because of the extremely effective preservation process used on them, do not rot quickly. Such sleepers make particularly strong and durable "walls" but do not always look pleasing. However, with careful planting, their square outline can be softened considerably.

Always obtain as good a quality of sleeper as possible (from a landscape contractor or alpine nursery): discard any that have a great deal of splintering or are split. Watch out, too, for any excess tarry substance that can ooze from the wood, making it very messy to handle.

Fixing

The easiest way to join planks together is with screws or large nails, although they can also be joined in any of the ways described below for sleepers.

Long coach bolts make a firm fixing for joining sleepers together. Alternatively, large staples can be hammered across the corners, though they will have to be manufactured specially. Another method is to bend thick wire around the corners, held by staples.

The simplest way to hold sleepers in position is with fairly heavy-duty tree stakes with their tops sawn off level. This, of course, is not possible on a paved area.

Lining

It is best to line built wooden containers with polythene sheeting in order to reduce wood rot.

Raised beds

Large containers of a more permanent nature can be constructed in various materials sympathetic to the area in which they are situated. The construction can be of brick or stone. Alternatively, proprietary walling can be used: many modern types are easy to build, and may have a natural stone finish. Such containers, or raised beds, can be made to any size and shape. They have several advantages: they give height to a display in an otherwise flat area; the working height is ideal for

Joining planks or sleepers

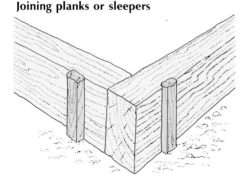

Heavy-duty tree stakes are one method of keeping together planks or sleepers at the corner of a raised bed.

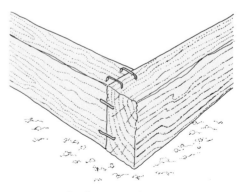

Large staples hammered across the joins at the corners are another method.

Types of raised beds

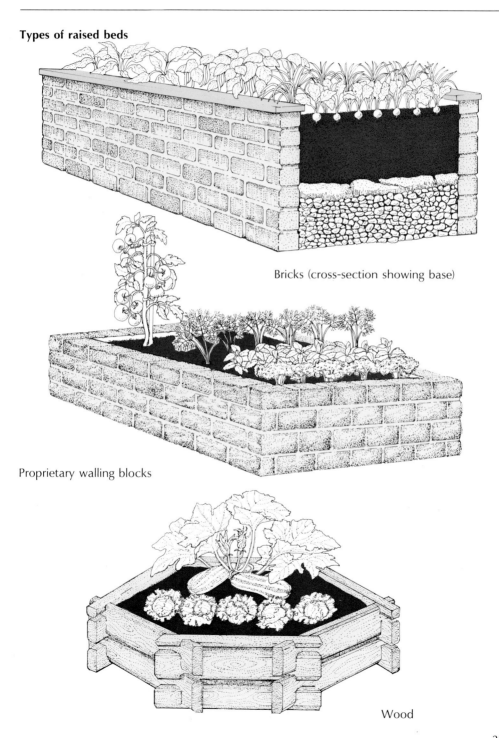

Bricks (cross-section showing base)

Proprietary walling blocks

Wood

Built containers 2

older people; and the disabled gardener can maintain plants even from a wheelchair. Where wheelchairs are to be used, make sure that all the paths to the bed(s) are smooth and wide enough for access.

Size
The dimensions of raised beds are all-important, and will have a bearing on the ease of maintenance. When large raised beds are made, the construction will need to be particularly robust. A good working height is 18-24in/45-60cm; the width of the container should be no more than 3ft/90cm, if it is accessible from only one side, or 6ft/1.8m if the bed has access from both sides.

Siting
There are no set rules on positioning, as plants can be selected to suit any location. A site that receives a good amount of direct sunlight will usually be the most satisfactory. However, if calcifuge (lime-hating) plants are to be grown in a bed filled with peat and retained with hard peat blocks, logs or stones, choose a shady site, against a wall, or in the shade

cast by trees and shrubs, although not directly under them. Avoid frost pockets.

A scree bed (a raised bed with much of the soil replaced by stone chippings and devoted to the cultivation of alpines requiring extremely sharp drainage) is best sited in an open, sunny position. Shelter from distant fences and trees will help cut down winds, but avoid heavy shade from trees (these would also shed leaves onto the plants).

Drainage and soil
Large raised beds should have a few holes left in the bottom course of bricks or stones to act as drainage weep-holes.

Fill raised beds with a 9in/23cm layer of rubble for drainage, followed by a layer of old turves grass-side down. Fill the remainder of the bed with good garden soil or compost.

Peat beds sitting on top of chalky soil will eventually become contaminated, so lay plastic sheeting between peat and soil. Enrich the soil in the bed to a depth of one spit with 50 per cent of its own bulk of moist peat (of a medium or coarse grade) and a light dusting of a lime-free general fertilizer such as blood,

Building a brick planter

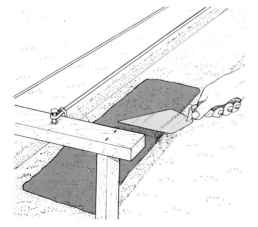

1 If the ground is soft, lay a screed of mortar over concrete strip foundations. Use stringlines to indicate the width of the trench.

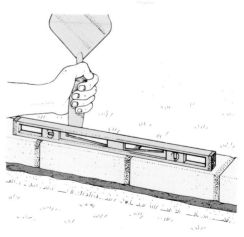

2 Check each course is level using a spirit level. Use the end of the trowel handle to tap the bricks horizontal.

bone and fishmeal.

Scree beds should be at least 24in/60cm high over clay soils to provide good drainage; and at least 12in/30cm high over sandy soils. Place a 4-6in/10-15cm layer of broken bricks and rubble in the bottom of the bed and fill the rest of the space with the following compost:

10 parts stone chippings
1 part loam
1 part peat or leaf-mould
1 part sand
plus a slow-release fertilizer.

Types of plants

Planting such containers for display can take many forms, but it is likely that these permanent built containers will be planted with equally permanent subjects.

Herb wheel

Another type of built container is a herb wheel (pages 82-5). This can also be attractive when used as a setting for a wide range of decorative plantings.

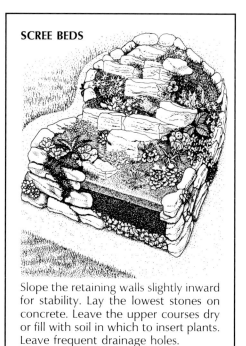

SCREE BEDS

Slope the retaining walls slightly inward for stability. Lay the lowest stones on concrete. Leave the upper courses dry or fill with soil in which to insert plants. Leave frequent drainage holes.

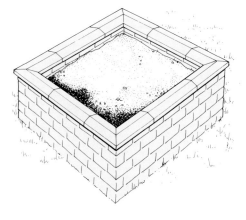

3 Continue laying bricks to the required height, alternating the bricks in stretcher bond. The structure need be no more than 6 or 8 courses high.

4 Add coping stones to finish off the structure neatly. Leave for four days before adding soil. (For more detailed instructions see the RHS volume on *Garden Structures*.)

Equipment 1

EQUIPMENT

Hand trowel

Rose

Long-spouted
watering can

Hand fork

Pruning knife

D-shaped spade
handle

Wheelbarrow

Step-
ladder

Secateurs

String

Hose on stand

YD-shaped spade handle

T-shaped spade handle

Container gardening requires very few tools, but, as always, it makes sense to buy the best quality that you can afford. However, some tools can be improvised: for example, a dibber from an old spade handle.

Always clean tools thoroughly after use, washing the metal parts with water, drying them, and then rubbing them over with an oily rag. This final operation is particularly important if the tools are not going to be used again for a long period.

Trowel

For general planting, especially for taking out small holes, a trowel will be invaluable. This can be used to scoop out compost, leaving a hole large enough for the plant's roots.

Short and long-handled trowels are available, but the former are more useful. Handles are made from wood or polypropylene, both quite durable. A stainless steel blade is the best buy, especially if there is a lot of planting to be done. Strong forged steel blades are adequate. Cheaper trowels bend too easily.

Hand fork

Hand forks are about the same size as trowels, with either three or four prongs. They can also be used for planting, and are better than trowels for levelling off the surface of the compost afterwards. They are ideal for weeding large containers.

Spade

A spade can be used both for soil preparation and for planting, but only in very large containers. Various sizes are available, but, because of the confined working space, a so-called "lady's" spade, or an even smaller border spade, will be ideal. Several types of suitable handle are available, and the choice is not too critical. Most people prefer "D"- or "YD"-shaped handles to "T"-shaped.

Fork

Forks will be needed only in the larger containers. The smaller border fork will be more useful than the standard size, especially for levelling compost or soil after planting.

Shovel

A shovel can be useful for mixing compost and for filling containers, but will only be needed if there is a number of containers to deal with. Otherwise, a spade will suffice. The shovel need not be over-large, but a distinct crank in the shaft will make work easier.

Secateurs

Secateurs are required where there is a lot of shaping and pruning to be done in a container permanently planted with shrubs and small trees. A medium-sized pair of secateurs should be adequate for most pruning purposes.

Two types are available: one with a blade that cuts onto an anvil of softer metal, and the other with two cutting blades. Make sure that the pivot pin of both types is strongly fixed and that the closing catch is well designed and that is easy to operate. Always clean the blade(s) after use and keep the pivot pin lightly oiled.

Knife

A small penknife or a budding knife is invaluable for trimming soft growths, cutting away old or decaying flowers and leaves, and cutting lengths of tying material. Although an inexpensive knife will cut, after a while the blade often becomes weak at the pivot and the edge soon wears because of the poorer quality steel.

Keep the blade clean after use. If a small drop of oil is put on the pivot end of the blade at fairly regular intervals, it will reduce the wear caused by the constant opening and closing, which can eventually result in the blade not seating properly.

Stepladder

For reaching hanging baskets and window boxes, a pair of steps will be handy, especially the type that converts to a short ladder. Most steps are constructed in aluminium. Metal or wooden steps with a top platform are equally useful.

Test for stability before purchase. Open up the steps and check for ease of climbing. Check that any ladder extension fits with ease and is sufficiently strong when at its full working height. Check, too, that the steps will reach the maximum height required. Also, ensure the safety catches are strong enough to prevent the ladder from collapsing in use.

Equipment 2/drainage

Wheelbarrow
A well-balanced wheelbarrow will be useful for moving containers from one position to another, especially if quantities of potting compost have to be shifted as well. A galvanized metal body is lighter than wood and therefore better for moving heavier weights.

Strong handles and a strong superstructure are vital. It is worth trying out the barrow in the store before making a purchase. Wheel it around with a load in it; if your arms feel the weight, the balance of the barrow is probably too far back.

A pneumatic or cushioned-tyred model

MOVING CONTAINERS

A wheelbarrow's superstructure should be constructed so that the framework surrounds the wheel to provide a guard in the front. When the handles are raised to an upright position, the guard will support the wheelbarrow and allow a heavy empty container to be tilted and loaded. The barrow can then be lowered and wheeled to the new location with its load. A second person will, of course, be needed to do the job safely. As a precaution against external damage to the container, it is wise to put an old sack or piece of matting inside the barrow.

Sack truck Moving empty containers is always much simpler than when they are filled with compost and fully planted. However, if a completed container *must*

be repositioned, a small sack truck will be ideal. Purchasing one for occasional use is not cost-effective; however, if the garden is large, a sack truck will be found to have many other uses.

Platform on castors A wooden platform on castors is suitable for moving fully planted containers, provided that the surface is fairly smooth. More importantly, such a platform allows all-round planting—for example, in a strawberry pot—to be turned at regular intervals to give the flowers or developing fruits an equal share of direct sunlight.

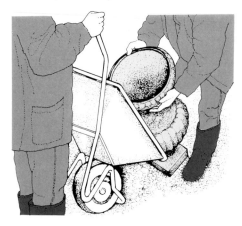

To move a heavy empty container, hold the wheelbarrow handles upright, while a second person tilts and loads the container.

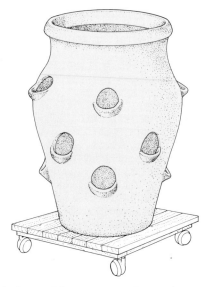

A platform with castors can be used to move a fully planted container over smooth ground.

will make it easier to push the barrow over uneven surfaces. The pneumatic type is prone to punctures but gives a much easier, smoother movement.

It is always a good idea to obtain a fairly large barrow, but bear in mind the width of gates and shed doors, and the amount of storage space available. Whenever possible, store the wheelbarrow under cover to prevent rust and general deterioration. If a barrow has to be left outside, turn it upside down, so that rain cannot accumulate in the body and cause it to rust or rot.

Hose
A length of garden hose may be required if several containers have to be maintained. A diameter of $\frac{1}{2}$in/1.25cm is perfectly adequate. The hose should be wound on a metal hose reel to store it neatly, and preferably under cover. Lay-flat hose, which stores very neatly on a small, hand-held reel, is also available.

Many hoses come with an adjustable nozzle, but these are not practicable for watering containers because the adjustment from a jet to a spray is not very fine. A thumb or finger held over the end of the hose can, with a little practice, be used to achieve accurate results.

Hose used in a drip system is very useful on a patio where there are several containers; it also allows liquid food to be applied using a "feed-in" attachment (see pages 40-1).

Watering can
Small numbers of containers can just as easily be watered by hand as with a hose. A long-spouted watering can is best for this. Plastic cans serve very well, but galvanized or painted metal ones are more durable.

DRAINAGE

The compost in containers easily becomes waterlogged unless good drainage is provided. It is essential to ensure that there are sufficient drainage holes at the base of a container to allow excess water to drain out freely. If a container is to be stood on a surface that does not drain freely, raise the base above ground level by placing bricks underneath.

The best way to determine whether there is sufficient drainage is to fill a container and flood it with water—if the water starts to drain through after a few minutes, the drainage is adequate.

Puncture any lining used for moisture retention to release excess water.

When large brick-built containers are constructed, a few gaps should be left in the bottom course to act as weep-holes.

Drainage holes in containers should be covered by a broken piece of clay flower pot placed concave-side downwards; smaller pieces can then be put round the hole and on top of the flower pot fragment, if loam-based compost is to be used. A thin layer of coarse peat should be placed on top of these crocks. If very sharp

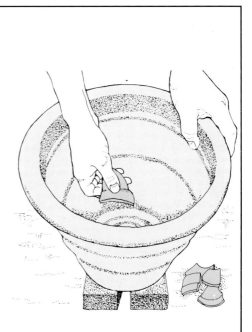

drainage is required, coarse gravel may be used instead of peat.

When refilling a container, always inspect the drainage and replace the crocks if necessary.

Composts

A potting compost for containers should be sterile and moisture-retentive. It should also be free-draining and able to supply sufficient nutrients to establish and sustain plants. Without sufficient nutrients, regular feeding would be necessary, and this is expensive and time-consuming. However, even where there are plenty of nutrients, some feeding is beneficial.

There are two types of compost available: one based on loam, and the other with peat or some other bulky organic material making up the major part of the formula.

Loam-based composts

Many gardeners mix loam-based composts to their own recipes and obtain good results, but it is still advisable to use the John Innes formulae; see chart (right). You can buy ready-made John Innes compost, or make it up at home. The main ingredients are loam, peat and sand.

Loam Strictly speaking, loam is derived from rotted-down top-spit turves; however, provided that it is in a good fertile condition, there is no reason why garden soil cannot be used instead.

Peat Peat derived from moss will always give the best results. It should be passed through a $\frac{3}{8}$in/10mm sieve. It must also be well moistened before being mixed with the other ingredients, as it is difficult to wet thoroughly once inside a container.

Sand Lime-free, coarse sand is essential and should pass through a $\frac{1}{8}$in/3mm sieve with not more than 30-40 per cent fine particles. Do not use silver sand or yellow builder's sand. Sand must be dry for easy mixing.

Sterilization Peat and sand are both naturally sterile, but the loam must be pasteurized to kill harmful organisms and, equally important, weed seeds. If a proprietary electric sterilizer is used, the soil must be put in while slightly moist and heated to 176°F/80°C for 10 minutes before being allowed to cool rapidly.

Small quantities of loam can be treated in a large saucepan. About $\frac{1}{2}$in/1.25cm of water should be brought to the boil. Pour in sieved, dust-dry soil and simmer for 20 minutes.

Unsterilized loam Although this has been used successfully, it is not to be recommended, as the likelihood of pests and diseases affecting plants is high, and weed seeds will always be present.

Mixing Make sure that the floor on which compost mixing is done is as clean as possible. The ingredients should be put out in layers, with the loam at the bottom, the peat in the middle and the sand on top. Keep a small amount of sand to one side so that chalk and fertilizer (see chart) can be mixed with it for easier incorporation into the heap. A clean shovel should be used to mix the ingredients, which should be turned four or five times for thorough mixing.

Peat-based/loamless composts

Composts with no loam and consisting of peat and other inert ingredients have become popular because of the difficulty in obtaining loam of a consistent quality and of sterilizing it adequately. Such loamless composts are light, clean, naturally sterile, and easy to handle, but have drawbacks, because the nutrients they contain are exhausted relatively quickly. It will be necessary to provide supplementary feeding sooner than with loam composts, usually about six weeks after you have done the planting.

Loamless compost is not heavy enough to support top-heavy plants, especially if they are allowed to dry out. The compost is then difficult to re-wet, even when a wetting agent is included. However, because of its lightness, loamless compost is ideal for hanging baskets and window boxes or other containers that need lifting and supporting.

Ordinary soil

Where small trees, conifers and shrubs are to be planted, it can be costly to fill a very large container with any of the special composts, although this would be ideal. Ordinary topsoil can give good results, provided that it is fertile and free of perennial weeds.

Well-rotted manure, mushroom compost or peat should be incorporated as well as coarse sand. The proportions will depend on the type of soil, but if the formula for the main ingredients of the John Innes Potting Compost is followed, a good growing medium will be produced. The fertilizer content is best provided by a general fertilizer, preferably one that releases nutrients over a long period.

POTTING COMPOSTS

John Innes Potting Compost:
7 parts by volume sterilized loam (passed through $\frac{3}{8}$in/10mm sieve)
3 parts by volume granulated moss peat (passed through $\frac{3}{8}$in/10mm sieve)
2 parts by volume lime-free sharp sand or grit $\frac{1}{8}$in/3mm diameter with not more than 30-40 per cent of it fine
Plus the following amounts of fertilizer per 1 bushel/36 litres to make the compost:

John Innes Potting No.1 (for rooted cuttings and seedlings)
4oz/114g John Innes Base Fertilizer
$\frac{3}{4}$oz/21g ground chalk or limestone

John Innes Potting No.2 (for a wide range of containers)
8oz/228g John Innes Base Fertilizer
$1\frac{1}{2}$oz/42g ground chalk or limestone

John Innes Potting No.3 (for vigorous plants)
12oz/342g John Innes Base Fertilizer
$2\frac{1}{4}$oz/63g ground chalk or limestone

John Innes Ericaceous Compost
4oz/114g John Innes Base Fertilizer. No ground chalk or limestone to be included.

John Innes Base Fertilizer (bought ready-mixed, but contains the following):
2 parts by weight hoof and horn
$\frac{1}{8}$in/3mm grit
2 parts by weight superphosphate of lime
1 part by weight sulphate of potash.
If hoof and horn is not available, nitroform, a urea derivative, can be substituted at one-third the weight for hoof and horn.

Cuttings Compost
1 part by volume granulated moss peat
1 part by volume sharp sand or Perlite

Soilless Potting Compost
3 parts by volume granulated moss peat ($\frac{3}{8}$in/10mm sieve)
1 part by volume sharp sand
4oz/114g John Innes Base Fertilizer per 1 bushel/36 litres
4oz/114g ground chalk or limestone
This approximates to John Innes Potting No.1. To make up to a No.2, double the Base Fertilizer but not the chalk or limestone. In all instances Vitax Q4 can be a substitute for John Innes Base Fertilizer.

John Innes Seed Compost (for sowing most seeds)
2 parts by volume sterilized loam ($\frac{3}{8}$in/10mm sieve)
1 part by volume granulated moss peat ($\frac{3}{8}$in/10mm sieve)
1 part by volume sharp sand as for the potting mixture
$1\frac{1}{2}$oz/42g superphosphate of lime per 1 bushel/36 litres
$\frac{3}{4}$oz/21g ground chalk or limestone per 1 bushel/36 litres.

Planting techniques 1

Buying plants

Select only plants that are robust, compact or well branched, with plenty of flowers to come. They should be well rooted in their containers, but not old plants that are so rootbound that they will not readily establish in their new positions. Plants may have been raised in boxes, unit packs or individual pots. The last two methods are those that give the least root disturbance on transplanting.

Spring planting

Containers for summer display should not be planted up out of doors until late frosts are finished. The end of May will usually be safe, and roots will then quickly establish with the increasing warmth. However, if an abnormally late frost is forecast, newspaper draped over the plants and secured to stop it falling off will protect against several degrees of frost.

Whether plants have been raised at home or bought, make sure that they have been hardened off well, even if it means a delay in planting: plants that are rather soft and tender are given the protection of a cold frame or even a wall or hedge, and covered with newspaper at night (see page 47).

Planting small containers

Preparation Start by filling the container with a suitable potting compost (pages 32-3), having made sure that the drainage hole has been covered (page 16). If the container is fairly large, it is best to fill it in layers, firming as the job proceeds. Loam-based composts can be firmed by lightly using a rammer (easily made from a short length of broom handle). To avoid over-compaction, it might be preferable to use your fingers. Peat-based composts do not need ramming as they can be consolidated adequately with the fingers. The surface needs to be about 1in/2.5cm below the rim to allow plenty of water to be given.

Make sure all the plants to be used have been well watered in their original pots, but left to drain so handling is not too messy.

Planting from pots Put the central plant in first, scooping out with a trowel a hole just large enough to take the root ball. Turn the plant upside down by supporting the root ball with one hand, and remove the pot with the other. If the plant does not come out readily, give the rim of the pot (still upside down) a sharp rap on a firm edge. Put the root system in the hole and firm with the

Planting from pots or boxes

1 Hold the plant stem between the fingers and invert the pot. Tap gently so that the root ball slides out into the palm of your hand.

2 With a trowel, dig out a hole large enough to accept the root ball. Insert the root system into the hole.

hands or the end of the trowel handle. Continue to plant the remaining subjects, finishing with the edging plants.

Planting from boxes Plants grown directly in boxes can be removed with the point of a trowel: take care not to damage the roots.

Another method is to tilt the box first one way and then the other, giving its bottom edges a sharp knock on a firm surface to make a slight gap between the compost and the inside walls of the box. Grasp the box with both hands, holding it level, and give it a quick jerk upwards: the whole contents should come out undamaged. Separate individual plants by gently teasing out their roots.

Watering

Once planting is complete, finish off the surface of the compost to make it neat and level. Then give it a thorough soaking, using a fine rose. Do not rely on rain to give sufficient water, but always water in by hand. After the initial watering, some time may elapse before more is required, but keep a careful check, especially during hot, dry weather. Water, not at regular intervals, but when the top inch of compost is fairly dry and before any signs of wilting.

Autumn planting

When containers are planted for spring effect, the work should be done in early autumn to give the plants plenty of time to establish themselves before the colder weather.

The compost in the container need not be renewed at this stage. After the old summer display plants have been removed and all the plant débris has been cleaned up, just loosen up the compost with a small hand fork or trowel. A dressing of a balanced, general fertilizer should then be given and thoroughly incorporated: a handful should be sufficient for a container with a diameter of 12in/30cm. A top-up of fresh compost should be added at this stage, either incorporated into the container compost or as a final top layer. (Summer plants will have fairly large root balls and some compost will have been removed with them; a fresh top-dressing is also beneficial to growth.)

Proceed with planting as described above, but any bulbs (pages 66-9) should be planted last, being placed in position before they are actually set in. Once again, be sure to give a

3 Firm the root ball and the compost around it with your hands or with the end of the trowel handle (but do not over-compact), in order to avoid air pockets.

4 Water the plants in thoroughly with a fine rose, after levelling off the surface of the compost.

Planting techniques 2

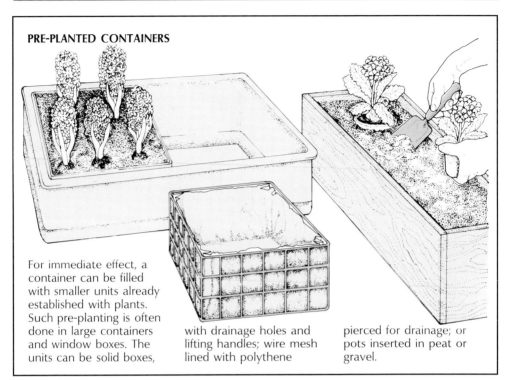

PRE-PLANTED CONTAINERS

For immediate effect, a container can be filled with smaller units already established with plants. Such pre-planting is often done in large containers and window boxes. The units can be solid boxes, with drainage holes and lifting handles; wire mesh lined with polythene pierced for drainage; or pots inserted in peat or gravel.

Planting large containers

1 Dig out a hole large enough to take the root ball. Allow space to spread out any extensive roots.

2 Knock in a short stake if necessary to stabilize a tree or shrub. In a raised bed, bang the stake down into the firm soil beneath.

thorough watering, followed by successive waterings if the weather is at all dry.

Renew compost annually, or after two batches of plants (summer and spring), to avoid disease, pests, lack of nutrition, etc.

Planting large containers

Large fixed containers are more usually planted with permanent, woody plants.

Preparation Consolidate the soil or compost lightly, so that the finished level is 1-2in/2.5-5cm below the top of the container. Settlement will lower the level quite appreciably, leaving the surface too low; this never looks good and reduces the volume of soil for sustaining the plants. Slightly overfill the container and consolidate by firming the layers of compost with hands or a flat board.

Ideally, the container should be filled in the autumn and left until spring, or even longer, to ensure that settlement is complete. Even then, it may be necessary to top-dress with compost to bring up the level.

Planting Put in the dominant plant(s) first. For small-growing trees, conifers, shrubs and herbaceous plants, take out a hole large enough to accept the root system when it is spread out. With a tree, insert a short stake in the hole; tie the trunk to it after planting.

Most woody plants will have been grown in pots by nurserymen. Remove these pots before planting, making sure that the root balls are moist and the roots teased out. Straighten out strong roots that have taken up the shape of the original container and spread them out in the planting hole.

Some conifers have their root balls wrapped in hessian. Cut this away and remove carefully once the plant is in the hole, disturbing the root ball as little as possible.

If the roots of bare-rooted trees and shrubs are at all dry, immerse them in a bucket of water before planting. Prune any broken or damaged roots.

Place the soil over and between the roots and firm it by treading gently with the heel. Continue this firming after the planting hole has been filled in, and neaten the surface. Water thoroughly and continue watering at intervals if planting has been done in spring.

In the first year, the effect of such permanent plants can be somewhat sparse, but as an interim measure they can be interplanted with seasonal bedding plants.

3 Tease out the roots of a containerized tree or shrub if they have become potbound. Then place in the hole and fill in with soil.

4 Firm the root area with the heel of your boot. Secure the trunk to the stake with a tree tie, allowing room for expansion.

Planting techniques 3

Hanging baskets
Ideally, a hanging basket should be made up in April or early May and allowed to establish itself in a greenhouse before it is placed out of doors at the end of May. If a severe frost is forecast, it is a fairly simple task to bring the basket under cover again.

Choosing plants Established plants in flower will provide an immediate effect, but younger plants will grow away quickly and often provide a longer-lasting display.

Preparation At least one recent design of basket is available with a flat base, so that the basket can stand without tilting while it is being planted or watered on the ground or on a bench.

To plant a hanging basket with a rounded base, place the basket in a large pot. This pot must be relatively small in diameter so that the basket sits high enough for easy planting in its sides.

Soilless composts are light and would therefore seem to be ideal for hanging baskets; however, they do tend to dry out rather quickly and can be difficult to recharge with water. John Innes No.2 Potting Compost, being loam-based, retains moisture well, but, of course, is much heavier.

There is increased interest in the use of polymer granules as a compost additive. These are capable of absorbing vast quantities of water and of giving this up over a period of time.

Lining and planting If moss alone is being used as a liner (pages 14-15), cover the bottom half of the basket with about a 1in/2.5cm thickness. Place an old saucer on the moss at the base of the basket to help retain some moisture. Add some moist compost; as you build this up, push the root balls of the plants through the holes of the basket, so that they come in contact with the compost. Place more compost on the top of the roots and lightly consolidate the compost with the tips of the fingers.

Add more moss lining, together with additional compost, so that you can plant on the top of the basket. Scoop out holes for this with your hand, put in the plants, then replace and firm the compost. Now place an extra thickness of moss all around the basket to make a firm rim a little above the top wire. Add more compost, to leave 1in/2.5cm below the rim for watering.

Watering Once the basket has been planted, give the compost a thorough soaking. In order to keep the basket level for this, once again place it in the pot if suspension is not yet

Planting a hanging basket with a moss lining

1 Line the hanging basket with damp sphagnum moss, then fill with compost, to about halfway.

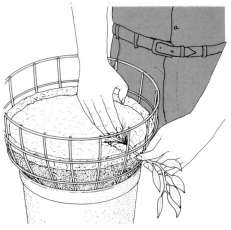

2 Fill the basket with compost to about halfway. Insert plants in the sides of the basket, so that they come in contact with the compost.

possible. When placing the basket in its flowering position, make sure that it is firmly supported (pages 12-13 and 100-1). For ideas to make watering easier, see opposite.

Window boxes
Planting a window box should be done *in situ*: it is foolish and dangerous to attempt to lift such a container full of moist compost and plants onto a high window sill.

Instead of planting directly into compost, you can place plants in pots in the box and surround the pots with gravel (page 19). Change the plants when the flowers fade for new ones prepared beforehand.

When selecting plants for window boxes, remember that windows may need to be opened, and that a plant that grows above the base of the window will become a nuisance. Always plant as generously as possible so that the edges and sides of the container are hidden.

Preparation for direct planting Place a layer of drainage material such as crocks or coarse gravel in the bottom of the box, to ensure adequate drainage. Fill with moist compost (John Innes No.2) or a soilless equivalent, and gently firm until the level is 2in/5cm below the rim.

Planting A trowel may be used to take out the small planting holes needed, but it will often be found more convenient to use the fingers. After planting, firm the plants in the compost.

Watering Once they are in place, give the plants a thorough watering. In very warm weather, several light sprinklings from overhead will help to establish the plants in their new positions (see page 41).

Autumn planting After the summer display has finished, remove the plants and loosen the compost with a small hand fork. It may be necessary to add more potting compost to give sufficient planting depth for the plants that are going to provide next spring's display. In any case, incorporate a general fertilizer (about a handful to each 24in/60cm of box length).

If the compost has become very dry, it should be soaked and allowed to drain through so that the whole window box becomes moist. However, do not water to excess, or the compost will be too messy for planting.

Make sure the compost is kept reasonably moist, as even in autumn and winter window boxes can dry out, especially if under an overhanging roof, so check regularly.

3 Add more moss and compost to within 1in/2.5cm of the rim. With your hand, scoop out holes in the compost on top and insert plants.

4 Water in thoroughly with a fine rose, after firming the compost and adding an extra thickness of moss to make a firm rim.

Special watering techniques

Hanging baskets

Hanging baskets are particularly vulnerable to drying out, so need special attention. In very dry, breezy weather, it is not uncommon for them to require watering twice a day. Even in rainy weather, never assume that enough water has penetrated into the compost, because much is shed off the foliage.

The simplest way to water one or two hanging baskets is often to use a long-spouted can. If the spout is grasped firmly in one hand, it is possible to raise the can above your head with your arm fully extended. A gallon watering can is not too difficult to hold in this position. Alternatively, a pair of lightweight steps will enable you to climb up to the required height.

A $\frac{1}{2}$in/1.25cm hose can also be held high enough to reach a hanging basket. If a length of bamboo cane is attached to the end of the hose, sufficient rigidity can be maintained to stretch up to a considerable height. Garden hose can also be extended rigidly by inserting a length of metal tubing, leaving the top of the hose bent over at an angle so that the water can be directed accurately. Special tubing extensions are available, as illustrated

in the diagram (below right), for extra height.

Where it is impossible to run a length of hose, water can be pumped from a tank mounted in a truck by means of a small immersible pump, provided that electric power is available nearby.

If there is only a small number of baskets, you could use a proprietary handheld lance that has a small reservoir emptied by means of a pumping action.

Tubing systems

For watering a window box, it may be convenient to erect overhead tubing into which are inserted spray jets positioned directly over the window (the same method could be used for a row of hanging baskets). Water can then be turned on at the household tap; with this remote-control technique, always make sure that sufficient time has elapsed to allow plenty of water through, so that the container receives a thorough soaking.

Another, similar method is to have very fine "drip tubing" leading from a main tube and going straight into the boxes or baskets. More than one tube will be required for larger containers.

Watering hanging baskets

A carefully directed hose works well for hanging baskets. An added length of cane will give the hose rigidity if needed.

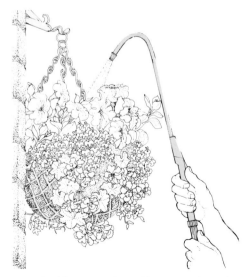

A metal tubing extension with a curved nozzle is useful if extra height is required.

Tubing irrigation

Position jets in overhead tubing above less easily accessible containers such as high window boxes or hanging baskets. Turn water on at a tap, allowing sufficient time for an adequate amount to penetrate the container.

Growing bags

Compost in a growing bag must be thoroughly watered at planting time. Strong-growing plants will make great demands on water in dry, breezy weather.

To prevent the bag from drying out, it is possible to obtain a trough into which the growing bag is put, and this to a certain extent acts as an automatic watering device.

Another simple method is to insert into the compost of the growing bag a couple of plastic lemonade bottles, neck downwards with the caps removed or partly unscrewed and with the bottoms cut off. Fill these bottles with water, which will gradually seep into the compost.

A long-spouted can should be held firmly in both hands, with the arms extended.

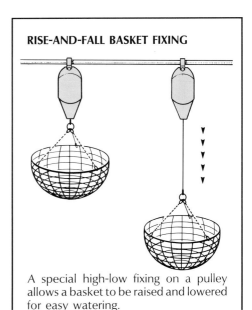

RISE-AND-FALL BASKET FIXING

A special high-low fixing on a pulley allows a basket to be raised and lowered for easy watering.

Staking and support

Wall-grown plants

A container placed near a wall or fence can have a backing of wooden trellis-work fixed to the vertical face. In such a situation, wires stretched between nails, screws or vine eyes are also suitable, especially as supports for woody plants whose main stems can be easily tied in. It is best to run the wires horizontally, 6-9in/15-23cm apart.

Galvanized or plastic-coated wire will last for many years, but should be inspected at regular intervals to check that none of the fixings or ties has worked loose.

Free-standing plants

Fixings for stakes in free-standing containers should be as unobtrusive as possible once the plants have reached their full height. Check how high a particular plant is likely to grow and put in a support of the height required, even if at the outset it looks somewhat out of proportion.

Canes Three or four bamboo canes pushed vertically into the compost at the edges of the container can be tied together lightly at the top to form a wigwam shape. Place the canes near to a plant so that, if the plant is self-climbing, it will have a chance of getting immediate support. A few initial ties will encourage the plant to grow upwards.

Netting Another useful support is a cylinder made of sheep fencing or chicken netting to a height suitable for the plants and with a diameter that fits neatly into the container. Support the fencing or netting with stout canes pushed in on either side and tied firmly to it. Plastic mesh can also be used.

Twiggy sticks A third method of staking is to insert twiggy sticks all the way around the container, trimming them lightly to make a neat shape. They can be tied in at the top.

If the sticks are bare at the base, short twiggy growths can be pushed in, or one or two lengths of tying material can be wound

Cane tripod

Netting cylinder

Twiggy sticks

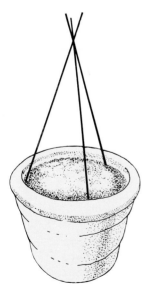

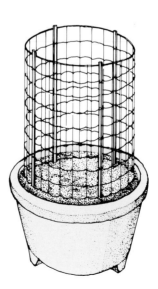

Insert three canes into the compost and tie them securely at the top.

Roll netting into a neatly fitting cylinder. Thread canes through and tie.

Insert twiggy sticks inside the container. Trim neatly; tie with twine if necessary.

SUPPORTS FOR USE WITH GROWING BAGS

Wire frames are available for growing bags: strings are stretched vertically from the top bar to the bottom, each providing a support for one plant.

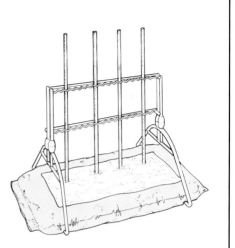

Alternatively, you could use a framework specially designed to hold a series of upright canes.

horizontally round the stakes a short distance apart, to give the plants some initial support.

Tying materials
A wide selection of tying materials is available.
Twine Garden twines come in a range of thicknesses and colours. Duller colours are less obtrusive. The thickness chosen will depend on the size of stem to be tied in, but thinner twine can always be doubled to make a stronger tie if necessary. Tarred twine will be best for a plant that is to be permanently fixed, as it lasts for several years.

Ties should be made neatly using a reef knot, cutting the remaining ends so that they are not too long and unsightly.
Raffia This is ideal for tying in thinner growths, and has the advantage that it can be split down to suit various thicknesses of stem.
Wire ties Paper-covered wire ties are ideal for securing plants quickly, but care is needed if they are not to look untidy. The wire may cut into the stems if the plant is grown for any length of time, so periodic inspection and replacement is necessary.
Plastic string Plastic string is often manufactured in lurid colours, but is very strong and extremely easy to use.
Plastic ties Special plastic ties can also be purchased, and these are particularly useful for permanent plants. They consist of a loop which passes through a buckle and automatically holds the plant in place.

Growing bags
Supporting plants in growing bags can often present a problem as the shallow depth of compost on a hard surface provides very little rigidity to the bottom of a cane. Canes must, therefore, be securely tied at the top to an overhead wire or alternatively tied to individual wall fixings.

When this is not possible, specially designed free-standing wire frames can be used effectively. Either the frames are made to hold canes upright so that each plant can be supported with a single cane, or several long strings are stretched vertically to allow stems to climb over them. The latter type is better for tall-growing plants. Both methods rely on the fact that the growing bag is placed in the space at the base of the frame to give a solid anchorage and to hold the vertical section in place.

Protection

Wind protection

Wind can cause much damage in the garden, especially to plants in containers that are sited on draughty corners. The plants and their supports may be blown down, or their roots may be loosened in the soil and consequently dry out. At the very least, the foliage may be spoilt.

Position containers near to walls, hedges, fences, or the house itself (but away from windy corners), in order to block, or preferably filter, wind. Siting the container with a hedge or fence 6ft/1.8m to the south and west will cut the force of the prevailing wind, yet will be far enough away to avoid a shadow falling over the plants.

If a windy site cannot be avoided, you could screen plants using cut-down fencing, neatly cut hardboard or Netlon (doubled if necessary) supported between two stakes.

Frost protection

Frost protection may need to be provided for some plants where young growth or flowers are liable to be damaged.

Free-standing plants Putting the plant and container inside a cold structure is often sufficient to stop any frost damage. The plant should be further protected by plunging its container in soil: this protects the root ball from very hard frosts and prevents the vulnerable roots from being killed. A plant under cover can be further protected by putting newspaper or sacking loosely over its branches: polythene is not advised as condensation may occur, leading to the growth of mould on branches.

Sometimes it is impossible or undesirable to move a plant inside for the winter, so protection has to be given to the plant *in situ*. This needs to be done as neatly and securely as possible. Tie straw or bracken to stakes pushed into the compost, until the container is completely enclosed.

Another method is to put a cylinder of chicken wire netting over and around the

Frost protection

Wind protection

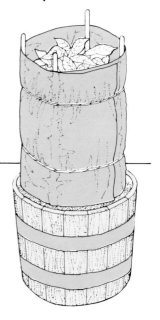

Wrap a plant under cover with a sack for protection against very cold weather.

Plunge a pot in a sheltered spot outside and cover with straw or bracken.

Use a plastic or hessian sack fixed to four canes around a free-standing plant.

FROST PROTECTION IN RAISED BEDS

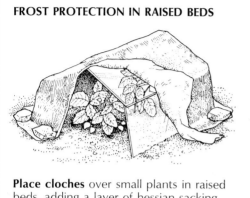

Place cloches over small plants in raised beds, adding a layer of hessian sacking when severe frost is threatened.

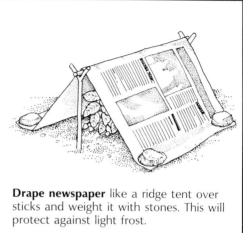

Drape newspaper like a ridge tent over sticks and weight it with stones. This will protect against light frost.

plant and fill in the middle with loosely packed straw or bracken.

Alternatively, hessian sacking can be draped around vertical canes and tied neatly and securely in position. Polythene sheeting can be used in the same way, but does not always give sufficient protection unless it encloses straw insulation. Such sheeting can also be difficult to fix as it offers much wind resistance and can soon become shredded.

Cloches will help to keep small plants in raised beds safe against mild frosts, but cover the glass with hessian sacking in the event of severe cold. Remove this during the day.

Wall-grown plants Plants permanently planted against walls will derive some protection from the walls, but it may be necessary to give them additional cover.

Chicken netting or plastic netting can be stretched over the front of the plant on a simple framework of bamboo canes which keeps the netting just away from the growths. Straw or bracken can then be pushed down in between the stems.

If the plant is fairly tall, it is easier to add the insulation in layers, in which case the netting should be gradually tied in place from the bottom upwards as the work proceeds.

Protecting containers

It is easy to forget that the containers themselves may be at risk during the winter. Unglazed terracotta pots and other, similar containers that have not been frost-proofed will need to be kept dry to avoid damage. Empty containers are best stored in a shed, greenhouse or even at the base of a hedge.

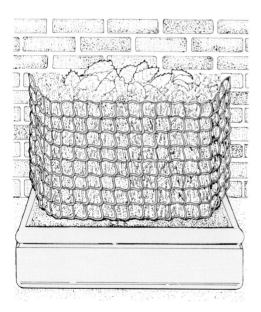

Cover a wall-grown plant with straw kept in place by netting stretched over a framework of canes.

Propagation by seed 1

A wide range of container plants can be grown inexpensively from seed, though attention to detail and cleanliness are needed for good results.

Sowing seeds indoors
If seeds are sown in trays or pots placed in a heated greenhouse or frame, a close watch can be kept on their development, and complete control can be exercised over their environment. It is, however, possible to germinate seeds of some of the easier plants in an airing cupboard or on a warm window sill, provided that they can be protected in the next stage of cultivation.

Preparation Slightly overfill clean trays with John Innes Seed Compost or soilless equivalent. Press the compost down level to $\frac{1}{2}$in/1.25cm below the rim. The compost, if loam-based, needs to be consolidated lightly all over with the fingertips. Water with a fine rose and drain thoroughly.

Sowing Sow evenly and thinly: do this direct from the packet, or by holding the seeds between finger and thumb, or by scattering from the palm of the hand. Mix very small seeds with a little dry silver sand for easier distribution. Very large seeds should be space-sown individually; simply press into the compost.

Covering Cover large and medium seeds with a thin layer of compost. Very fine, dust-like seeds need not be covered at all. Place black polythene sheeting over the top of the seed tray and keep at 65-70°F/18-21°C. Do not allow the compost to dry out. Remove the polythene when the first seedlings emerge. Stand the tray in a good light to minimize fungal attack which can make the tiny plants damp off. Water occasionally with diluted Cheshunt compound to combat fungal disease.

Pricking off As soon as the cotyledons (seed leaves) have expanded, you need to "prick off" (transplant) into another container. If the seedlings are allowed to become too dense, they will become spindly and prone to disease. Small seedlings will grow away more quickly than larger ones.

Fill plastic seed trays with compost exactly as for sowing seeds, but use John Innes No.2 Potting Compost or its equivalent. Prise out a clump of seedlings with the point of a plant label or a small dibber. Separate the seedlings,

Sowing seeds indoors

1 Fill a seed tray or small pot with moist compost and firm it level. Water and drain.

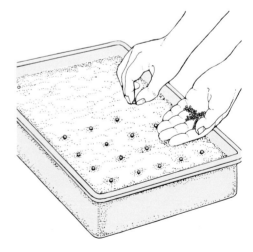

2 Sow seeds, scattering small ones evenly over the surface. Mix very tiny seeds with dry silver sand. Space-sow larger seeds.

and make a hole for each with a dibber.

Pick up a seedling by one seed leaf and hold in position. Make sure the root goes far enough down the hole so that the plant rests at least at the same depth as in the original container, preferably even lower so the cotyledons almost touch the compost's surface.

In a standard-sized tray 35 or 48 seedlings can be grown. Put the name on a label in the tray. Water in the seedlings using a can fitted with a fine rose.

Hardening off Plants raised in warmth must be hardened off—that is, gradually accustomed to the cooler conditions that will be encountered later on. The best way to reduce the heat gradually is to move the plants into an unheated garden frame (a box-like structure with a removable glazed lid, called a light) which can be easily positioned on open ground. Gradually, provide more ventilation during the day, keeping the lid on until the danger of frost has passed; then the lid can be removed completely. A wall or hedge gives some extra protection if a frame is not available, but cover the plants against frost.

Once hardened off, the plants will be ready to be planted in their flowering positions.

Sowing out of doors

Seeds for spring-flowering plants can be sown out of doors the previous summer, and later transferred to their containers.

Preparation Rake the surface of the soil level and break it down to a reasonably fine tilth. It should be moist, but not stick to footwear. Take out drills (V-shaped furrows) to the required depth (this will vary with seed type) with the corner of a hoe blade or a pointed stick. Keep the furrows straight by following a line stretched tautly across the plot.

If the soil is very dry, water with a long-spouted can held close to the bottom of the furrow. Allow to drain through before sowing.

Sowing Pour the seeds into an old cup or bowl. Remove them a pinch at a time, rather than sowing direct from the packet, or too much seed may suddenly spill out.

Stand at the side of the drill, sowing seeds thinly and evenly to the appropriate depth. A good way to measure the sowing rate is to keep the legs fairly wide apart and sow a pinch of seed between each foot; move along the drill, sowing each time you change position.

Covering Lightly cover the seeds by carefully

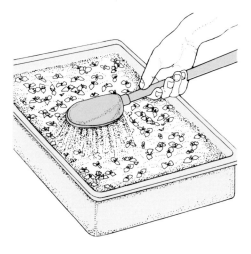

3 Cover seeds evenly with a thin layer of compost. Leave very small, dust-like seeds uncovered. Cover container with polythene.

4 When the seedings appear, remove the polythene and stand in a good light. Keep the compost moist.

Propagation by seed 2

raking the soil down the length of the drill. Press the soil firm with a flat rake head (held downwards with the handle vertical).

Watering If the weather turns hot and dry, water the emerging seedlings, continuing to water regularly, even when the seedlings become quite large. Whenever the soil is dry, hoe between the rows to keep weed-free.

Transplanting Once seedlings are large enough to handle, with a good root system, transplant them into nursery rows, to grow on for planting out in the autumn. Loosen the roots with a fork and prise the plants out of the ground. Water well and allow to drain. During very dry weather it is a good plan, especially on light, sandy soil, to dip the roots in thin mud (made by stirring soil into a quantity of water in a bucket or old bowl). This operation is known as puddling. Deal with a handful of plants at a time, just prior to planting: the plants will withstand the shock of transplanting more readily and establish themselves more quickly.

On lighter soils, plants often grow away better if transplanted into a drill (which will hold more water than a flat surface). Make rows about 12in/30cm apart.

Straddle the line, making holes with a large

Sowing out of doors

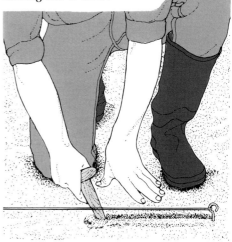

1 Take out a V-shaped drill with a pointed stick or a hoe blade, following a line.

dibber and planting as you progress down the row. A dibber with a metal tip is heavier and will enter the soil more easily. Make holes

Pricking off

5 Prise a clump of seedlings from the compost with a label or dibber. Separate carefully, holding gently by a seed leaf.

6 Make holes 2 in/5 cm apart in moist compost. Transplant each seedling into a hole, holding one leaf. Firm in and water.

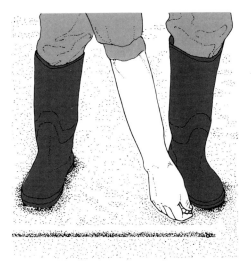

2 Sow the seeds thinly and evenly spaced in the bottom of the drill. Rake soil over and water.

3 Transplant into nursery rows when the seedlings are large enough. Loosen roots with a fork. Plant and firm in.

deep enough to take the root system without longer roots having to curl round.

Firm the plants in by pushing the dibber

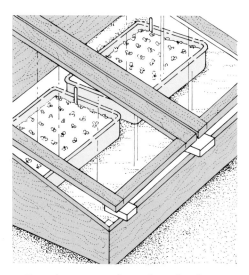

7 Transfer to an unheated garden frame. Gradually lift the frame lights to provide increasing daytime ventilation.

into the soil a little distance away from the plants and at a slight angle. Your feet moving along the row will do additional firming, but it will be necessary to hoe out any footprints.

Watering Water in thoroughly. On a large area, irrigate with a lawn sprinkler.

Weeding Hoeing between the rows and also between plants will keep weeds down.

Sowing in cold frames

Some plants are better raised in a cold frame.

Preparation Prepare the ground well in advance before placing the frame in position. A layer of sterilized compost on top will help to prevent weeds. Lightly consolidate the surface, taking out drills with a pointed stick.

Sowing Sow seeds thinly in rows, raking soil over them. Water with a fine rose. Shade the frame lights to prevent the soil from drying out too rapidly. However, some ventilation is essential, or the temperature will rise excessively. As soon as the seedlings have germinated, remove the frame lights and let the plants develop.

Transplanting Plants propagated in this way are more conveniently transplanted into shallow planting holes with a trowel.

49

Propagation by cuttings 1

Many plants are best propagated from cuttings taken in spring or autumn, so long as the young plants can be grown on or overwintered in a light, frost-free place.

For spring cuttings, it will be necessary to have brought through the winter stock plants from which to take cuttings as soon as suitable growths can be obtained. However, when propagating on a window sill or in an unheated greenhouse, it is a mistake to take cuttings too early in the spring.

Cuttings taken in late summer or early autumn will root very readily and can remain in their rooting containers throughout the winter.

Preparation Mix up a suitable rooting compost (pages 32-3) or purchase a recommended rooting medium. Fill up a pot or small seed tray with compost, consolidating the surface with the fingertips. Press the compost level with a flat board cut to the size of the container.

Choosing the cutting material Next select the cutting material; this is best done in the morning. Plant materials should be soft and in active growth: these are known as softwood cuttings. Avoid, if at all possible, stems coming into flower, as this tends to inhibit rooting. If this is not possible, make sure that all flowers and buds are removed.

Never select wilting stems. Make sure, too, that the material is free from pests and diseases, and is true to the type of plant to be propagated: if the plant has variegated foliage, the stems selected for cuttings should be well variegated.

Later in the growing season (say, from late summer to early autumn) the cutting material will be somewhat firmer at the base; such cuttings are referred to as semi-ripe cuttings. They are treated in just the same way as softwood cuttings, as described above, but take somewhat longer to root than softwood cuttings.

Taking the cuttings Depending on the plant, cuttings should be 1-3in/2.5-7.5cm long. The leaves should be removed from the lower section to one-third of the distance up the stem. Make a clean, straight cut immediately below a joint where a leaf joins the stem (called a "node"). It is important to use a sharp knife or razor blade, so that a clean

Taking cuttings

1 Remove the cutting material with a sharp knife or razor blade, making sure the cut is just above a node. Fill a pot or tray with compost, pressing it level.

2 Trim off bottom leaves and dip cut ends of semi-ripe cuttings into rooting powder. With a dibber make holes in the compost. Insert, firm and water the cuttings.

cut is made and no ragged tissue is left through which rot fungi may enter.

Hormone rooting powder Softwood cuttings usually root readily, and it is seldom worth while using a hormone rooting powder to promote rooting. However, hormone rooting powders may be used beneficially to improve rooting of semi-ripe cuttings. Dip the end of the cut stem into the powder and remove any surplus which may adhere to it by lightly tapping the stem against the powder's container.

Planting With a small dibber or pencil make a hole just deep enough to accept the bottom third of the cutting. Lightly firm it in by pushing the point of the dibber down into the compost at a slight distance away and at an angle. Water in well, using a fine rose.

Growing conditions Cuttings must never be allowed to wilt, so make sure that they are kept in humid conditions and also shaded from direct sunlight. A south-facing window sill can be very hot and should be avoided, but it is, nonetheless, important to select a warm position so that rooting takes place as quickly as possible. A sheet of newspaper will give extra shade, but condensation on the polythene in itself will exclude some light.

Covering A humid atmosphere should be provided by covering the container. One method is to enclose it with a polythene bag, tying the top lightly to seal it. The inside of the bag will become covered with drops of condensation which may drip onto the cuttings, providing conditions ideal for fungi to develop. Change the polythene bag for a dry one every day or two, using the original bag, once dry, for replacement.

As an alternative to a conventional propagator with a rigid plastic top, a convenient cover for cuttings can be made from the top of a plastic lemonade bottle. Cut this off with a sharp knife about 5in/12.5cm down from the cap. If the cut is made as level as possible, the top will fit snugly down on the compost surface: take care not to damage any of the foliage. Removing or replacing the screw cap provides a ready-made ventilation system.

A tinted plastic bottle provides ready-made shading, but watch carefully as cuttings can become somewhat lanky and weak if rooting takes a long time.

3a Cover with a polythene bag and place on a warm window sill or in a greenhouse. If condensation develops, change the bag for a dry one every day or two.

3b The top of a plastic lemonade bottle makes an alternative cover. Cut with a sharp knife about 5in/12.5cm down from the cap. Open and shut the cap for ventilation.

Propagation by cuttings 2

Fungicides Spray the cuttings once a week with fungicide to keep down fungal attack. The longer cuttings take to root, the more chance there is of them rotting off.

Potting off If a sample cutting offers some resistance when given a slight tug, it can be safely assumed that all have rooted. They should now be gradually weaned from their enclosed environment by increasing the amount of air until the polythene bag is completely removed. Once the root system has really established, it is time for the cuttings to be individually potted off. Spring cuttings will require potting into John Innes Potting Compost No.2 or equivalent compost. Semi-ripe cuttings are best left to grow through the winter in as cool a position as possible without frost damage, and then potted off in the spring when conditions have improved.

Pinching out Sometimes cuttings will make an appreciable amount of growth during the autumn. Pinch out the tip of the shoot with finger and thumb, so that the new plant will make more side shoots and become sturdier and evenly shaped.

Special propagators

Cuttings may be rooted by inserting them directly into compost in individual trays without bottom heat, provided that the surroundings can be kept reasonably warm by artificial or sun heat. However, a specially made propagator can make the job even easier and widen the range of plants that can be propagated successfully. Its bottom heat contributes to quicker rooting and lessens the chances of rotting off.

Propagators are also very useful for germinating seeds, especially if a controlled higher temperature is required. The thermostat will give a reasonably precise control and generally should be set at 65-70°F/18-21°C.

Most propagators are made to hold a layer of fine sand which retains the bottom heat and distributes it evenly. For plant hygiene, the sand should be changed each year.

Some propagators have a removable inner tray divided into sections, but one that can accommodate pots and trays of various sizes will often be found to be more convenient.

Position Electric propagators can be used in the home, but if a number of plants are to

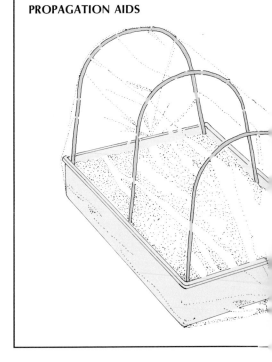

PROPAGATION AIDS

be raised, space in a suitable environment will be needed. The best position is a heated greenhouse where early-propagated young plants removed from the closed environment can grow on without check. An unheated greenhouse can also be extremely useful, although it is better to delay propagation until later in the spring when the warmer weather will offer better growing conditions for newly rooted plants removed from the propagator.

Safety If electricity is to be run from the house to a greenhouse, make sure that it is done competently by a qualified electrician. Waterproof connections are vitally important, and need also to be easily accessible.

Ventilation Proprietary propagators are made with transparent rigid tops which can be easily removed for carrying out any necessary work. The propagators also have several small ventilators which can be opened or closed depending on the environment required. Generally, a humid atmosphere is needed, so it is unlikely that much ventilation will be

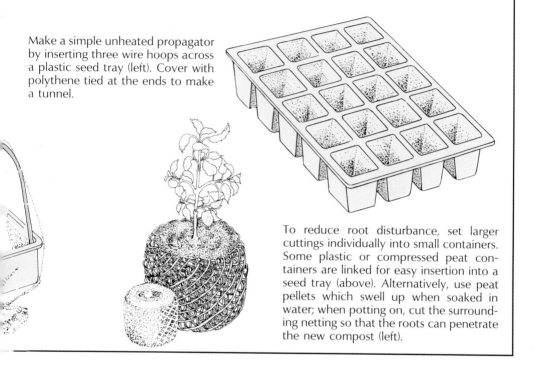

Make a simple unheated propagator by inserting three wire hoops across a plastic seed tray (left). Cover with polythene tied at the ends to make a tunnel.

To reduce root disturbance, set larger cuttings individually into small containers. Some plastic or compressed peat containers are linked for easy insertion into a seed tray (above). Alternatively, use peat pellets which swell up when soaked in water; when potting on, cut the surrounding netting so that the roots can penetrate the new compost (left).

required except to help dry off any excess condensation. The aim, at all times, is to keep cuttings turgid: if they flag and become limp, it is often impossible for them to recover. At best they may take a longer time to root, and the resultant plants may be less vigorous.

Shading In bright, sunny weather it will be necessary to shade the transparent cover of the propagator, but the material used for this should not be so dense that it excludes light completely. If the shading can be left off in the early or latter part of the daylight hours or on a dull day, so much the better. Once the cuttings have rooted, they should be potted and moved onto the greenhouse staging, but still may need shading for a few days if the sun is very strong.

Seeds Seeds germinated in a propagator should also be removed and shaded, once the seedlings show their fully expanded cotyledons. Some plants (such as begonias) may require longer in the propagator than others (such as petunias), as the extra warmth is necessary in the initial stages of growth.

Making propagators
Wooden boxes It is possible to make a large, heated propagator by constructing a wooden box to fit onto the greenhouse staging. The top covering should be clear polythene sheeting fixed on to a rigid framework for easy removal, or attached to a short length of wood so that it can be rolled on and off from side to side.

Bottom heat can be provided by an electric soil-warming cable bedded firmly in sand according to the manufacturer's instructions. A thermostat is essential: the rod type will give more accurate control. A small paraffin heater positioned underneath the propagation space can also provide bottom heat, but this has no fine temperature control.

Seed tray and hoops A very simple unheated propagator can be made from an ordinary plastic seed tray with three wire hoops inserted across the narrow part to form a mini tunnel. Cover the hoops with clear polythene sheeting, the ends tied tightly to keep it firmly in place.

Popular container plants 1

There are certain annuals, biennials and perennials that are especially favoured for containers.

All of the subjects here will give a good display over a long period, provided that they are kept fed and watered at regular intervals, and the old flowerheads and seed pods are removed as soon as they begin to form. All are annuals, or best treated as such, unless otherwise specified.

These plants are readily available from garden centres and nurseries. However, many are easily raised from seed and, unless otherwise indicated, will flower a few months after sowing. Most will require gentle heat (61-65°F/16-18°C) for germination, but many will germinate at a slightly lower temperature. Some of the plants are more easily raised from cuttings.

The seedlings should be pricked off into seed trays, using a suitable compost (pages 32-3), but in some instances are best grown individually in small pots.

Ageratum. Although there are pink and white forms of *Ageratum*, the blue ones are most commonly grown. They make fluffy-headed plants, up to 8in/20cm high, ideal as edging and filler plants. However, the cultivar 'Tall Blue' will attain a height of 18in/45cm, so is good for intermingling with other taller plants. Grow in full sun. Cultivars: 'Adriatic', mid blue; 'Blue Danube', lavender blue; 'Pacific', violet-purple. Sow seeds from February to March in gentle heat.

Alyssum. A prolific and sweetly scented edging plant, attaining a height of only 4in/10cm. Full sun. Cultivars: 'Rosie O'Day', rose pink; 'Snowdrift White'; 'Wonderland', violet-purple. Sow March to April in gentle heat.

Antirrhinum (snapdragon). Forms dense spikes of flowers in a wide range of colours: red, yellow, pink, orange or white. Up to 14-18in/35-45cm, though the dwarfer kinds are particularly useful. Use as a main feature. Full sun. Recommended: Coronette Series (mixed) and 'Floral Carpet'. Sow seeds February to March, in gentle heat.

Arabis. Biennials to use for carpeting or fillers in spring displays, with slender, fairly loose spikes of cross-shaped flowers in pink or white. 6in/15cm. Sun. Cultivar: 'Spring Charm'. Sow in spring in gentle heat or out of doors in summer.

Aubrieta. Cross-shaped flowers with rounded petals in shades of rose, red, lilac and purple. Perennial. Ideal for spring colour as an edging or trailer. 4in/10cm. Recommended: Bengal Series (mixed) and 'Novalis Blue'. Full sun. Can be sown outdoors from April to June and transplanted into a garden plot for autumn planting in containers.

Begonia. Both fibrous-rooted and tuberous types make excellent main plants in containers. Sun or partial shade. Fibrous-rooted cultivars: *Begonia semperflorens* and hybrids, providing masses of small flowers on compact growth; 'Pink Avalanche', 12in/30cm; 'Danica Red', 'Danica Rose', 'Danica White', all with bronze foliage and heights 9-12in/23-30cm; 'Frilly Pink', 'Frilly Red', with large, wavy-edged flowers, 12in/30cm high.

Tuberous hybrids: Nonstop Series (mixed), medium-sized double flowers in white, orange, red, pink and yellow, 12in/30cm; Finale Series (mixed), long pendent stems; Lloydii Series, a perennial with graceful, pendulous stems, double flowers in mixed colours.

Tuberous begonias can be raised from seed sown in January and February and germinated at 65-75°F/18-25°C. After flowering, the dormant tubers can be stored during the winter in frost-free conditions for flowering the following summer. Tubers should be started into growth in gentle heat.

Bellis (daisy). Spring-flowering biennials used as fillers or for edging. Sun or partial shade. Recommended: Carpet Series (mixed) in red, rose and white, 8-10in/20-25cm; Pomponette Series (mixed), red, rose and white, 6-8in/15-20cm; Goliath Series (mixed) in red, rose and white, 6in/15cm. All can be obtained as separate as well as mixed colours. Sow out of doors in open ground from June to July for autumn planting.

Busy lizzie. See *Impatiens*.

Calceolaria. Small, pouch-shaped flowers in yellow, orange and red. Use as main feature in partial shade as well as full sun. Recommended: Sunshine Series (mixed). 8-10in/20-25cm. Sow January to March in gentle heat. Best grown individually in small pots.

Calocephalus brownii. A half-hardy, wiry, silver-leaved perennial that is not at all rampant and makes a good filler, particularly in hanging baskets. 12-15in/30-38cm. Full sun. Cuttings taken in autumn should be rooted in pots kept on an open bench, as rotting can soon occur if they are kept in humid conditions.

Campanula isophylla (trailing bellflower). A perennial, not hardy, but easily grown and bearing small, open, bell-like flowers in either blue or white on short, trailing stems. Good for hanging baskets. 9in/23cm. Sun or partial shade. Take cuttings in autumn or spring.

Carnation. See *Dianthus caryophyllus*.

Centaurea candidissima. A half-hardy, low-growing edging plant with silver foliage. Sow from February to March in gentle heat.

Centaurea gymnocarpa. A half-hardy silver-leaved foliage plant for height and emphasis that acts as a foil for bright colours. 18in/45cm. Full sun. Sow from February to March.

Cheiranthus cheiri (wallflower). Very widely grown, delightfully fragrant main feature plant for spring flowering. Biennial. Full sun or partial shade. Cultivars: 'Fire King', scarlet, 15in/38cm; 'Orange Bedder', 12in/30cm; 'Cloth of Gold', 15in/38cm; 'Primrose Monarch', 15in/38cm; 'Vulcan', deep crimson, 12in/30cm. Sow out of doors in June and transplant for growing on until transferred in autumn to flowering positions.

Chrysanthemum (Argyranthemum) frutescens (Paris daisy or Marguerite). The popular form of this half-hardy perennial has white, daisy-like flowerheads, but pink variants with cushion-like centres, such as 'Mary Wootton', are also frequently grown. 'Jamaican Primrose' is another cultivar, with large yellow flowerheads. 2-3ft/60-80cm. Superb as dot or feature plants in large containers. Cuttings should be taken in autumn or spring.

Convolvulus sabiatus. Although this beautiful perennial trails, it is never rampant. Masses of fairly small, round, blue flowers. Good for hanging baskets. 9in/23cm. Full sun. Not fully hardy, so take cuttings in autumn.

Cordyline australis and **C. indivisa**. Long, sword-shaped leaves make these half-hardy, foliage plants (perennial) ideal as either central features or lone specimens. There are green and bronze-leaved cultivars. 24in/60cm 20ft/4.5-6m in frost-free areas where they can be grown without protection). Sow in March

in gentle heat for planting the following year.

Dianthus caryophyllus (carnation). Carnations are hybrids with *D. caryophyllus* as the main parent. Bright grey-green foliage, and a tremendous range of flower colour. Sow February to March. Variety: 'Trailing', with long, thin stems that cascade. Use as a main feature or as an edging plant. Full sun.

Dorotheanthus bellidiformis (Syn. *Mesembryanthemum criniflorum*). A brightly coloured, tender, ground-hugging feature or edging plant. White, pink to crimson, orange-red to buff. 4in/10cm. Full sun. Cultivars: Magic Carpet Series (mixed); 'Sparkles'. Sow March in gentle heat.

Erysimum hieraciifolium (Syn. *Cheiranthus* x *allionii*) (Siberian wallflower). A main feature plant for spring flowering, with spikes of brilliant orange or yellow flowers. Biennial. 12in/30cm. Full sun. Sow out of doors in July and thin out rather than transplant, especially on sandy soils, to avoid premature flowering.

Euonymus fortunei. A hardy, evergreen, spreading or trailing shrub, ideal for winter display, especially in hanging baskets. 6in/15cm. Cultivars: 'Emerald 'n' Gold' and 'Emerald Gaiety' are golden- and silver-variegated. Cuttings root easily at any time.

Felicia amelloides. A half-hardy sub-shrub, with blue, daisy-like flowerheads. Suitable for hanging baskets. There is also a variegated form. 12in/30cm. Full sun. Take cuttings in autumn or spring.

Forget-me-not. See *Myosotis*.

Fuchsia. Some of the more compact cultivars of this perennial, with their attractive pendulous flowers in combinations of red, lilac, pink and white, are ideal as main feature plants. The trailing kinds are particularly suitable for hanging baskets. Fuchsias grow well in sun but also thrive in light shade. They respond well to generous watering and feeding when in full growth. During the winter, some frost protection must be given. There are many cultivars of both upright and trailing forms. The following are recommended:

Compact cultivars: 'Alice Hoffman', white and red; 'Blush of Dawn', white and lilac; 'Charming', deep pink; 'Golden Treasure', green and gold variegated leaves, scarlet and magenta flowers; 'Leverkusen', deep rose pink; 'Sunray', leaves with yellow and pink

Popular container plants 2

CONTAINER PLANTS

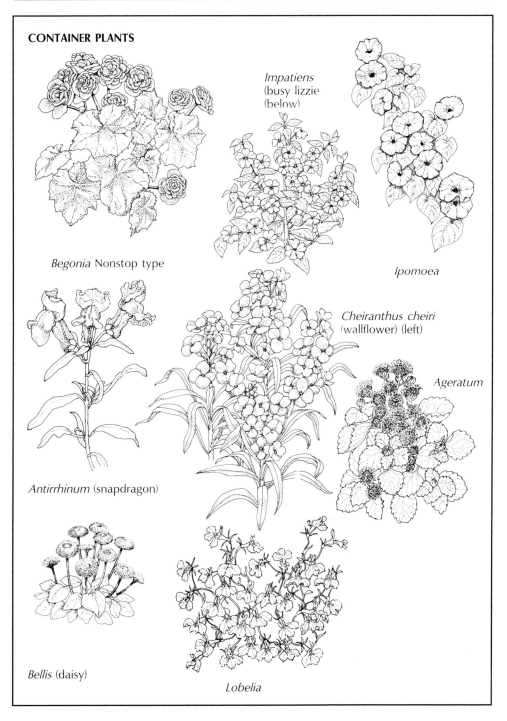

Begonia Nonstop type

Impatiens (busy lizzie (below)

Ipomoea

Cheiranthus cheiri (wallflower) (left)

Ageratum

Antirrhinum (snapdragon)

Bellis (daisy)

Lobelia

variegation, red flowers; 'Tom Thumb', carmine and violet.

Trailing varieties: 'Cascade', pink and crimson; 'Golden Marinka,' red flowers and yellow foliage; 'Marinka', red; 'Red Spider', crimson and rose; 'Summer Snow', white; 'White Spider', white; 'Tom West', deep red flowers, variegated foliage.

Softwood cuttings of fuchsias root quickly in the spring and the resultant plants soon build up to flower that summer.

Gazania. Broad-petalled, daisy-like flowerheads. An ideal edging and filler plant. Full sun. Recommended: Daybreak Series (mixed) in yellow, orange, pink, bronze and white, 9in/23cm; Mini Star Series (mixed), yellow, orange, pink, bronze and white, 8in/20cm. Sow February to March in gentle heat.

Geranium. See *Pelargonium*.

Hedera helix (common ivy). This ivy and its variants are very hardy and ideal for winter interest, especially in hanging baskets. They do well in a fairly shady position. Perennials. 6in/15cm. Cultivars: 'Adam', white and cream variegation; 'Glacier', silver variegation; 'Green Ripple', rippling deep green foliage; 'Kolibri', heavy white speckles on rich green leaves; 'Midas Touch', golden foliage; 'Parsley Crested', curled leaves; 'Manders Crested', long cascading growth. Cuttings can be taken at most times of the year.

Helichrysum microphyllum. This is a small-leaved, half-hardy, silver-grey foliage perennial which makes a good filler. If planted in the side of a hanging basket, it will tumble down for about 12in/30cm. Take cuttings in autumn or spring. All helichrysums are best in full sun.

H. petiolare. A more robust but slightly more tender plant than the above, with larger silver foliage. Ideal for larger hanging baskets, being 3ft/90cm long when trailing. Variegated and yellow-leaved forms also available and equally attractive. Cuttings in autumn or spring.

Heliotropium (heliotrope, cherry pie). Used as a main feature plant, with flat heads of densely packed small flowers. Full sun. Cultivar: 'Marine', violet-purple, 12in/30cm. Sow seeds February to March.

Impatiens (busy lizzie). Continuously flowering, half-hardy perennials, grown as annuals, with cup-shaped or flat blossoms in shades of red, pink, lilac and white. Use as a main feature or for edging. Excellent in partial shade as well as sun. Up to 12in/30cm. Many cultivars are available; some, such as the Zigzag Series, have striped flowers. Sow March to April at 65-70°F/18-21°C and maintain high humidity.

Ipomoea (morning glory). A vigorous climber (up to 8ft/2.4m), useful as a main feature plant. Large trumpet-shaped flowers. Full sun. Cultivars: 'Flying Saucers', sky blue; 'Scarlett O'Hara', brilliant scarlet; 'Heavenly Blue'; 'Mini-bar Rose', dwarf habit, variegated foliage with white-margined, rosy flowers, making a good trailer. Sow during April in gentle heat.

Ivy. See *Hedera helix*.

Kochia scoparia forma **trichophylla** (summer cypress, burning bush). An emphasis plant, with feathery green foliage that changes to crimson in the autumn. 3ft/90cm. Full sun. Sow during April in gentle heat.

Lantana camara. A tender perennial shrub with orange, yellow, red or white flower clusters borne continuously in summer. Good in hanging baskets. Full sun. 12in/30cm. Easily increased from cuttings in the spring.

Lathyrus odoratus (sweet pea). A popular annual climbing plant with large, pea-like flowers in many colours, used as a main feature. The shorter types are excellent container plants as they do not require staking; taller cultivars require the support of twigs or netting or may be allowed to cascade. Full sun. Cultivars: Knee Hi Series (mixed) and Jet Set Series (mixed), both 3ft/90cm; 'Bijou', 'Snoopey', 'Supersnoop', all 12in/30cm. Sow February to March in gentle heat.

Lobelia. Masses of small flowers on compact or trailing plants for sun or partial shade. Compact cultivars for edging or fillers: 'Cambridge Blue', sky blue; 'Crystal Palace', deep blue flowers, bronze foliage; 'Mrs Clibran', deep blue, white eye; 'Rosamond', carmine red, white eye; 'White Lady'; all 4in/10cm. Cultivars to use as trailing and filler plants: 'Light Blue Basket'; 'Blue Basket'; 'Sapphire', deep blue with white eye; 'Red Cascade'. Sow February to March at 70°F/21°C.

Marguerite. See *Chrysanthemum frutescens*.

Marigold. See *Tagetes*.

Mesembryanthemum. See *Dorotheanthus*.

Mimulus (musk). Large cheerful flowers in

Popular container plants 3

warm colours, used as main feature or edging plant in sun or partial shade. Varieties: Malibu Series, ivory, orange, red or yellow, all 6in/15cm; Calypso Series (mixed), 12in/30cm; 'Royal Velvet', mahogany red with golden throats speckled red, 12in/30cm. Sow during March in gentle heat.

Myosotis (forget-me-not). Biennial. Small flowers appearing in great profusion, used as edging or filler plants for sun or partial shade. Cultivars: 'Royal Blue', 12in/30cm: 'Blue Basket', 12in/30cm; 'Carmine King', 8in/20cm. Sow these biennials May to July and grow on out of doors for planting in the autumn in their spring-flowering positions.

Nasturtium. See *Tropaeolum majus*.

Nemesia. Loose spikes of flowers, used as a main feature or edging plant. Full sun. Cultivars: 'Carnival', weather-tolerant, in white, yellow, orange, pink and red, 7in/18cm; 'Blue Gem', 8in/20cm. Sow in March in gentle heat.

Nicotiana (tobacco plant). Spikes of large flat flowers with long tubes. Use as a main feature plant. Unfortunately the dwarf types have no scent, but, unlike the older cultivars, stay open during the day. Sun and light shade. Cultivars: Domino Series (mixed), white, pink, red and lime green, 12in/30cm; Nicki Series (mixed), 15in/38cm; 'Crimson Bedder', 15in/38cm. Sow March to April in gentle heat.

Osteospermum. There are several different forms of this half-hardy perennial with daisy-like flowerheads. Especially suitable for large hanging baskets. 24in/60cm. Full sun is essential. Cultivars: 'Blue Streak', blue and white; 'Buttermilk', yellow; 'Nairobi Purple' (Syn. 'Tresco Purple'); 'Whirlygig', white, with the reverse side blue, and petals shaped like little spoons. Take cuttings in the autumn.

Pansy. See *Viola*.

Paris daisy. See *Chrysanthemum frutescens*.

Pelargonium. Also commonly called *Geranium*. Several groups of pelargoniums with differing characters are available. The ivy-leaved, pendulous cultivars are particularly useful for hanging baskets. The common zonal pelargonium can also be used in baskets, but is probably best used as a dominant main feature plant with other filler and trailing plants. Full sun. There are many cultivars, with both single and double flowers, and in colours ranging through white, pink and red

CONTAINER PLANTS

Nicotiana (tobacco plant)

Nemesia

to purple. Some have attractive foliage, either white or yellow-variegated, or even tri-coloured. Annuals or perennials.

Cultivars to use as feature plants: a wide range is available, but 'Hollywood Star' (rose-pink and white) and the Century and Pulsar Series are particularly good, 12in/30cm; Video Series, red and pink shades or white, with dark foliage, 8in/20cm; Breakaway Series, with cascading flowers in salmon, red or coral; Summer Showers Series, red, pink, lavender, magenta or white, trailing ivy-leaved type.

Thunbergia alata
(black-eyed Susan)
(left)

Salvia splendens

Petunia

Primula × polyanthus   *Tagetes patula*

All these are single-flowered and can be raised from seed but require some heat to be really successful. Sow in September and overwinter in slight heat, growing them on the following spring and planting out in early summer. Alternatively, sow January to February at 65-70°F/18-21°C to flower the same year. Grow individually in pots.

Cultivars particularly useful for hanging baskets: 'Ailsa Garland', deep pink; 'Galilee', double rose pink; 'L'Elegante', variegated foliage, very pale pink, almost white, flowers; 'Madame Crousse', pale pink; 'Rouletta', white with red streaks; 'Snowdrift', white; 'White Mesh', cream-netted foliage; 'Mini Cascade', masses of pink flowers. All can be raised from cuttings in autumn or spring.

'Lady Plymouth' has white-variegated, much divided leaves and pink flowers. Its growth is fairly slender, making it ideal as a filler. Also: 'Frank Headley', red, silver-variegated foliage. Raise both from cuttings.

Perilla frutescens. A good purple-leaved accent plant attaining about 24in/60cm. There are cultivars with curly-edged and deeply cut leaves. Full sun. Sow in March in gentle heat.

Petunia. A vast range of bright colours makes this adaptable plant almost unequalled as an edging or filler plant for containers. Modern cultivars have been selected for weather resistance. Cultivars: 'Blue Cloud'; 'Pink Cloud'; 'Red Cloud'; 'Snow Clad'; Frenzy Series and Resisto Series (dwarf mixed), white, pink, red, blue and purple. 9in/23cm. Sow March to April in gentle heat.

Polyanthus. See *Primula*.

Primula × polyanthus (*Polyanthus*). Outstanding for spring bedding, with scented white, yellow, pink, red or blue flowers. 8in/20cm. Full sun or partial shade. Varieties: Triumph Strain Series and Pacific Giants Series. Sow this biennial in gentle heat January to March, or in a cold frame April to May. Prick off into boxes and grow on in rows out of doors before planting out in their flowering positions.

Pyrethrum ptarmaciflorum. See *Tanacetum ptarmaciflorum*.

Salvia farinacea. A vigorous feature or emphasis plant, producing dense, narrow spikes of violet-blue or white flowers, 24in/60cm. Full sun. Cultivar: 'Victoria', violet-blue. Sow dur-

Popular container plants 4

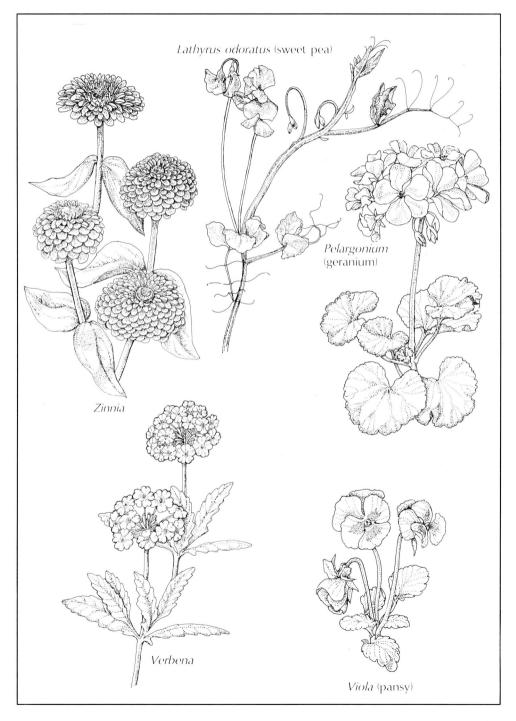

Lathyrus odoratus (sweet pea)

Pelargonium
(geranium)

Zinnia

Verbena

Viola (pansy)

ing March in gentle heat.

S. splendens. Unequalled for producing a display of intense scarlet flower spikes. Use as a main feature in full sun. Cultivars: 'Blaze of Fire', 9in/23cm; Carabiniere Series (red, pink or white), 12in/30cm; 'Vanguard', 9in/23cm. Sow in March in gentle heat. Best pricked out into individual pots.

Senecio. A half-hardy silver-leaved plant. The yellow flowerheads from July to September are best removed. Makes a good foliage contrast as an emphasis plant or a filler. Cultivar: 'Silver Dust'. 8in/20cm. Sow in spring.

Snapdragon. See *Antirrhinum*.

Sweetpea. See *Lathyrus odoratus*.

Tagetes (marigold). African, French and Afro-French types are available in an almost bewildering number, but all come in shades of yellow, orange or red-bronze. Use as main features for full sun. 6in-3ft/15cm-1m. Sow March to April in gentle heat.

Tanacetum (Pyrethrum) ptarmaciflorum. Finely cut silver foliage on compact plants, 12in/30cm. An excellent foil for bright colours. Full sun. Sow February to March in gentle heat. Grow on individually in pots.

Thunbergia alata (black-eyed Susan). A climber with white, yellow or orange flowers, usually with a black centre; sometimes grown as a trailer. Another cultivar, 'Susie', lacks the dark eye. Full sun. Up to 10ft/3m. Sow March to April in gentle heat and grow on individually in pots.

Tithonia rotundifolia (Syn. *T. speciosa*). Bold, somewhat stiff, erect flowerheads, in yellow or orange. Used as main subject. Full sun. Cultivars: 'Goldfinger', golden orange, 2ft 6in/75cm; 'Torch', orange, 2ft 6in/75cm. Sow March to April in gentle heat.

Tobacco plant. See *Nicotiana*.

Tropaeolum majus (nasturtium). Cup-shaped flowers with a prominent "tail". Use as a main feature, filler or edging plant. Best in a free-draining and sunny position. Cultivars: Gleam Series, double yellow, orange or red flowers, trailing to about 15in/38cm; 'Alaska', the same range of colours but with variegated foliage, 12in/30cm; 'Empress of India', crimson, dark foliage, 6-9in/15-23cm; Whirlybird Series, single flowers, wide range of colours, 12in/30cm. Easily grown and can be sown direct into flowering container, April to May.

T. peregrinum (Canary creeper). A vigorous climber with many small, clear yellow flowers. Use as a main feature. Full sun. Sow during April in gentle heat.

Verbena. Flattish heads of brightly coloured flowers. There are upright or spreading forms, both in a range of colours (white, pink, red, blue and purple); some are very vigorous. Full sun. Annual or perennial. Cultivars to use as main subjects or fillers: 'Showtime', 'Springtime', 8in/20cm. As a main feature: Derby Series (mixed), 8in/20cm. Sow February to March 60°F/15°C.

Several other kinds are worth growing: *V.canadensis* (*V.aubletia*) has magenta flowers, 12in/30cm. *V.rigida* (*V.venosa*) is erect, attaining 12in/30cm, with violet-blue flowers. Useful as a feature or filler plant. Full sun. Sow during March in gentle heat.

Some verbenas are good for hanging baskets, but require winter protection. Cultivars: 'Lawrence Johnston', scarlet; 'Loveliness', violet; 'Pink Bouquet', deep pink.

Viola × wittrockiana (pansy). Round, flat, velvety flowers that are very weather-tolerant and bloom continuously for months. Biennial. Some have been especially bred for spring flowering and will even be colourful in the winter if there is a mild spell. Ideal as main feature, edging or filler plants in full sun or partial shade. Cultivars: 'Majestic Giants', good colour range, 4½in/11cm; 'Swiss Giants', yellow, rose, red, white to blue shades. Crystal Bowl Series and Universal Series are particularly recommended for spring flowering. Sow February to March in gentle heat to flower the same year, or outdoors in June or July in a cold frame or seed bed to bloom the following spring.

Wallflower. See *Cheiranthus cheiri*.

Zea mays (ornamental sweet corn). Use as an emphasis plant in full sun. The striped-leaved cultivar gives a tropical effect. Sow in April and grow on individually in pots.

Zinnia. Use as a main feature in full sun, with broad-petalled, daisy-like flowerheads having a prominent central boss. Long-lasting, in a wide range of colours. Cultivars: 'State Fair Mixed', 2ft 6in/75cm; Peter Pan Series (mixed), 10in/25cm: 'Pucchino', 9in/23cm; Thumbelina Series (mixed), 6in/15cm; Lilliput Series (mixed), 9in/23cm. Sow March to April.

Grouping plants 1

The way plants are grouped in containers is just as important as the grouping of the containers themselves. Much is a matter of individual taste, but there are certain points it is helpful to bear in mind.

Free-standing containers
One well-chosen plant can often look better than a mixed planting. Always aim for as bold an effect as possible. It is usually preferable to plant a group of colourful seasonal plants in one large container rather than spreading them more sparsely between various smaller containers.

The planting, too, needs to be in scale with the containers themselves. For example, low, flat-growing plants will look lost if planted alone in a wide-topped vase or urn, whereas if they are dominated by a tall central plant, the whole design comes into proportion. Medium-sized main feature plants can be grown with stronger-growing trailing plants to keep the display well in scale.

Trailing plants will help to soften harsh outlines, but remember to leave sufficiently exposed any container with a pleasing shape, especially if it has prominent decoration.

On pages 62-5 are some suggested designs for planting typical shapes and sizes of containers.

Planting ideas for outdoor containers
(3ft/90cm across)

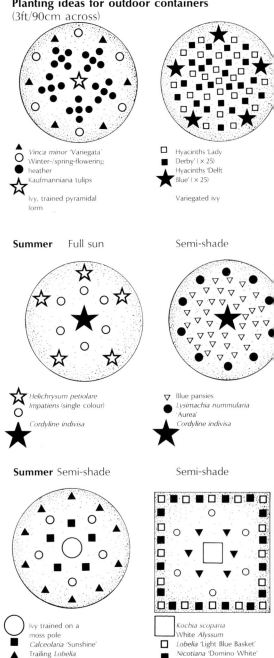

▲ *Vinca minor* 'Variegata'
○ Winter-/spring-flowering
● heather
☆ *Kaufmanniana* tulips

   Ivy, trained pyramidal form

☐ Hyacinths 'Lady Derby' (× 25)
■ Hyacinths 'Delft Blue' (× 25)

   Variegated ivy

Summer   Full sun   Semi-shade

☆ *Helichrysum petiolare*
   Impatiens (single colour)
○ *Cordyline indivisa*
★

▽ Blue pansies
● *Lysimachia nummularia* 'Aurea'
★ *Cordyline indivisa*

Summer Semi-shade   Semi-shade

○ Ivy trained on a moss pole
■ *Calceolaria* 'Sunshine'
▲ Trailing *Lobelia*
○ *Mimulus* 'Royal Velvet'

☐ *Kochia scoparia*
   White *Alyssum*
☐ *Lobelia* 'Light Blue Basket'
■ *Nicotiana* 'Domino White'
▼ Ivy-leaved *Pelargonium* 'Cascade'
○

Spring—sun or shade

◇ *Euonymus fortunei*
▼ *Myosotis* 'Blue Ball'
○ *Narcissus* 'Tête-à-Tête'

Dwarf conifer

Semi-shade

△ *Verbena* (trailing)
▲ *Heliotrope* 'Marine'
◇ French marigold

☆ *Centaurea gymnocarpa*

Semi-shade

● Standard *Fuchsia*
◇ Trailing *Fuchsia* 'Tom West'
● *Begonia* 'Pink Avalanche'
    (× 16)

Composition

Adding a tall main plant to the low-growing plants (right) brings the whole design into proportion with its container.

Trailing plants soften an outline (above), but should not obscure decoration: the main subject is large enough to be in proportion. A tall, thin container (right) always looks better if generously planted with trailing subjects.

Keep planting in scale with the container. Often one well-chosen plant looks better than a fussy planting. Flat, low-growing plants (left) are acceptable only if the container is well below eye-level.

Grouping plants 2

Hanging baskets

When grouping plants in a hanging basket, it is usual to have one larger central plant surrounded by smaller-growing kinds, but planting several of a single kind can be equally effective. The side plants in a basket will usually be trailing types, with taller, bushier plants set in the top.

Opposite are some suggested plans for hanging baskets.

The following plants are especially suitable for hanging baskets. For descriptive and cultivation details, see pages 54-61.

Begonia (fibrous and tuberous); *Calceolaria; Gazania; Impatiens* (busy lizzie); *Lathyrus odoratus* (sweet pea, dwarf kinds); *Lobelia; Mimulus* (musk); *Pelargonium* (geranium); *Petunia; Thunbergia; Tropaeolum majus* (nasturtium); *Verbena; Viola* (pansy).

Window boxes

To counteract the long narrow shape of a window box, every attempt should be made to avoid planting in straight rows. More informality can be given to the display by varying the heights of the main plants and by softening the effect with filler plants. One way to make an attractive planting is to group main feature plants first and then put fillers in between.

A succession of seasonal displays is a worthwhile approach. Separate units can be made up in advance and inserted as the plants come into flower (page 36). However, most gardeners will find it more convenient to rely on two main displays in spring and summer, planted the previous autumn and spring.

All the plants recommended for hanging baskets (above and right) are equally good for window boxes, but there are notable additions, especially for edging and filler plants. For descriptive and cultivation details, see pages 54-61.

Ageratum; Alyssum; Arabis; Bellis (daisy); *Centaurea gymnocarpa; Erysimum hieraclifolium (Cheiranthus × allionii)* (Siberian wallflower); *C.cheiri* (wallflower); *Dianthus caryophyllus* (carnation); *Heliotropium* (heliotrope); *Mimulus* (musk); *Myosotis* (forget-me-not); *Nicotiana* (tobacco plant); *Primula* (polyanthus); *Salvia farinacea; S. splendens; Tagetes* (marigold); *Tanacetum (Pyrethrum) ptarmaciflorum; Zinnia.*

Planting suggestions for window boxes (length 6ft 6in/2m): **Spring**

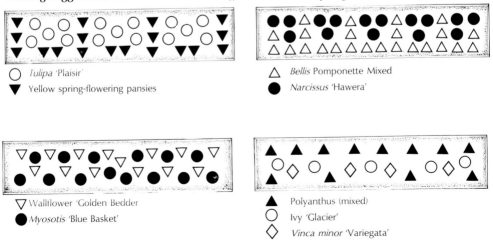

○ *Tulipa* 'Plaisir'
▼ Yellow spring-flowering pansies

△ *Bellis* Pomponette Mixed
● *Narcissus* 'Hawera'

▽ Wallflower 'Golden Bedder'
● *Myosotis* 'Blue Basket'

▲ Polyanthus (mixed)
○ Ivy 'Glacier'
◇ *Vinca minor* 'Variegata'

Planting suggestions for hanging baskets (diameter 14in/36cm)
Spring

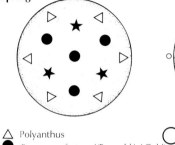

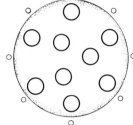

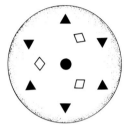

△ Polyanthus
● *Euonymus fortunei* 'Emerald 'n' Gold'
★ Ivy

○ Pansies, either single-colour or mixed (with additional plants in the sides)

▲ *Myosotis* 'Royal Blue'
● *Aucuba japonica* 'Variegata'
◇ Ivy 'Buttercup'

Summer

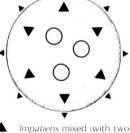

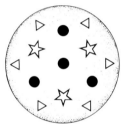

▲ *Petunia* Resisto Mixed
○ *Pelargonium* 'Frank Headley'
☆ *Lobelia* 'Light Blue Basket'

▲ *Impatiens* mixed (with two rows in the sides)
○ *Begonia* 'Frilly Red' or 'Frilly Pink'

● *Calceolaria* 'Sunshine'
☆ *Helichrysum petiolare*
△ *Petunia* 'Blue Cloud'

Planting suggestions for window boxes: Summer

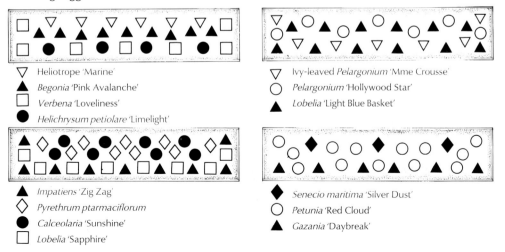

▽ Heliotrope 'Marine'
▲ *Begonia* 'Pink Avalanche'
□ *Verbena* 'Loveliness'
● *Helichrysum petiolare* 'Limelight'

▽ Ivy-leaved *Pelargonium* 'Mme Crousse'
○ *Pelargonium* 'Hollywood Star'
▲ *Lobelia* 'Light Blue Basket'

▲ *Impatiens* 'Zig Zag'
◇ *Pyrethrum ptarmaciflorum*
● *Calceolaria* 'Sunshine'
□ *Lobelia* 'Sapphire'

◆ *Senecio maritima* 'Silver Dust'
○ *Petunia* 'Red Cloud'
▲ *Gazania* 'Daybreak'

Bulb and corms 1

For colour in the spring there is nothing that quite matches the impact of flowering bulbs. Different species and cultivars can be planted in the autumn, or grown in pots to be replaced continuously, giving a succession of displays from February to May (see box on page 36).

In smaller containers and window boxes it is easier to insert pots of bulbs (page 36). Because of the limited space in such containers, it is also useful to plant layers of different kinds of bulbs, both to blend in with the other planting and also to have a succession of flowers. For example, tulips can be planted just below the surface, with daffodils somewhat deeper.

Buying bulbs
When purchasing bulbs, always go to a reputable source, even if this means paying slightly more for good quality. Bulbs should be firm to the touch.

Planting spring-flowering bulbs
Spring-flowering bulbs are planted in the autumn, as soon as possible after they have been purchased.

Preparation Soil preparation is not too critical for the range of bulbs that are likely to be the most useful in container gardening. It is always better, however, to use new compost, which must be free-draining, rather than compost that has already been used for growing summer bedding plants. If it is essential to use the same compost, just remove the plants, break up the soil with a small hand fork, and top up with new compost.

If the soil has become very dry, water thoroughly before the bulbs are planted. Allow to drain.

Planting Set the bulbs firmly in the pots or bowls at the depths indicated in the list below. Fill in with compost or bulb fibre.

Then stand the containers in a cold greenhouse or frame, or out of doors in a sheltered spot, and keep the compost moist.

Bulbs and corms for containers
Crocus*.* The spring-flowering crocuses associate well in containers with large permanent plants and look particularly well with conifers; they are useful as carpeting plants or fillers.

The Dutch crocuses are probably the best for containers as they have large, bold flowers growing to 4-5in/10-13cm in height. Cultivars: 'Jeanne d'Arc', snow white; 'Remembrance', violet-purple; 'Vanguard', pale lilac; 'Yellow Mammoth', golden yellow.

The free-flowering cultivars of *Crocus chrysanthus* and *C. biflorus* are also excellent container plants with smaller but more numerous flowers than the Dutch crocus. Cultivars: 'E.A. Bowles', deep yellow; 'Snow Bunting', white; 'Blue Pearl'; 'Lady Killer', purple and white; 'Cream Beauty'.

Crocus sieberi, quite vigorous, has several forms, usually pale mauve; but a good white one is 'Bowles White'. Flowers in February. 4in/10cm.

Plant with the "nose" of the corm just below the surface, with the corms 2in/5cm apart. Mice and voles are rather fond of crocus corms, so cover the compost with small-meshed chicken netting.

Fritillaria imperialis (crown imperial). A dramatic plant that flowers in April-May and is suitable for large tubs and other containers, as it grows up to 4ft/1.2m high. There are red and yellow forms, and one with orange flowers and white-variegated foliage. Plant 6in/15cm deep and 9in/23cm apart.

Galanthus (snowdrop). This most popular of all the spring-flowering bulbs can be planted

Crocus sieberi

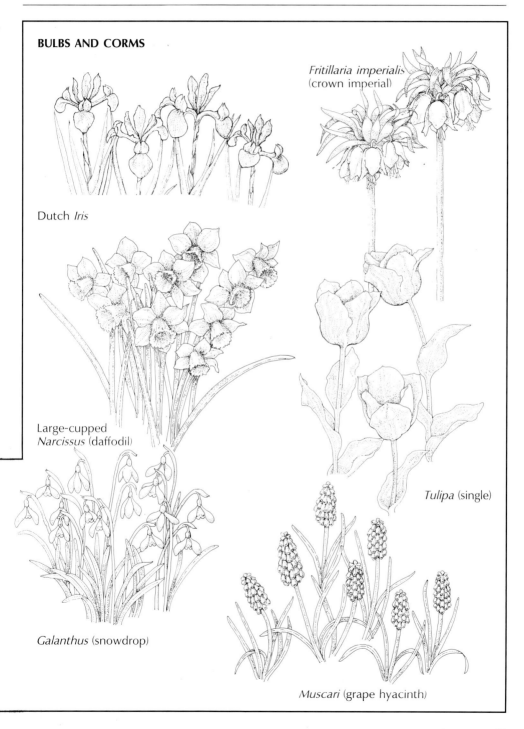

BULBS AND CORMS

Fritillaria imperialis
(crown imperial)

Dutch *Iris*

Large-cupped
Narcissus (daffodil)

Tulipa (single)

Galanthus (snowdrop)

Muscari (grape hyacinth)

Bulbs and corms 2

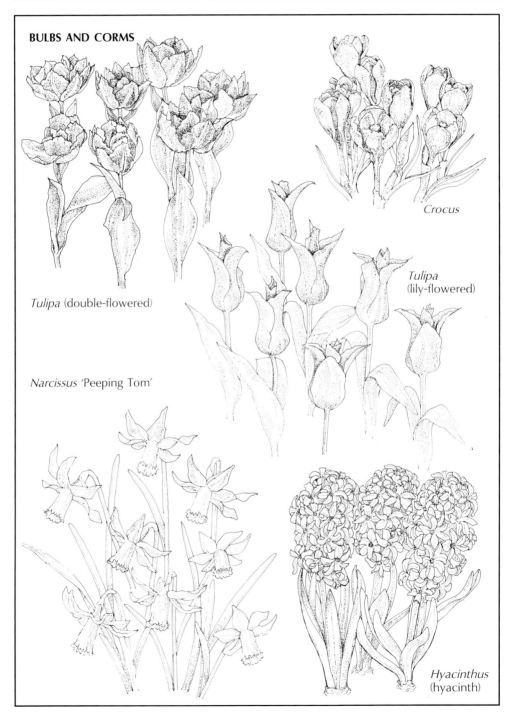

BULBS AND CORMS

Crocus

Tulipa (double-flowered)

Tulipa (lily-flowered)

Narcissus 'Peeping Tom'

Hyacinthus (hyacinth)

directly in a container, or pre-planted in pots and then inserted when flowering. Ideally, they should be planted just before the leaves die down; so long as good quality, plump, dry bulbs are selected, they should flower well if planted in the autumn.

There are many cultivars available, including ones with double flowers, but for general purposes the ordinary *Galanthus nivalis* is as good as any.

Plant snowdrops 2-4in/5-10cm deep and about 1in/2.5cm apart.

Hyacinthus (hyacinth). Rather formal when in flower, hyacinths make an early splash of colour and are most effective when planted in groups. Their heavy perfume makes them particularly attractive when planted near the house. Cultivars: 'Delft Blue', porcelain blue; 'Ostara', deep blue; 'L'Innocence', white; 'Jan Bos', deep red; 'Lady Derby', rose pink; 'Pink Pearl', deep rose pink; 'Gypsy Queen', salmon-orange; 'Yellow Hammer', yellow. All grow to about 9in/23cm high. Plant 4in/10cm deep and 5in/13cm apart.

Iris. There are many different kinds of iris, and several of the bulbous species and cultivars are excellent for window boxes or containers. The dainty *Iris reticulata* flowers in February and March, and has purple, scented flowers, with golden markings, 6in/15cm. 'Cantab' is pale blue with orange markings, 4-6in/10-15cm. 'Harmony' is sky blue with yellow markings, 4-5in/10-12.5cm. 'J.S. Dijt' is reddish-purple, 4-5 in/10-12.5cm.

Plant about 3in/7.5cm deep and 4in/10cm apart.

All the Dutch irises are good, as are *I. danfordiae* (yellow, 2-4in/5-10cm) and *I. histrioides* (light or deep blue, 4-5in/10-12cm).

Muscari (grape hyacinth). These associate well with other bulbs, especially daffodils and tulips, and in full sun or partial shade their bright blue flowers can be very effective. *M. armeniacum* is very frequently grown, with each bulb sending up several flower spikes 6-8in/15-20cm; 'Blue Spike', deep blue with white edge.

Plant 3in/7.5cm deep and 2in/5cm apart.

Narcissus (daffodil). Unless the container is reasonably large, the shorter-growing daffodils will be best. Despite their upright growth, daffodils can be effective in hanging baskets, but are rather vulnerable to wind damage, so need a sheltered spot.

There are many hundreds to choose from, in varied forms and heights, but all can be relied upon. Cultivars: 'Hawera', 8in/20cm, clear lemon yellow; 'Dove Wings', 12in/30cm, white, turned back petals, pale yellow trumpet; 'February Gold', 10in/25cm, clear yellow, long-lasting; 'February Silver', as 'February Gold' but with white petals; 'Peeping Tom', 14in/35cm, deep yellow, long-lasting; 'Tête à Tête', 6in/15cm, lemon yellow, two or more flowers on a stem, very early-flowering.

Plant the smaller bulbs listed above 2-3in/5-7.5cm deep, the larger ones 4in/10cm deep; 2-4in/5-10cm apart.

Tulipa (tulip). This has the widest colour range of all the spring-flowering bulbs, comes in varying heights and flower forms, and can be relied upon to make a dazzling display. By carefully choosing heights it is possible to obtain a double layer of colour. Tulips may also be interplanted with daffodils to give a succession of flowering. Plant 4in/10cm deep and 3-4in/7.5-10cm apart.

There are many cultivars to choose from within the various types described below:

Single Early. These begin flowering in April on short, sturdy stems about 10in/25cm high.

Double Early. Fully double flowers, particularly suitable for window boxes and tubs, 10in/25cm.

Triumph. Flowering mid-April on taller, strong stems up to 18in/45cm high.

Darwin hybrids. Late April to early May, with large, rounded flowers on stems 24in/60cm high.

Single Late. May-flowering, similar to Darwin hybrids. 24in/60cm.

Double Late. These flower in May and will give a long display in a sheltered position. Similar to the above, but with fully double flowers. 24in/60cm.

Lily-flowered. Graceful flowers with pointed petals. Can grow to 24in/60cm or higher. May-flowering.

Kaufmanniana hybrids. Dwarf and early-flowering. Can be left *in situ* to flower year after year. 12in/30cm.

Greigii hybrids. Dwarf and April-flowering with strikingly mottled and striped foliage which is attractive in itself. 12in/30cm.

Trees

Small trees, especially conifers, can be planted to give height in containers, and with care and attention can last for many years. The choice is somewhat limited, as there are few really suitable short-growing trees available.

Planting
Always purchase trees from a reputable source. Most will come already growing in pots, so transferring them to a large container is simple (page 36). Plant at most times of the year; however, generally, early autumn or late winter is better.

Watering When planting a tree in full growth, it is essential to water thoroughly and regularly, so that the tree is established as quickly as possible. If the root ball is at all dry, immerse it in water before planting. Bare-rooted or balled specimens should be treated in the same way before planting if the roots are dry.

Staking Some support may be necessary (pages 36-7 and 42-3). The stake should be at least twice as thick as the stem of the tree to be planted but should not be so tall.

Pruning Little pruning is necessary other than for cosmetic shaping if required. However, *Laurus* will require clipping at least once a year to keep it within bounds.

Deciduous trees for containers
Acer palmatum. There are many cultivars of this very attractive maple, short enough at 6ft/1.8m to be suitable for containers. Their effect can be very dramatic, with oriental overtones. Some have finely divided leaves in soft green, red or purple. Some also have coloured stems and branches. Protect from cold winds, which can damage young foliage. Always water generously. Spring-flowering bulbs associate well with maples.

Caragana arborescens 'Pendula'. A very tough small tree with yellow, pea-shaped flowers and dark green foliage on weeping branches. 5ft/1.6m.

Laurus nobilis (sweet bay). An evergreen easily clipped into shape. Maintain at 6ft/1.8m: it will reach 30ft/9m easily. Protect from frost damage in winter. The aromatic foliage can be used in cooking. Any pruning should be done in April and again in August.

Magnolia stellata (star magnolia). A relatively slow-growing magnolia making a fairly compact but well-branched large shrub. 4ft/1.2m: will grow to more than 12ft/3.6m if left unpruned. The narrow-petalled, white flowers in March and April can sometimes be damaged by frost. A cultivar called 'Royal Star' flowers slightly later and is therefore less prone to frost damage. Young plants require only limited pruning to shape; other specimens may need more severe restriction if they outgrow their container.

Salix caprea 'Pendula' (Kilmarnock willow). Another weeping tree that will stay fairly small (about 6ft/1.8m) when the roots are confined. Particularly attractive in early spring with a profusion of white, fluffy catkins on its stiff, pendulous branches.

Conifers for containers
These valuable and interesting plants are almost all evergreen, and their beauty and form can be appreciated all through the year. Although some grow very large and are grown as timber trees, many are quite small and slow-growing, and so ideal for containers. Even some of the larger ones can be useful if discarded after several years when either their condition begins to deteriorate or they become too large.

Conifers are generally thought of as being upright and pyramidal in shape, but some can be spreading and low-growing and therefore used as bold edging plants. Very little pruning is required except in August to keep them in shape.

The upright, straight-growing types are best planted in a large container such as a tub and underplanted with small permanent plantings or seasonal bedding plants: spring-flowering bulbs look particularly good.

In the list below, the measurements given are the likely heights after about ten years, provided that the plant has been kept fed and watered. Feed in spring with a slow-release general fertilizer.

Chamaecyparis lawsoniana (Lawson's cypress). This has given rise to many forms, but the following are particularly recommended: 'Ellwoodii', compact, pyramidal shape, with grey-green foliage darkening in the winter, 6ft/2m; 'Ellwood's Gold', growing like 'Ellwoodii' above but even slower; only the tips of the growth are yellow, 4ft/1.2m; *C.* 'Minima Aurea', rounded growth, with pale gold foliage, 24in/60cm; *C. obtusa* 'Crippsii', a more open shape with golden yellow growths slightly drooping at the ends, may require light pruning, 6ft/2m; *C. obtusa* 'Nana Gracilis', dense, globular shape, deep, glossy green leaves in small, fan-like sprays, 2ft 6in/75cm in 10 years; *C. pisifera* 'Boulevard', a broad pyramid with silvery blue foliage, year-round attractiveness, best in a shadier situation, may require light pruning, 3ft/1m; *C. pisifera* 'Sungold', dense, round-headed shape with golden yellow, thin, overlapping branches, rarely suffers from sun scorch, 24in/60cm.

Juniperus (juniper). Tough and hardy, tending to withstand dry conditions better than most conifers. Some grow quite upright, while others are "spreaders", which can, however, be pruned to keep within bounds. Cultivars: *Juniperus* x *media* 'Blaauw', spreading habit with blue-grey foliage, 3ft/1m; *J. chinensis* 'Pyramidalis', columnar with dense bluish-green growth, 4ft/1.2m; *J. horizontalis*, blue-green or grey-green foliage, keeps very low, 8in/20cm, spread 3ft/1m; *J.* x *media* 'Old Gold', spreading, golden foliage all the year round, height 3ft/1m, spread 3ft/1m; *J. squamata* 'Blue Carpet', almost prostrate, silvery blue foliage, fairly quick-growing, height 12in/30cm, spread about 4ft/1.2m; *J. squamata* 'Blue Star', bushy habit, intense blue-grey foliage, 12in/30cm; *J. squamata* 'Meyeri', somewhat irregular, spreading outline, blue-grey foliage, height 3ft/1m, spread 3ft/1m.

Tsuga canadensis '**Jeddeloh**'. Spreading, bun-shaped plant with light green leaves. Height 12in/30cm, spread 24in/60cm.

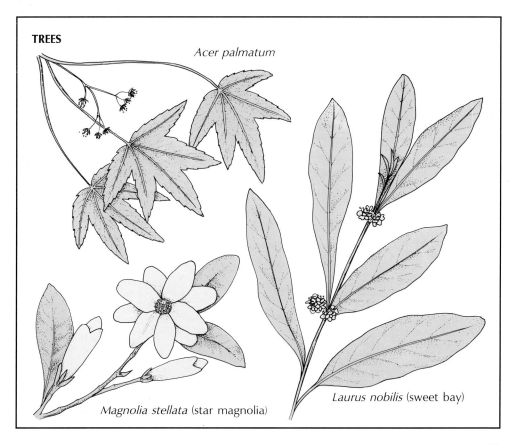

TREES

Acer palmatum

Magnolia stellata (star magnolia)

Laurus nobilis (sweet bay)

Shrubs 1

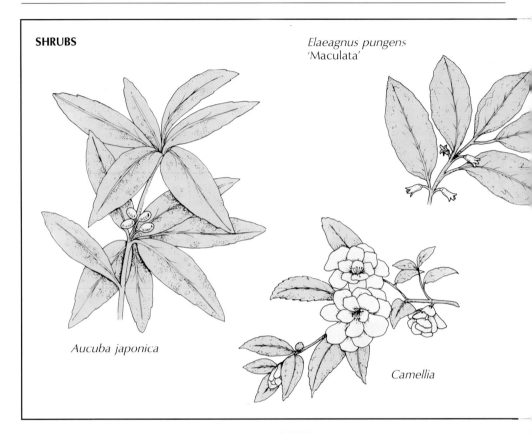

SHRUBS

Elaeagnus pungens 'Maculata'

Aucuba japonica

Camellia

Many shrubs offer long-lasting effect in containers, either with flowers or foliage, and sometimes with both. The shorter-growing shrubs can be planted in association with a tree or conifer in a large container. Plant as described on pages 36-7. It is essential to keep container shrubs watered and fed during the growing season. The foliage and roots of some may need protection in winter: containers raise root systems into an elevated position and thus make them more vulnerable to frost damage.

The following is a list of suitable shrubs for containers:

Aucuba japonica. Happy in sun or semi-shade. Large, glossy evergreen leaves. Red berries form on female plants, so long as a male plant is nearby. Cultivars: 'Picturata', male, leaves with golden centres, green margin; 'Variegata', female, leaves flecked yellow.

Height around 5ft/1.5m.
Berberis buxifolia '**Nana**'. Semi-evergreen, rounded leaves and yellow flowers in spring, forming a mound 24in/60cm high, with a spread of 24in/60cm; *B.* 'Irwinii', dense and compact, bearing small, narrow, evergreen leaves with short spines. Orange flowers in May and June. Height 2ft 6in/75cm, spread 24in/60cm.
***B.* × *stenophylla* 'Corallina Compacta'**, a small plant with golden yellow flowers and narrow, spiny evergreen leaves, 12in/30cm, spread 12in/30cm.
Buxus sempervirens (common box). An evergreen shrub with small leaves, which is often clipped to make formal shapes. Grows well in a tub, provided that it is kept regularly watered and fed. Clip during July and August.
Calluna vulgaris. Hardy evergreen, some with fine winter foliage in shades of yellow, orange and red. Flower colours range from white

Buxus sempervirens

through pinks and mauves to purple. Late summer to autumn. Up to 18in/45cm. Not lime-tolerant.

Camellia. A choice evergreen shrub which flowers in late winter and early spring. The forms *C. japonica* and *C. x williamsii* are hardy, but the beautiful flowers can be damaged by frost. Camellias are very suitable for container culture, but the receptacle should not be too large. The compost should be for acid-loving plants, and a top-dressing of new compost given each spring. Pruning in April should be just sufficient to keep in a neat shape.

C. *japonica* has many different cultivars and grows a little slower than the *C. x williamsii* group, which are often freer- and longer-flowering. *C. japonica* cultivars: 'Elegans', pink; 'Jupiter', single, deep red; 'Mathatiana', large double, dark red; 'Adolphe Audusson', red; 'Lady Vansittart', double, pink and white, often striped. *C. x williamsii* cultivars:

'Donation', semi-double pink; 'J.C. Williams', single, pale pink; 'Water Lily', semi-double, pink.

Convolvulus cneorum. A low-growing evergreen with silvery leaves that requires a warm sunny situation and some protection in cold districts. White trumpet flowers flushed with pink throughout summer. A good individual plant for a small container. Height 24in/60cm, spread 2ft 6in/75cm. Prune the shrub to shape in spring.

Elaeagnus pungens 'Maculata'. A popular evergreen with gold-centred, green-edged leaves. Spreading habit, and once established requires pruning to keep within bounds. Restrict to 4ft/1.2m in a tub.

Erica (heathers). There are numerous types of heathers which offer flower and foliage interest throughout the year, but the winter- and spring-flowering kinds are best for containers, including hanging baskets. Flowers are white, pink, purple or bicoloured, leaves are green, occasionally orange, red or yellow. The soil should not be limey, although some of the winter-flowerers will tolerate this. All heathers prefer full sun, but accept light shade. Light pruning should be given after flowering each year to retain bushy habit. Recommended: *Erica carnea* cultivars, flowering winter to early spring, lime-tolerant, 12in/30cm; *E. x darleyensis* cultivars, winter to spring, 24in/60cm; *E. cinerea* cultivars, summer-flowering, lime-tolerant, up to 18in/45cm.

Euonymus fortunei. A valuable plant with many cultivars which tend to trail or climb but which can be trimmed to keep within bounds. Without a background support, most grow to about 24in/60cm tall; they can spread up to 3ft/90cm or more. The glossy, evergreen leaves are small. All are good in shady conditions. The following cultivars are particularly recommended: 'Coloratus', trails or climbs, glossy green leaves with purple tints in winter; 'Emerald Cushion', dwarf mounded growth with emerald green foliage; 'Emerald Gaiety', silver and green variegated foliage, sometimes with pink tints in winter; 'Emerald 'n' Gold', golden and green variegation, bronzy shades in winter; 'Kewensis', a very small form with leaves to match, slow-growing; 'Silver Queen', cream variegation, fairly slow-growing.

Shrubs 2

Fatsia japonica. A superb shrub that can make a large plant 10ft/3m or more high. Tolerates shady situations. Very large, glossy evergreen foliage, with sprays of small rounded heads of white flowers in October and November. 4ft 6in/1.5m.

Fuchsia. The fuchsias listed below are hardy in mild areas, where they make shrubs; however, in cold districts they may be cut to soil level by frost in winter, so protection will be needed. Water generously in summer. Fuchsias tolerate light shade and flower in summer and autumn. In large containers a height of approximately 2ft 6in/75cm can be expected. Cultivars: 'Madame Cornelissen', red and white; 'Mrs Popple', red and purple; 'Versicolor', pink, red and white-variegated foliage, crimson flowers, reaches more than 3ft/90cm.

Hebe Evergreens, but not hardy in the coldest areas. Sun or light shade. Recommended species and cultivars: *Hebe albicans*, white flowers, fairly hardy, 18in/45cm, spread 24in/60cm; *H. armstrongii*, low-growing with long, narrow, greenish-yellow, "whipcord" shoots, 18in/45cm, spread 24in/60cm; *H.* 'Autumn Glory', erect growth, glossy green foliage, violet-blue flowers, 18in/45cm, spread 2ft 6in/75cm; *H. cupressoides* 'Boughton Dome', dense, compact, rounded mounds, which have fresh green tips to the growths during spring and summer, 3ft/90cm, spread 2ft 6in/75cm; *H.* 'Carl Teschner', forms mounds of small dark green foliage, violet flowers; *H.* x *franciscana* (often grown incorrectly as a form of *H. elliptica*) 'Variegata', mounds of small leaves with cream variegation, violet flowers, requires a sheltered situation, 12in/30cm, spread 24in/60cm; *H.* x *franciscana* 'Blue Gem', dome-shaped, with bright blue flowers, 24in/60cm, spread 24in/60cm; 'Great Orme', compact growth, with spikes of pink flowers, 2ft 6in/75cm, spread 2ft 6in/75cm; *H.* 'Marjorie', rounded shrub, hardy, pale violet and white flowers, 2ft 6in/75cm, spread 2ft 6in/75cm; 'Midsummer Beauty', rounded bush, fairly strong-growing and moderately hardy, with dark lilac flowers; *H. pinguifolia* 'Pagei', small mounds with silver-grey foliage and white flowers, hardier than 'Great Orme', but not reliably hardy, height 12in/30cm, spread 24in/60cm.

Hydrangea. Valuable late-flowering shrubs

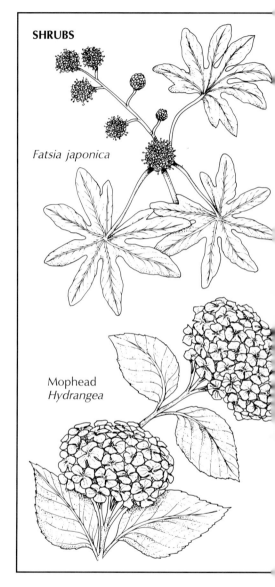

SHRUBS

Fatsia japonica

Mophead
Hydrangea

requiring plenty of moisture and generous feeding. A sheltered, lightly shaded site is best. Up to 5ft/1.5m high and as much across with plenty of root run. The old flowerheads should not be removed until March in order to give protection to the buds in winter. Prune out weak growths at the same time.

Two main forms are available: lacecap hydrangeas, with flat flowerheads edged with

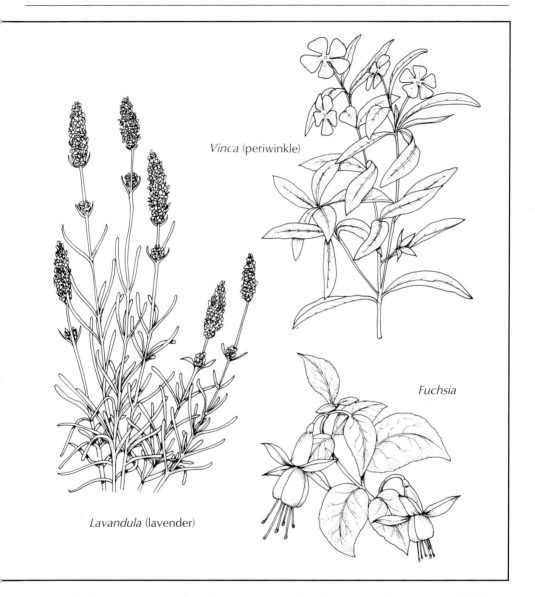

Vinca (periwinkle)

Fuchsia

Lavandula (lavender)

large sterile flowers; and mophead hydrangeas with dome-shaped flowerheads. Both types have white, pink, reddish or blue flowered cultivars. A special blueing powder may be required to keep this colour constant.

Hypericum. Clear yellow, cup-shaped flowers held on fairly stiff stems, blooming profusely throughout the summer and on into early autumn. Little pruning is required. Cultivars and hybrids for containers include: *H*. 'Hidcote', a semi-evergreen which, although growing quite large, can be kept smaller by spring pruning, up to 4ft 6in/1.5m; *H.* x *moserianum*, a first-rate, dwarf shrub with large yellow flowers, 24in/40cm, spread 2ft 6in/75cm; H. x *moserianum* 'Tricolor', with leaves variegated white, pink and green, best in a sheltered position as slightly tender, 24in/60cm, spread

Shrubs 3

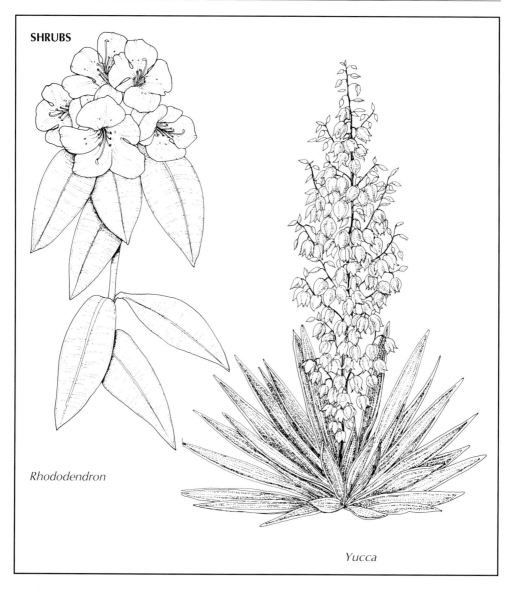

SHRUBS

Rhododendron

Yucca

24in/60cm.
Lavender. See *Lavandula*.
Lavandula (lavender). Evergreen shrubs varying from plants 12in/30cm or so high to 3ft/90cm. Mauve or purple flowers, grey foliage. Enjoy full sun. Prune fairly hard in the spring. Cultivars: 'Grappenhall', long spikes of lavender-purple flowers, 4ft/1.2m; 'Hidcote', 12in/30cm; 'Munstead Dwarf', 24in/60cm.

Nandina domestica (sacred bamboo). Lovely bronze foliage in spring, turning green in summer, and red and purple in the autumn. White flowers. A smaller form has foliage that remains reddish-purple all the time. Requires a well-drained soil in full sun, with root protection in winter, height 3ft/90cm, spread 24in/60cm.
Periwinkle. See *Vinca*.

Phlomis fruticosa (Jerusalem sage). Grey-green foliage and yellow flowers appearing in whorls all the way up the stem. Withstands drought well but may be damaged by severe frost. Full sun. Height 2ft 6in/75cm, spread 3ft/90cm.

Phormium tenax. Tall, sword-shaped leaves, some with bronze foliage, others vividly variegated. Winter protection under cover is a wise precaution in cold areas. Some cultivars are dwarf at 12in/30cm, while the tallest can attain over 6ft/1.8m. In flower may reach 10ft/3m.

Rhododendron. Whereas the larger-growing kinds of rhododendrons can be regarded as short-term container plants, the dwarf and compact hybrids of *R. yakushimanum* in white and shades of pink, red and pale mauve are ideal for growing in large containers. The flowers open in May and early June and should be removed, complete with the old stalks, as they fade, to prevent seed pods from forming.

The Japanese evergreen and semi-evergreen rhododendrons—better known as azaleas—also make superb specimens in pots or tubs. They are low-growing, spreading out their branches in horizontal layers which become completely covered in flowers of white, pink, red, orange or violet. Partial shade is ideal and shelter from cold winds preferable. Height 3ft/90cm, spread 3ft/90cm.

All rhododendrons require a lime-free soil and need regular watering in the growing season.

Rosa (rose). The miniature kinds of roses with white, pink, red, yellow and orange flowers bloom for a long period in summer and are ideal for troughs and tubs. Prune by simply removing flowers as they fade and any weak growth in spring. Height 12in/30cm, spread 12in/30cm.

Rose. See *Rosa*.

Rue. See *Ruta*.

Ruta graveolens (common rue). Very hardy and ideal as a specimen plant. Blue-green leaves, yellow flowers in summer. Full sun is best. Can grow to about 3ft/90cm. 'Jackman's Blue' is more compact and 'Variegata' has leaves splashed creamy-white.

Sage. See *Salvia officinalis*.

Salvia officinalis (common sage) The leaves are grey-green and used for seasoning (see also pages 83 and 85). Bluish-purple flowers in summer. The following varieties are very decorative: 'Icterina', leaves variegated green and yellow; 'Purpurascens', purple foliage; 'Tricolor', creamy-white variegation splashed with purple and pink, 24in/60cm, spread 2ft 6in/75cm. Sage may be damaged by frost but soon recovers. Prune hard in spring to retain the shrub's shape.

Santolina chamaecyparisus. Silvery, aromatic foliage with yellow, button-like flowerheads in summer. Requires full sun. 1ft 6in/45cm, spread 1ft 6in/45cm. Prune hard in spring.

Senecio 'Sunshine'. Has yellow daisy-like flowerheads throughout the summer and silvery, evergreen foliage. Full sun and restriction of the roots will keep it to a manageable size in a large container, though hard pruning may be needed every third spring to retain a neat shape. Height 3ft/90cm, spread 3ft/90cm.

Vinca (periwinkle). A low, prostrate shrub, with evergreen foliage on long, arching growths. The blue flowers are borne on shorter, more upright growths. Tolerant of full or partial shade but best in full sun. Species and cultivars: *Vinca major*, blue flowers, glossy leaves; *V. major* 'Maculata', central splash of yellow on the leaves; *V. major* 'Variegata', foliage marginally bordered creamy-white, 16in/40cm, spread indefinite; *V. minor*, not so vigorous as *V. major*, with smaller leaves and flowers; *V. minor* 'Alba Variegata', leaves edged pale yellowish-white, height 8in/20cm, spread indefinite. Prune all hard in the spring.

Weigela florida. A deciduous shrub somewhat uninteresting in winter, but with attractive pink or red flowers in early summer. Variegated and purple-leaved forms are also available. Sun or partial shade. Height 3ft/90cm, spread 3ft/90cm.

Yucca. Sword-shaped leaves give a tropical effect, but their sharp points should be borne in mind when siting the container. Yuccas grow well in tubs. Several cultivars are available, some with variegated leaves. Imposing clusters of bell-shaped white flowers on long stems well above the foliage. Full sun. Height 2ft 6in/75cm, spread 3ft/90cm. No pruning is required.

Hardy perennials 1

Hardy herbaceous perennials tend to be used in more permanent container plantings, either associated with shrubs or as a main feature. Their top growth dies down each winter to a perennial root system which sends up new shoots and flowers the following year.

Propagation

Generally, the best method of increasing is by division. This is a simple operation in which the root system is split down into smaller clumps during the dormant season. The strong outside growths should be retained and replanted in their flowering positions.

Some may be grown from seed sown in autumn or spring either out of doors or in gentle heat in a greenhouse. They are subsequently grown on out of doors for flowering the following year. The following is a list of plants suitable for containers.

Acanthus spinosus. Grown mainly for its large, arching, glossy green foliage with bold-toothed edges and spines. Purple and white flowers in July. Full sun. 4ft/1.2m high, foliage a little shorter; spread 3ft/90cm.
Achillea 'Moonshine'. Sulphur-yellow flowers from June to August, with feathery silver foliage. Full sun. Height 24in/60cm, spread 12in/30cm. Also: *A. millefolium* hybrids (white, pink, cerise).
Agapanthus. Imposing, especially when grown as a specimen plant, with globular heads of blue or white flowers on long stems and long, narrow, basal leaves. Flowering July and August. Full sun. Height 2ft 6in/75cm, spread 2ft 6in/75cm. Although the Headbourne Hybrids are hardy, some winter protection should be given to *Agapanthus* grown in containers.
Ajuga reptans. Carpet plant tolerant of sun or shade, bearing blue flower spikes in May and June. 6in/15cm. Various coloured-leaved cultivars are particularly attractive: 'Atropurpurea', purplish leaves; 'Burgundy Glow', reddish-purple with bronze and yellow variegation; 'Multicolor', red and bronze variegation; 'Variegata', vigorous, with white and grey-green variegation.
Aquilegia vulgaris. The modern hybrids of the columbine have large flowers with long spurs on each petal. Relatively short-lived,

and should be raised from seed every four years. Aquilegias tolerate sun or shade. Flowering May and June. Cultivars: 'McKana Hybrids' have a wide colour range, are 24in/60cm high with a spread of 18in/45cm; Music Series is slightly shorter but with larger flowers; Star Series is available in blue, red or white.

Aquilegias are easily raised from seed sown outdoors or in a greenhouse in the spring and then grown on out of doors to flower the following year in May and June.
Astrantia major. Thick clumps of lobed leaves

HARDY HERBACEOUS PERENNIALS

Acanthus spinosus

Achillea millefolium hybrid

in semi-shade or shade. 'Sunningdale Variegated' has leaves variegated cream and pale yellow. White flowerheads with a green tinge; variants with purplish-red flowerheads are also available. June to August. Height 24in/60cm, spread 18in/45cm.

Doronicum. Valuable early-flowering plants with golden-yellow, daisy-like flowers from April to June. Sun or shade. Cultivars: 'Miss Mason', 18in/45cm, spread 12in/30cm; 'Spring Beauty', fully double and slightly shorter.

Euphorbia myrsinites. Grey-green leaves on arching, eventually spreading stems and lime-green flowerheads in March and April. Full sun. 6in/15cm. *E. polychroma* has sulphur-yellow flowerheads in March and April, which fade green. The whole plant looks well throughout the summer, even after flowering. Sun or semi-shade. Height 18in/45cm, spread 18in/45cm.

Helianthemum (sun rose). Helianthemums are available in a range of colours: yellow, orange, pink and red. May to July. Full sun. 6-12in/15-30cm, spread 12-24in/30-60cm. Cut hard back

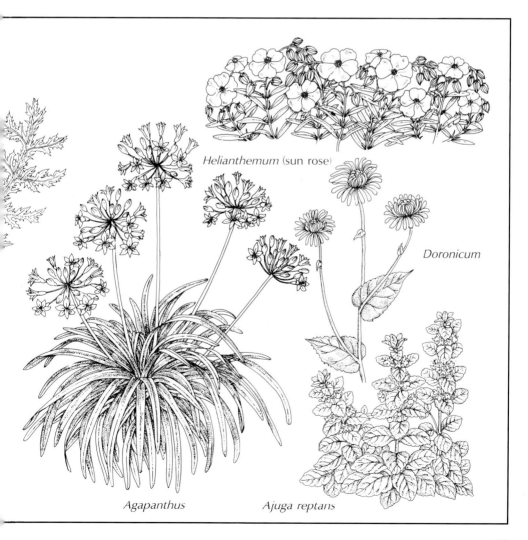

Helianthemum (sun rose)

Doronicum

Agapanthus

Ajuga reptans

Hardy perennials 2

after flowering to keep neat and bushy.

Hosta (plantain lily). Broad, imposing foliage and mauve or lavender, lily-like flowers in July and August. Some hostas have attractive variegated leaves. Particularly fine as specimen plants, but also associate well with other plants in semi-shade or shade. Flower spikes can reach 3ft/90cm, spread 24in/60cm.

Incarvillea delavayi. The rosy-red, trumpet-shaped flowers last for a long time, but the plant may need protection in winter. Sun. May to July. Height 18in/45cm, spread 12in/30cm.

Lamium maculatum. Tolerant of sun or shade, flowering April to June, up to 6in/15cm high and creeping. Various cultivars with differently coloured flowers and usually variegated foliage. 'Beacon Silver' has silvery, purple-tinted leaves and mauve-pink flowers; 'Chequers' has marbled foliage and deep pink flowers.

Lysimachia nummularia (creeping Jenny). An excellent trailing plant for sun or shade, and a good hanging basket plant. Yellow, broad-petalled, star-shaped flowers from June to August. 2in/5cm. A golden-leaved form

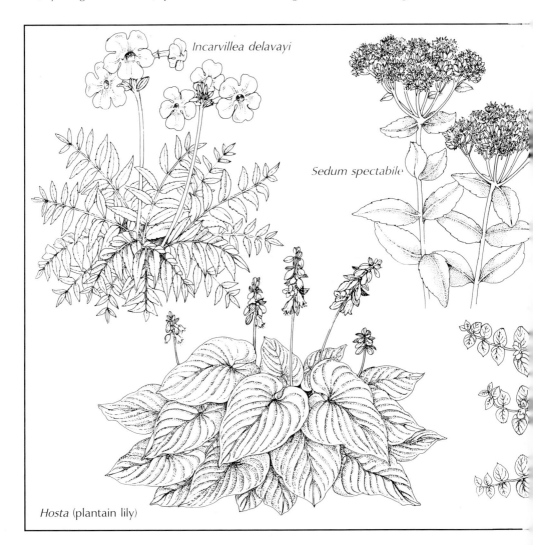

Incarvillea delavayi

Sedum spectabile

Hosta (plantain lily)

'Aurea' is also recommended.

Melissa officinalis (balm) Very aromatic foliage and upright habit. Sun or semi-shade, height 24in/60cm, spread 12in/30cm. Golden-leaved and yellow-variegated forms are available. See also page 82.

Phalaris arundinacea var. ***picta***. Commonly called 'gardener's garters'. A white-striped grass attractive throughout the growing season. Sun or semi-shade, height 32in/80cm, spread 24in/60cm.

Pulmonaria (lungwort). Early-flowering plants (March to May) with green or silvery-grey, often spotted foliage, and blue, red, white or rosy pink flowers depending on variety. Semi-shade or shade, 8in/20cm, spread 12in/30cm.

Sedum spectabile. Autumn-flowering plant (August to October) with cool green succulent leaves handsome all summer. Drought-resistant. Flat flowerheads that are particularly attractive to butterflies. Sun, height 18in/45cm, spread 18in/45cm. Cultivars: 'Autumn Joy', bright rose flowers, purplish stems; 'Brilliant', pink flowers.

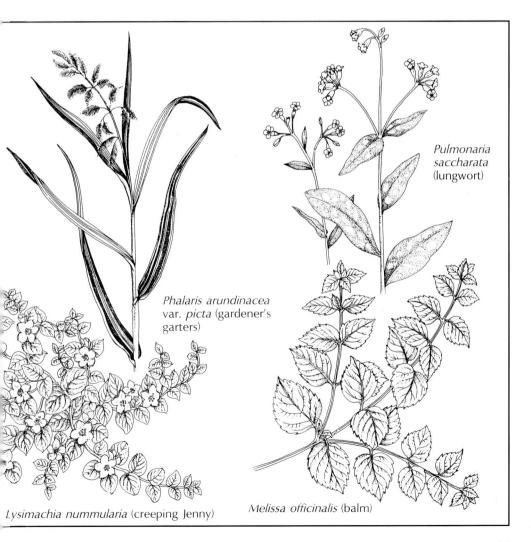

Pulmonaria saccharata (lungwort)

Phalaris arundinacea var. *picta* (gardener's garters)

Lysimachia nummularia (creeping Jenny)

Melissa officinalis (balm)

Herbs 1

Many herbs make ideal container plants and can be attractive as well as useful.

Site
Almost all herbs grow well in a sunny position, but some tolerate semi-shade and dry conditions. As container plants, they require reasonably moist soil to thrive. For easy harvesting, herbs should be sited as near to the kitchen as possible, especially when they are needed regularly. They can also be cultivated in growing bags, under glass if preferred (page 116).

Sowing seeds
Herbs can be bought as plants, but also raised from seed sown either directly out of doors or in pots and boxes on a window sill. A wide range of containers can be used.

Parsley pot
A parsley pot is a popular way of growing window sill herbs. It is rather like a miniature strawberry pot (page 22), about 15in/43cm high and 5in/13cm in diameter, perforated with a number of holes (without the protruding lower lips that are found on strawberry pots).

The pot should be filled with compost, and a tiny pinch of seed then sown in each hole and seed also scattered on the top surface. The compost should be kept moist. After germination, the seedlings in each hole are reduced to one.

By this method, fresh parsley can be grown on a window sill—particularly useful during the winter when none is available out of doors.

Making a herb wheel
An attractive and novel way to grow herbs is to construct a herb "wheel". This makes a special feature in a garden or on a patio. Its individual compartments, between the "spokes" of the wheel, help to confine the more invasive herbs such as mint. Evenly cut pieces of stone can be used, but ordinary house bricks will be easier to lay.

A short length of large-diameter drainpipe or a short chimney pot in the centre forms the wheel's "hub". As an alternative, a clay flower pot can be used, but a straight-sided container looks best. A central plant can be grown in this.

Fill in the sections made by the "spokes" with good garden soil mixed with a little peat, or, better still, John Innes Potting Compost No.2. Make sure that the soil is gently firmed during the filling, and bring the level right to the top of the bricks to allow for settlement.

Water the newly planted herbs thoroughly. The wheel may also be used as a permanent container for other plants and looks very attractive planted with low-growing bedding plants.

Herbs for containers
Balm. A perennial with lemon-scented leaves. 24in/60cm. Sow outdoors April to May and either thin out the seedlings or transplant them to their final position.
Borage. Oval green leaves and pendent blue flowers. 3ft/90cm. Better in a large container. Sow outdoors April to May.
Chives. The fine, onion-flavoured leaves appear early in the year and the highly decorative mauve flowerheads are an added bonus in early summer. 18in/45cm. Sow outdoors April to June.
Coriander. An annual with finely divided foliage and clusters of aromatic seeds. 12in/30cm. Sow in May, thinning out seedlings later.
Fennel. Although a perennial, fennel is often treated as an annual. The feathery foliage and stems have a distinct aniseed flavour. It can grow quite tall: 4ft/1.2m. A purple-leaved variant makes a decorative foil for other plants, especially in the spring. Sow April to May, thinning out later.
Marjoram. Pot marjoram is a perennial, with small green leaves and clusters of tiny rose-purple flowers. 15in/38cm. Sow outdoors April to May.
Mint. There are several kinds of this popular perennial, including several variegated forms. 24in/60cm. The latter, and several others with different flavours such as 'Apple Mint' and 'Peppermint', are best bought as small plants. The ordinary mint (spearmint) can, however, be grown successfully from seed sown out of doors in March and April. Because of its spreading nature, mint is best grown in a confined space such as a herb wheel, or in a

container, rather than in open ground where it becomes invasive. Tolerates light shade.

Parsley. The curly-leaved cultivars are very decorative, but some people consider the plain-leaved type has a superior flavour. Can be grown in specially made containers (see page 22), which facilitate gathering if they are sited in the kitchen. 9in/23cm. Cultivators: 'Moss Curled'; 'Consort'; 'Hamburg', with long fleshy, edible roots. With exception of last, all are easy to cultivate in growing bags. Sow seed from March to July. Germination is slow, so it is best to keep the container in a shady position. When in full growth parsley will tolerate some shade. Thin the seedlings down to one plant, as parsley resents being transplanted.

Rosemary. The cultivar 'Miss Jessop's Upright' is an ideal shrub for the centre of a herb wheel. 4ft/1.2m. Perennial. It is more usual to obtain grown plants, as these are propagated from a known cultivar, but it is also possible to raise from seed. Sow in March in a greenhouse or on a warm window sill, and grow the plants on in separate small pots.

Sage. Another small shrub thriving in a sunny situation. Grey-green, wrinkled leaves, and small tubular violet-blue flowers. 24in/60cm. Sow out of doors April to May.

Savory. Summer savory is an annual with green leaves and tiny, tubular, lilac flowers. Sow out of doors in April. Winter savory is a perennial with grey-green leaves, and tiny, rose-purple, tubular flowers; it prefers dry, fairly poor soil. Both 12in/30cm. Sow outdoors April to May.

Sweet basil. This annual with oval green leaves should be sown in a greenhouse or on a sunny window sill for early use. There is a purple-leaved variety which is attractive when used in association with decorative plants. Will tolerate semi-shade. 9in/23cm.

Tarragon. A perennial with grey-green leaves and loose clusters of tiny, greenish-white flowerheads. Grows to about 24in/60cm high. Tarragon can be propagated by division in March and April; grow the pieces on out of doors in open ground or in pots. Cuttings of the new growth root easily in the spring.

Thyme. Short-growing perennial with aromatic, dark green leaves and clusters of tiny mauve flowers. Sun or semi-shade. 9in/23cm. Sow outdoors April to May.

Making a herb wheel

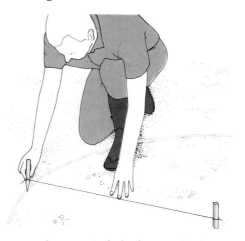

1 Mark out a circle by hammering in a peg and marking the circumference with a pencil (or stick) and a length of string, used like a pair of compasses. (*continues on page 84*)

Borage
(*Borago officinalis*)

Herbs 2

Making a herb wheel (continued)

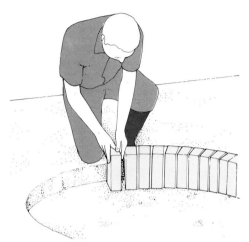

2 Dig out the soil inside the circle to a depth of approximately 6 in/15 cm. Remove the loose earth, and tread and firm the base to make a flat surface.

3 Lay a row of bricks vertically on the inside of the circle. Keep the tops of the bricks level, a few inches above the surrounding area. Cement the bricks.

Chives (*Allium schoenoprasum*)

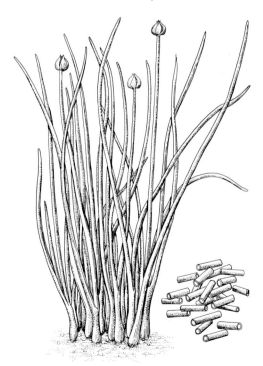

Fennel (*Foeniculum vulgare*)

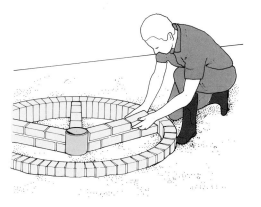

4 Place a length of drainpipe or a chimney pot in the middle of the circle. Mark lines for the "spokes". Lay and cement together rows of bricks on these lines.

5 Fill in the segments with potting compost or a mixture of soil and peat. Firm gently during filling, bringing the level to the top of the bricks to allow for settlement.

Rosemary (*Rosemarinus officinalis*)

Sage (*Salvia officinalis*)

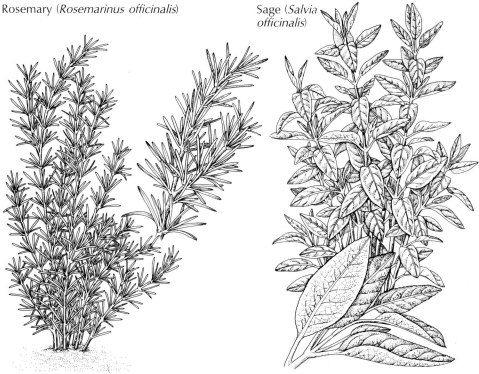

Plants for a sink garden 1

A careful choice of alpines, rock plants and small bulbs can create a most attractive and interesting display in a stone sink. If the sink is raised on bricks, the effect can be further enhanced by underplanting.

Planting a sink

Do not plant later than July: it is necessary to give the plants long enough to establish their root systems before the onset of winter weather.

Preparation Place some drainage material in the base of the sink and cover the plughole with a large piece of old clay flower pot placed concave-side downwards. Drainage material can consist of old clay pots, broken bricks, gravel or washed ashes to a depth of about 2in/5cm.

The compost will differ according to the type of plant grown. Plants requiring more moisture (and sometimes shade) need John Innes Potting Compost No.2, with the addition of 25 percent peat and 25 percent coarse sand. Plants with a sharper drainage requirement need the same compost, with just the 25 percent extra peat.

The sink needs to be filled almost to the brim, as this will allow for natural settlement. Firm the layers of compost as the work proceeds. When the sink is full, small pieces of stone can be strategically placed on top to create a miniature landscape setting.

Planting Grouping of the plants will need to be done with care to create a balanced effect. Most sinks are planted with a range of suitable dwarf plants of different genera; however, variants of a single genus, such as the house leek (Sempervivum), can also be attractive.

After planting, sprinkle a layer of gravel or stone chippings on the surface. This will not only make the planting more attractive, but will help to conserve moisture.

On pages 88 and 89 are a few ideas for layouts, and below is a list of suitable plants for sink gardens. Most should be available from good garden centres and specialist nurserymen.

"Outcrops" of stone can be positioned in the sink for additional interest. Where stones are placed together the crevices so formed can be planted with suitable plants—for example, cushion-forming plants. Position them as the "landscaping" proceeds.

Alpines

Allium amabile, tufts of fine leaves, reddish-purple flowers, flower stem about 6in/15cm.
Androsace sarmentosa, silvery leaves in tufts, pink flowers; *A. carnea*, tufts of very small green, narrow leaves, with pink or red flowers; *A. chamaejasme*, silvery, pointed leaves growing in rosettes, with white, yellow-eyed flowers; *A. sempervivoides*, overlapping, smooth green leaves, pink flowers; *A.villosa*, mats of greyish leaves and white flowers. All grow to approximately 6in/15cm when in flower.
Armeria juniperifolia, dense-growing hummocks of narrow, dark leaves, stemless heads of pink flowers, 4in/10cm.
Asperula lilaciflora, dwarf, cushion-like growth, green leaves, pink flowers 2-3in/5-7cm; *A. nitida*, dense tangled growth of dark green leaves, clusters of pink flowers, 2in/5cm; *A. suberosa*, mats of greyish foliage smothered in pink flowers, 3in/7.5cm.
Campanula arvatica, rosettes of small leaves. Bears starry, rich violet flowers, 2in/5cm.
C. 'Elizabeth Oliver', compact mat of pale green leaves, blue flowers June to August.
C. fenestrellata, a rock-hugging plant with radiating stems, white-centred blue flowers.
C. garganica 'Dickson's Gold', crevice plant,

Planting a sink

1 Insert drainage material (such as gravel) up to a depth of 2in/5cm.

radiating stems, with masses of star-shaped flowers.

***C. pilosa* 'Superba'**, foliage in rosettes, flowers bell-shaped, light blue on 3in/7cm stems.

Centaurium scilloides, shiny green leaves, flowers clear pink on short stems.

Cyananthus microphyllus, stems prostrate forming mats on the edge of which appear purple flowers.

Dianthus alpinus, mats of narrow green leaves, rose-crimson flowers, 2in/5cm; *D. freynii*, tufted grey-green leaves smothered in pale pink flowers during the summer, 1in/2.5cm; *D. microlepis*, neat, rounded tufts of tiny grey leaves, many small pink flowers, 1in/2.5cm; *D. myrtinerius*, tight cushions of foliage with many bright pink flowers, 1in/2.5cm.

Draba rigida, small hummocky growth, yellow flowers, 2in/5cm.

***Dryas octopetala* 'Minor'**, compact form with oak-shaped leaves and large white flowers on short stems.

Erodium reichardii (Syn. *E. chamaedryoides*), white, pink-veined flowers held above mats of dark green leaves, 1in/2.5cm. *E. corsicum*, downy foliage growing in tufts, pink flowers veined deep pink, 1in/2.5cm.

Gentiana acaulis (*G. excisa*), large, azure blue trumpets, 3in/7.5cm, requires lime-free soil.

G. farreri, light blue flowers appearing in autumn. Slightly lime-tolerant.

G. saxosa, very dark green foliage in rosettes, flowers white marked with purple veining, 4in/10cm.

G. verna, deep blue flowers which appear in spring, 3in/7.5cm.

Geranium farreri, grey-green leaves in tufts, pink cup-shaped flowers.

***Hypericum empetrifolium* 'Prostratum'**, evergreen with woody trailing stems, rich yellow flowers.

Petrocallis pyrenaica, neat cushions of downy shoots, white, fragrant flowers, 1in/2.5cm.

Phlox caespitosa, cushion of close-growing shoots, flowers white or lavender, scented.

P. douglasii, many hybrids, all suitable cushion-forming plants, flowers white, pink, red and mauve.

P. hoodii, prostrate with almost stemless white flowers.

Polygala calcarea, prostrate with dark green leaves, blue flowers.

***P. chamaebuxus* 'Purpurea'**, firm, small leaves, flowers carmine and yellow. Light shade.

Potentilla eriocarpa, grey-green foliage growing in mats, short-stemmed yellow flowers.

2 Fill with the appropriate compost, firming as you proceed. Landscape with small stones.

3 Plant, and then sprinkle a layer of gravel or stone chippings on the surface. This will help conserve moisture.

Plants for a sink garden 2

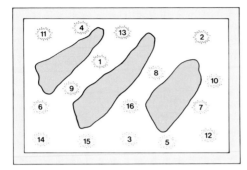

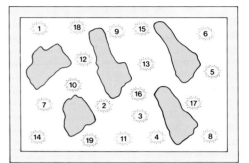

1	Campanula pilosa 'Superba'	9	Primula minima
2	Chamaecyparis obtusa 'Nana'	10	Ramonda myconi
		11	Rhododendron campylogynum var. myrtilloides
3	Cyananthus microphyllus	12	Rhododendron prostratum/radicans
4	Cyclamen coum	13	Salix x boydii
5	Gentiana saxosa	14	Salix reticulata
6	Iris lacustris	15	Saxifraga cochleacis 'Minor'
7	Narcissus asturiensis	16	Soldanella minima
8	Polygala chamaebuxus 'Purpurea'		

1	Allium amabile	12	Gentiana verna
2	Androsace carnea	13	Petrophytum hendersonii
3	Asperula nitida		
4	Campanula arvatica	14	Phlox douglasii 'Violet Queen'
5	Campanula 'Elizabeth Oliver'	15	Potentilla verna 'Nana'
6	Chamaecyparis obtusa 'Nana'	16	Saxifraga 'Boston Spa'
7	Cyclamen cilicium	17	Saxifraga 'Jenkinsae'
8	Dianthus myrtinervis	18	Saxifraga paniculata 'Baldensis'
9	Dianthus subacaulis	19	Viola adunca
10	Douglasia laevigata		
11	Genista delphinensis		

P. verna **'Nana'**, mat-forming, small yellow flowers on trailing stems.

P. marginata, jagged, silver-edged foliage growing in rosettes, flowers ranging from lavender, blue and purple.

Primula minima, low-growing, with pale pink or white flowers, in spring, 2in/5cm.

Raoulia australis, flat carpets of tiny silvery leaves, very small yellow flowers, 1in/2.5cm.

Ramonda myconi, flowers, flat, wide-petalled, purple-blue, on short stems.

Rhodohypoxis baurii, narrow stems, flowers white, pink to deep red on very short stems.

Saponaria x *olivana*, cushions of green stems, large pink flowers.

Saxifraga **'Boston Spa'**, mat-forming with rich yellow flowers.

S. **'Bridget'**, tight rosettes of silvery leaves, pink flowers.

S. cochlearis **'Minor'**, tight cushions of silver-grey leaves, white flowers, 6-9in/15-23cm.

S. **'Jenkinsae'**, foliage bluish-grey growing in rosettes, stemless blue-pink flowers.

S. paniculata **'Baldensis'**, compact growth, white flowers, 2in/5cm.

S. x *petraschii*, grey-green mounds with large

white flowers on 2in/5cm stems.

S. **'Winifred Bevington'** flat-growing, tufts of dark green foliage, stemless large pink flowers.

Sedum: many dwarf species are suitable.

Sempervivum: many species and cultivars are suitable.

Soldanella alpina, tufts of small, leathery leaves, with lavender, bell-shaped flowers, 1in/2.5cm, suitable for semi-shade; *S. minima*, spoon-shaped leaves, blue flowers, 2in/5cm, suitable for semi-shade.

Teucrium subspinosum, spiky, mat-forming stems, leaves silvery, crimson flowers.

Veronica bombycina, silvery-white foliage, with short-stemmed, porcelain-blue flowers, 2in/5cm.

V. caespitosa, dense tufted growth, with pink, star-shaped flowers, 1in/2.5cm.

V. prostrata **'Nana'**, evergreen foliage, very dwarf form, flowers blue.

Viola adunca, compact growth with somewhat woody but leafy stems, violet or lavender flowers with white centres.

Viola aetolica, Neat tufts of toothed leaves, yellow flowers, 2in/5cm.

Viola pedata, quite large short-stemmed flow-

and March. Cultivars: 'Amsterdam Forcing', 'Early French Frame', 'Rondo'.

Courgette. Seeds can be sown individually in small pots in April and early May in warmth, or directly into a growing bag placed outdoors in May or June. Two plants can be grown in a bag. Plenty of water must be given at all times. Varieties: 'Green Bush' and 'Zucchini'. See also under Marrow (page 92).

Cucumber. Sow singly in pots in April or May in heated conditions. Do not plant out into raised beds until all frosts have finished. Ridge cucumbers are low-growing and trailing, but their leading shoots can be cut back to keep the plant within bounds. Cultivars: 'Long Green' and 'Tasty Green', both producing fruits comparable to greenhouse cultivars; 'Venlo Pickling', small-fruited and therefore good for preserving in small jars; 'Crystal Apple', with pale-skinned, round fruits. The latter will require training up a support.

Cucumbers are easy to cultivate in growing bags, from sowings made at the same time as for raised beds. All the cultivars mentioned above do well in growing bags.

French bean. Dwarf French beans are vigorous bushy plants and produce a large quantity of beans if picked regularly. Sow in raised beds April to July. Cultivars: 'Masterpiece', 'Sprite' and 'Tendergreen'.

For growing bags, sow in June directly into the bag to give eight evenly distributed plants. For a slightly earlier crop, sow seeds in warmth in April and transplant. Cultivars: 'Kinghorn Wax'; 'Masterpiece'; 'Sprite'; 'The Prince'.

In growing bags, the climbing type of French bean attains a height of around 5ft/1.5m, so will need support. Sow seeds as for dwarf beans. Cultivars: 'Blue Lake', 'Hunter' and 'Purple Podded'.

Kohl rabi. The small, bulbous stem which grows above the soil should be eaten when young. Sow in raised beds mid-April to mid-July. Cultivars: 'Purple Vienna' and 'White Vienna' have a cabbage/turnip flavour.

Lettuce. Sow in raised beds between March and June depending on cultivar. There are so many cultivars to choose from, but the following can be relied upon when sown in succession at fortnightly intervals. 'Fortune' and 'Unrivalled', ideal for summer use; 'Avondefiance', sow June to July for harvesting September and October; 'Tom Thumb', smaller type; 'Continuity', reddish foliage; 'Webb's Wonderful', 'Windermere' and 'Lake Nyah', crisp heads of good quality; 'Salad Bowl' and 'Red Salad Bowl' are non-hearting and produce leaves that can be picked as

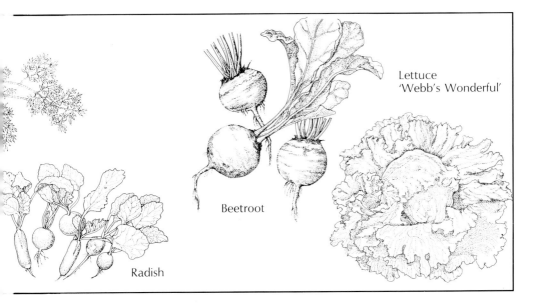

Radish

Beetroot

Lettuce 'Webb's Wonderful'

Vegetables 2

required; 'Lollo Rosso', fringed foliage, tinged with red; 'Lobjoits Cos Green' is a useful cos type; 'Little Gem', small-growing and intermediate between cabbage and cos types of lettuce, quick to mature and succeeding well in dry, hot conditions; 'Valdor', sown in autumn to mature in spring.

All of these cultivars of lettuce are very easily cultivated in growing bags; eight or more plants can be accommodated in each bag. Sow from March to July, or in September for those varieties which stand the winter and can be cut the following spring. Regular watering is important in dry weather.

Marrow. One plant can produce many fruits, especially when cut young, as with courgettes (see above). Sow in raised beds May to June, or singly in small pots in April and early May for planting out 2ft 6in/75cm apart. Can be grown as single plants in a growing bag. Cultivars: 'Green Bush'; 'Zucchini'.

Onion. The salad type (often called spring onions) is the most useful in a small area. Sow March to early May in raised beds or growing bags. Cultivar: 'White Lisbon'.

Pea. Sow the following cultivars in raised beds either November or January to March: 'Meteor'; 'Piklot'; 'Feltham First'. Sow the following March to June: 'Hurst's Green Shaft';

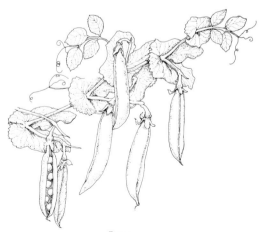

Peas

'Onward'.

Radish. Radishes will tolerate some light shade and cooler conditions. Sow in raised beds March to September. Keep well watered. Cultivars: 'Scarlet Globe', 'Saxa', 'French Breakfast' and 'Long White Icicle', all maturing very quickly; 'Black Spanish Round', 'China Rose' and 'Mino Early' have very large roots which can be left *in situ*. Some protection with straw may be required in severe weather.

For growing bags, sow a few seeds at a time from March to September in three rows running the length of the bag. Cultivars: 'Crystal Ball', 'Scarlet Globe' and 'Saxa'.

Runner bean. These will require support in growing bags. Only three or four plants should be grown to a bag, as they are vigorous. Sow in warmth during April for transplanting in May, or directly into the growing bag in May. When sowing direct, place two beans in position and thin to one plant when fully germinated. Cultivars: 'Achievement'; 'Pickwick', a dwarf grower requiring quite short supports and therefore also suitable for raised beds; 'Sunset', pink flowers; 'White Achievement', with white flowers that are not susceptible to bird damage.

Shallot. Plant the bulbs 9in/23cm apart in either raised beds or growing bags during February to March. Push the bulbs into the soil, leaving just the tips showing. Shallots tend to push themselves out of the soil, so watch out for any that need replanting.

Tomato. Requires a sunny position. Sow under glass in April or early May at a temperature of 65°F/18°C or obtain plants from a nurseryman. Plants should not be put out of doors until all threat of frost has gone. Cultivars for raised beds: 'Alicante'; 'Gardener's Delight', small fruits; 'Sweet 100'; 'Tiny Tim', very dwarf. Bush types recommended are 'Tornado' and 'Sigmabush'.

Allow two plants per growing bag (although most manufacturers suggest three per bag). Cultivars: 'Alicante'; 'Gardener's Delight'; 'Marmande'; and 'Red Alert'. The last two are dwarf-growing, so plant three to a bag.

Turnip. Sow in raised beds and growing bags May to July. Cultivars: 'Snowball'; 'Veitch's Red Globe'; 'Green Globe'.

Tomatoes

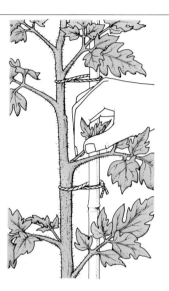

Supporting. Use bamboo canes for supporting tomatoes. Tie the plant on loosely with soft garden string to protect stems.

De-leafing. Snap off side shoots between thumb and forefinger. De-leaf by making a cut near to the main stem.

Fruit setting. Spray the flowers with a fine droplet spray or shake the plant gently. This disperses pollen and improves fruit setting.

Feeding. Give liquid feed to growing plants to improve growth and quality, following manufacturer's instructions. Water as necessary.

Stopping. Pinch out growing point two leaves above top truss when 6-7 trusses have set fruit. Remove any yellowing lower leaves.

Picking. Pick ripe fruit by snapping the stalk, leaving the calyx on the fruit. Ripened fruit left under hot sun will lose firmness.

Fruit

Certain soft fruits can be grown in containers, especially in raised beds. Strawberries are the easiest to grow successfully.

Gooseberries

Gooseberries lend themselves to growing in large containers. If the container is next to a wall, plants can be trained in a fan shape. A sunny site is ideal, but gooseberries can also be grown on a north-facing wall.

The following cultivars are successful in containers. Green fruit: 'Keepsake'; 'Careless'; 'Lancer'. Red fruit: 'Whinham's Industry'; 'Lancashire Lad'. White fruit: 'Whitesmith'. Yellow fruit: 'Golden Drop', 'Leveller'.

Planting Bushes can be planted in autumn or winter in well-prepared soil dressed with sulphate of potash at $\frac{3}{4}$oz per sq yd/25g per sq m.

Mulching with farmyard manure after planting helps to conserve moisture.

Pruning The aim of pruning gooseberries is to build up short fruiting branch systems known as spurs. Begin at the end of June by shortening new growths to five leaves. Leading growths should be pruned in the winter by removing about a quarter of the summer growth; in this way fruiting spurs are more readily formed.

Red and white currants

These fruits grow in much the same way as gooseberries, producing fruit on short spurs. The plants can be trained as a fan against a wall or other support. Birds sometimes damage the fruit buds in the winter, so it may be necessary to use netting as a protection. Although a sunny position is best, currants are quite successful in partial shade.

Cultivars of red currants: 'Jonkers van Tets'; 'Red Lake'; and 'Stanza'. Cultivars of white currants: 'White Grape' and 'White Versailles'.

Planting Plant from autumn to early spring in fertile, well-drained soil to which a dressing of a good general fertilizer has been applied at 2oz per sq yd/65g per sq m, with the addition of sulphate of potash at $\frac{1}{2}$oz per sq yd/15g per sq m.

Water regularly in the growing season and apply fertilizers annually in the winter as described above.

Pruning At planting time, reduce the leading growths by half and tie them on to wires to form an open fan shape.

At the end of June each year the new growths should be summer-pruned to about five leaves, but the leading growths must be left until the full length has been reached.

Each winter, reduce the length of the

Strawberries: strawing down

When the fruits begin to swell, scatter slug pellets along the rows, then cover the ground between the berries and between rows with barley or wheat straw to keep the fruits clean.

Alternatives to strawing down

Lay black polythene over a 3 in/7.5 cm high, well-watered ridge of soil, if straw is not available. Tuck the edges under the soil. Insert strawberry plants through slits in the polythene at 18 in/45 cm intervals. Leave a

leaders by a quarter and cut back the lower side shoots to one or two buds. As the plant gets larger, more leading growths will have to be retained in order to cover the wired support fully, but these leaders in turn will need pruning to build up fruiting spurs. After some years these spurs will need to be pruned quite hard to rejuvenate growth.

Strawberries

Strawberries are very popular container plants, whether in raised beds or in specialized containers such as strawberry pots (page 22). Good cultivars are: 'Tamella', heavy cropper, large fruits; 'Red Gauntlet', heavy cropper, producing a second crop in the autumn; 'Hapil', good for light, dry soils.

Small-fruited alpine types are also useful and make a good edge planting for a larger built container. Cultivars: 'Baron Solemacher', easily raised from seed in a warm greenhouse; 'Alexandra'; 'Alpine Yellow', yellow-fruited.

Preparation The soil should be well drained, with plenty of organic material worked into the top 9in/23cm. It is important to make sure that there are no perennial weed roots. Apply Growmore fertilizer at a good handful per square yard/metre before planting.

Planting Plant strawberries from late June to September. Young plants should be spaced 15-18in/35-40cm apart. Plant firmly, spreading the roots out in a shallow hole. It is important to have the crown at the surface of the soil, or the plants may rot.

Watering Water the plants well in. Yields are increased when generous watering is given to the ripening fruits.

Protection As the fruits grow larger, they come in contact with the soil, and this can make them dirty. Straw placed around the plants is useful for keeping the fruits clean, but first scatter slug pellets sparingly on the ground.

Proprietary mats, or a layer of black polythene positioned down either side of the row, can be used instead of straw.

Some protection can be given against birds by draping netting over string stretched tightly between short stakes.

Care after fruiting After picking, cut off all the foliage with a pair of garden shears and remove unwanted runners. A further application of Growmore fertilizer will help the plants build up again quickly, ready for the following year. To prevent disease it is wise to keep the plants for just three years, then discard them and plant new stock in a different position.

Clearing up the bed

6 in/15 cm run of soil between polythene sheets to enable rain to permeate easily to the roots.

Another alternative is to place mats around individual plants, like collars (above).

In August, after cropping, cut off the old leaves and unwanted runners 3 in/7.5 cm above the crowns. Rake off and burn leaves, old straw and other débris. Fork up and weed compacted earth between rows.

Seasonal chart of tasks

JANUARY
- Where containers have been planted for spring or winter effect, pick off any decaying foliage and remove old flowerheads of plants such as winter-flowering pansies.

- Hanging baskets or window boxes may have become quite dry, so water thoroughly as required.

- If a heated greenhouse is available, sow seeds of fibrous-rooted begonias and zonal pelargoniums (geraniums).

- Check that protection of tender plants is still effective.

- Sow under glass quick-maturing vegetables such as radishes and spring onions.

FEBRUARY
- Continue to pick off decaying foliage and flowers. During snowy weather do not remove snow from containers, as it affords some protection to many plants.

- Sow lobelias in heat.

- Make sowings of broad beans, peas and lettuce in slight heat for planting outdoors in March.

MARCH
- Greater demands for watering can now be expected, especially for hanging baskets. As early bulbs finish flowering, cut off the old flower stems as close to the base of the foliage as possible.

- A wide range of flowering plants can be sown this month in a heated greenhouse, but delay until the end of the month if window sill germination is all that is available. If weather conditions are poor, delay sowings of *Petunia, Alyssum, Nicotiana* and French marigold until April.

- Many vegetables can be sown outdoors.

- Planting of bare-rooted trees, shrubs and fruit in containers should be completed this month.

APRIL
- If frost-free conditions can be provided, make up hanging baskets.

- Many excellent plants for hanging baskets can be bought from garden centres. Look for young fresh plants that are only just coming into flower.

- Hanging baskets already made up and purchased during the month should be given protection.

- Check stakes, supports and ties.

- Complete pricking off of bedding plants for summer display.

- Pot on houseplants at the end of the month.

MAY
- Plant up window boxes and other containers. Stand out of doors at the end of the month.

- If there is a threat of late frost, it may be necessary to bring hanging baskets under cover. Sheets of newspaper draped over plants will give some frost protection, but need to be secured in position because they can be dislodged by the slightest breeze.

- Harden off tender plants before planting them out when frosts have finished.

- Apply a balanced fertilizer to trees and shrubs in containers.

JUNE
- Water and feed seasonal displays, as plants will now be in full growth.

- Remove faded flowers and decaying foliage.

- Plant out courgettes, cucumbers and marrows in raised beds or growing bags.

- Spray conifers in containers with water during warm, still weather.

- Give permanent plantings a thorough watering.

JULY
- Continue watering and feeding.

- Sow suitable plants for spring display. Wallflowers can be sown out of doors. Daisies, winter-flowering pansies and forget-me-nots can be sown in boxes, using a shaded cold frame.

- Attend to summer pruning of fruit.

- Continue to water trees and shrubs in dry weather, especially those planted earlier in the year.

AUGUST
- All plants will have reached full maturity and be making the greatest demands on water and food.

- Continue picking over flowers and foliage to keep displays fresh and healthy.

- If pelargoniums can be overwintered in a heated greenhouse, now is a good time to sow seeds or take cuttings.

- Bulbs for forcing should be potted as soon as purchased and then plunged outdoors.

SEPTEMBER
- Take cuttings of half-hardy perennial plants for overwintering in frost-free conditions. At this time of year, cuttings of many plants will root readily even on a window sill in a small propagator.

- Plant up containers for winter and spring display.

- Plant strawberries.

- Cuttings of semi-hardwood plant material should be taken.

OCTOBER
- Make sure that all spring-flowering bulbs are planted or potted this month as soon as they are purchased.

- Repot or pot on fruit grown in containers.

- Plant evergreens in containers.

- Collect together protective materials.

NOVEMBER
- Before the onset of really severe weather, susceptible plants such as bay trees in containers should be given some protection against frost damage. Overwinter in a cold greenhouse, or a sheltered corner, or even under trees.

- Terracotta containers, if not frost-proofed, should be kept as dry as possible.

- Bare-rooted deciduous trees and shrubs should be planted between now and March.

- Look through seed and plant catalogues and place early orders to avoid disappointment.

DECEMBER
- Continue to inspect plants and remove decaying foliage and flowers.

- Look at gardening diary notes. Assess successes and failures so that necessary changes can be made next year regarding choice of plants, colour schemes and cultural requirements.

- Check over containers for next year's display.

- Prune vines grown under glass.

Containers under glass 1

This section of the book covers plants that can be grown in the conservatory and greenhouse, either in conventional containers or in structures such as raised beds.

Conservatories are generally attached to dwellings. Some are quite ornate structures, whereas others are just adapted greenhouses. Some conservatories and greenhouses are heated, some are not, but all do the same job of growing plants that are not hardy enough to stay outside, or do better in the greater warmth and protection afforded them.

Extending the house's living space, a conservatory can be a garden room, in which many more plants can be grown than would normally be the case in an ordinary room. Alternatively, a conservatory can be devoted entirely to growing plants.

Whether a greenhouse or conservatory is being used for container plants, some understanding of this growing environment is necessary, especially as regards ventilation, shading, humidity, watering and feeding. It should be remembered that the entire wellbeing of plants grown under glass depends very much on the care and skill of the gardener in providing a suitably balanced environment.

Ventilation

The admission of air through ventilators is an important factor in cultivating plants under glass successfully. A free flow of air is essential to maintain a cooling effect on the interior of the conservatory or greenhouse in hot weather. It also helps to cut down on the incidence of diseases that thrive in stagnant air conditions.

Ventilation must be carefully controlled, especially when the wind is gusting or cold. Ideally, air flow should be increased and decreased gradually, so that there is not a rapid fluctuation in temperature.

It is possible to fix automatic ventilator controls, which can be very useful if the conservatory has to be left unattended during the day. Alternatively, electrically operated extractor fans can be fitted.

A further cooling effect is produced by damping down the floor with liberal amounts of water. This may need to be done three times a day in very hot weather. It is, of course, only feasible on a solid, uncarpeted surface and where there is suitable furniture.

Shading

Some shading is always necessary. Blinds fixed on the outside of the roof of the conservatory or greenhouse are most effective. These can be rolled up and down according to the prevailing weather conditions. However, proprietary "whitewash" shading painted on the glass is perfectly satisfactory and considerably less expensive. It is, however, time-consuming to put on and remove annually.

As a compromise between these extremes of expense, shading material in the form of tinted polythene sheeting or close-woven netting can be stretched inside the structure, but the cooling effect is never so efficient as when the shading is on the outside.

A good canopy of foliage from climbing plants can also give shade.

Watering

Regular watering will be necessary in a conservatory or greenhouse, since the plants are wholly dependent for moisture on the gardener's efforts. During the summer, the liberal use of water on floors and staging, if this is possible, helps to create humidity, and for most plants a good growing atmosphere.

Watering is the single most skilled job to be mastered in the conservatory or greenhouse. Close observation is important, combined with an understanding of how the pattern of watering can change with various factors— the type of crop, its maturity, the time of year, the size and position of container, and the type of compost. As a general rule, it is better always to underwater slightly rather than run the risk of drowning the plants.

Use rainwater if it can be collected but, if not, ordinary tap water is perfectly satisfactory for the vast majority of plants.

Feeding

Very closely linked with watering is feeding, which also should be done regularly. Applications of proprietary fertilizer should be given according to the manufacturer's instructions. This usually means every week or ten days during the growing season.

Opening systems

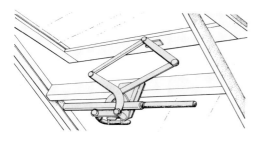

Ventilators can be opened manually or automatically.

Fans

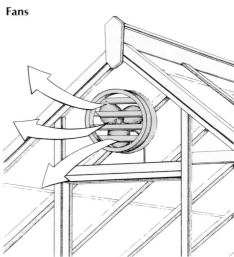

An extractor fan specially designed for greenhouses should be positioned above the door to cool the air.

Methods of shading

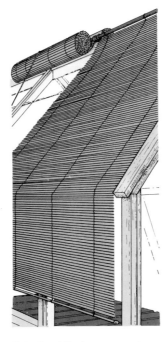

Apply shading paint to the outside of the glass in late spring or early summer.

Exterior blinds prevent heat build-up, cut down light, and protect against frost.

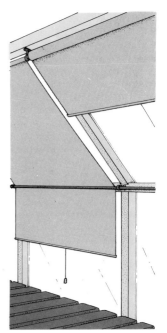

Interior blinds are less effective than exterior, but neat and easily used.

Containers under glass 2

Benches, staging and support

Metal or wood shelves can be fixed to glazing bars on the sides and roof of the greenhouse. Use special clips in alloy frames. Make shelves at least 6 in deep.

Tiered staging displays large numbers of pot plants attractively. It is available in wood or metal and can be placed on the ground or on staging.

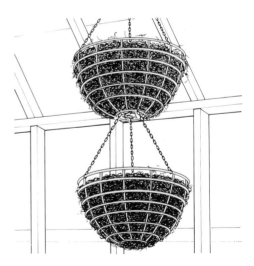

Decorative brackets attached to a strong wooden framework can be used for hanging baskets, but check first that they are able to bear the load.

Double hanging baskets can be effective, but the fixings must be very secure. The mesh type of basket is suited to this approach.

Smells and toxicity

Pests can be a problem in some conservatories and greenhouses: good growing conditions for plants are often those in which insects thrive. Chemical control is seldom easy, and in conservatories or greenhouses built onto houses the unpleasant smell of some chemicals may seep into the house.

If chemicals are used for pest control, they should be non-toxic and applied strictly in accordance with manufacturers' instructions.

The conservatory should be kept as clean as possible, making sure that all plant débris and weeds are removed regularly. This will remove possible insect hiding places as well as sources of disease. Infestations of pests or diseases on only a few plants can be cleared by taking them outside and applying a suitable pesticide there.

The use of microscopic predators against some of the main pests, such as red spider mite, mealybug, scale insects and whitefly, is gaining in popularity; and, although there are some drawbacks, they are effective, if correctly managed, in controlling these pests in the conservatory or greenhouse.

Types of container

Many of the same kinds of containers used in outdoor situations (pages 6-27) and in the home (pages 126-9) are suitable for growing and display purposes in conservatories. The more ornamental types are especially attractive, provided that they are chosen to complement their surroundings. Unglazed and other frost-vulnerable containers are perfectly satisfactory in this protected situation.

Most of the plants listed on pages 102-9 are perennial, so it is necessary for their containers to be large enough for the plants to develop without restriction for two or three years. Although ready-made containers can readily be purchased, it is relatively easy to construct square or rectangular wooden boxes or raised beds for use in a conservatory.

Making conservatory containers

Boxes can be made of well-preserved wood: the depth should be no less than 12in/30cm. Drill a few holes in the bottom for drainage. To ensure that the holes are working efficiently and to give more protection to the wood, raise the container slightly on bricks or stones.

Permanent containers such as raised beds can also be made entirely from bricks or stone (pages 24-7). The materials used should match the floor surfacing and walls of the conservatory if possible. It is not essential to cement together the bricks or proprietary walling: if left uncemented they can be taken apart quite easily to allow the bed to be extended if necessary.

Hanging baskets

Hanging baskets are no less suitable for conservatories than they are for outdoor situations. Hanging baskets sited in the greenhouse or conservatory can be planted with more permanent subjects and will only need to be replanted when the plants have begun to deteriorate or their growth becomes too congested.

Keep the baskets away from doorways, as water drips and long pendulous growths can be a nuisance.

Plastic baskets with a reservoir attached or built into the base are ideal to reduce water spillage to a minimum. However, where there is a paved floor and the conservatory is devoted entirely to growing plants, rather than used as a living space, there is no real problem with any type of basket (see pages 12-15).

Containers suspended in macramé work look very attractive, but it may be necessary to have a drip tray underneath.

Care is needed when positioning and fixing hanging baskets in conservatories. In a conservatory that backs onto the house, use firmly secured brackets on the solid wall. Fixing a basket can be difficult if it is to be suspended in the centre of a structure. Modern conservatory and greenhouse designs in lightweight metals such as aluminium generally have few, if any, horizontal bracings. Baskets can become quite heavy when the plants are in full growth and charged with water. If hung on glazing bars they may place considerable stress on the structure. If the conservatory has a strong wooden frame, however, suitable hooks for suspending hanging baskets can be screwed into various sections without causing damage.

Climbers and pillar plants 1

A wide range of flowering and foliage plants is available for growing in warm and semi-warm conditions. In order to furnish a new conservatory, it is often best to obtain reasonably large subjects for immediate effect. Many of the indoor plants listed on pages 142-65 and 178-81 are also good for conservatories. Indoor bulbs, too, make colourful, if temporary, subjects (pages 168-76). Also suitable, of course, are the outdoor plants listed on pages 54-61; they will flourish especially well in the protected and warmer situation of even a cold conservatory or greenhouse.

Described below are some ornamental plants that are especially suitable for growing under glass, needing, on the whole, a minimum winter temperature of 50°F/10°C.

CLIMBERS AND OTHER PILLAR PLANTS

Climbers and tall, willowy shrubs are excellent for clothing pillars in a conservatory. Climbers may also be trained along wires stretched below the roof glass. The resultant overhead growth helps to keep the structure cool and create a pleasant, relaxing atmosphere. Larger plants will need to be grown in raised beds or very large pots.

Abutilon. Vigorous shrubs, often with willowy branches which may be tied on to a pillar or trained to a backing. 6ft/1.8m. Sun or semi-shade. Generally, open, bell-like flowers in white, pink, red or orange. There are several cultivars, some with pleasantly variegated foliage and all with attractive flowers. *A. megapotamicum* and its variegated form 'Variegata' have slender growth and pendulous, light cream flowers, with red calyxes, throughout the summer; respond well to hard pruning. *A. pictum* 'Thompsonii' (*A. striatum* 'Thompsonii'), upright and fairly free-branching, produces orange, bell-shaped flowers almost continuously; foliage is heavily variegated with irregular yellow blotches. *A. striatum* 'Souvenir de Bonn' has cream-edged leaves.

A. x *hybridum* is available in a range of flower colours and can be raised from seed. It reaches 8ft/2.4m or more in 2-3 years. A cream-variegated form known as 'Savitzii' is less strong-growing. It roots easily from cuttings in spring and summer.

Asarina (Maurandia) barclaiana. A tender perennial usually treated as an annual, with small purple flowers in summer. Not a strong grower and therefore ideal for pots, vases and urns. *Asarina (Maurandia) erubescens* is similar, but is stronger-growing and has rose-pink flowers.

Bougainvillea. Flamboyant heads of paper-like flowers, in pink, red, purple, white, orange and shades between, produced in great profusion over a long period. To keep this rampant climber within bounds, prune the

CONSERVATORY CLIMBERS AND PILLAR PLANTS

Abutilon megapotamicum

previous year's growth back hard to one or two buds in March each year, and tie in new growth to pillars and wires. Indefinite height. Sun or semi-shade. Also makes a good subject for growing in free-standing pots.

Cestrum aurantiacum and **C. elegans**. Strong-growing plants for training on walls, pillars and overhead wires. 8ft/2.4m. Sun or semi-shade. They are quite happy with a minimum winter temperature of 40°F/5°C. The tubular flowers are orange and reddish-purple respect-ively. As they flower on new growths, prune the previous year's flowering stems hard each spring.

Cobaea scandens. A very rampant climber, especially if its roots are not too restricted. Clings by tendrils, so needs very little tying. Bluish-purple trumpet flowers all summer; there is also a white-flowered cultivar. Height variable. Sun or semi-shade. Almost hardy, so needs very little heat in the winter. Although this may be grown as a part of a

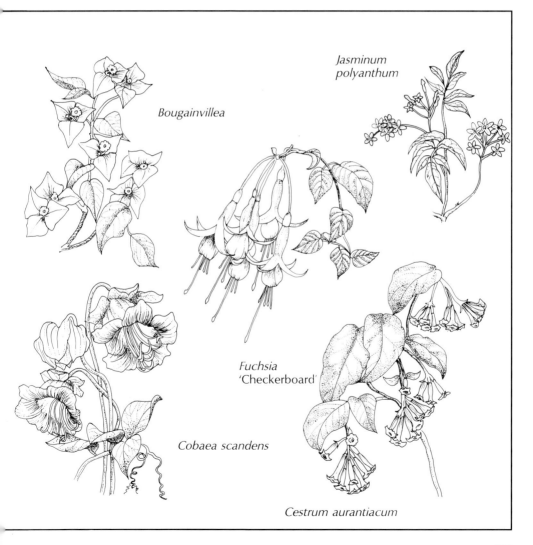

Bougainvillea

Jasminum polyanthum

Fuchsia 'Checkerboard'

Cobaea scandens

Cestrum aurantiacum

Climbers and pillar plants 2

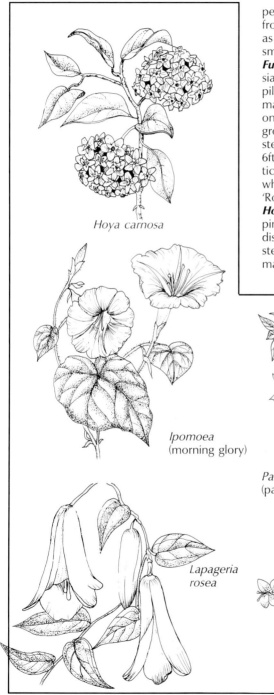

Hoya carnosa

permanent planting, it is very readily raised from seed in the spring each year; if grown as a perennial, the plant will rapidly cover a small greenhouse.

Fuchsia. Some of the stronger-growing fuchsias can be very effective when trained up a pillar. It may take two or more years for the main stems to reach the required height, but once the position is fully covered with main growth, prune the previous year's flowering stems back to one or two buds each spring. 6ft/1.8m or more. Semi-shade. Cultivars particularly recommended: 'Checkerboard', white and red; 'Preston Guild', pink and lilac; 'Rose of Castille Improved', pink and purple.

Hoya carnosa. Waxy, white flowers ageing to pink, with deep pink centres, make a good display in early to midsummer. Self-climbing stems also intertwine to produce a dense mass of growth. Variable height. Prefers fairly

Ipomoea
(morning glory)

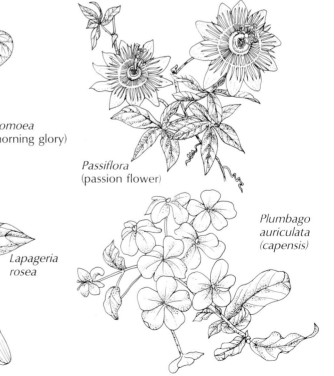

Passiflora
(passion flower)

Lapageria
rosea

Plumbago
auriculata
(capensis)

light conditions. The old flower stalks should not be removed, as flowers are produced on these the following year as well as on the new growth.

Ipomoea (morning glory). A tender annual with blue or purple (occasionally pink or white) flowers, raised from seed each year. Variable height. Full sun. To aid germination, soak seeds in warm water for about twelve hours before sowing. There are many cultivars, some with very large flowers. An interesting variant is 'Minibar Rose', which is less strong-growing and makes a good trailing plant for an urn. It has deep pink flowers with a white edge and variegated leaves.

Jasminum polyanthum. A climber with very sweet-scented, white flowers from winter to early summer. The young growth tends to be self-climbing, but the stronger shoots require tying into position. 10-13ft/3-4m. Sun or semi-shade. Prune after flowering, cutting the strongest growths back quite hard. *J. mesnyi* has semi-double, yellow, unscented flowers, but is very showy in the spring. It is less rampant, but should be pruned after flowering to keep it in shape.

Lapageria rosea. A very beautiful climber, with pendent, tubular, waxy flowers in red, pink or white. Needs a cool position with some shade and an acid soil. Best in a permanent container. The growths intertwine but are not self-supporting. Virtually no pruning is required, although old plants can, if necessary, be hard-pruned to rejuvenate them.

Oxypetalum (Tweedia) caeruleum. A blue-flowered, slender, perennial twiner or climber which requires support. 3ft/90cm. Easily raised from seed in warmth, and may be grown as an annual.

Passiflora (passion flower). There are many kinds of passion flower, some requiring fairly high winter temperatures to be really successful. The common *P. caerulea* produces blue flowers in summer, followed by unpalatable orange fruits. Variable height. Sun or semi-shade. Soak the seeds for twelve hours before sowing; without this treatment germination can be slow and sporadic.

Plumbago auriculata (P. capensis). Ideal for training up pillars or as a pot plant, when it will require some support. Height 9ft/2.7m. Sun or semi-shade. Blue flowers from spring to autumn; there is also a white-flowered cultivar. Both can readily be raised from cuttings or from seed sown in a warm greenhouse in the spring. Flowering will begin in the second season. Prune weak or unwanted growths to base each spring.

Thunbergia alata (black-eyed Susan). This popular plant climbs or trails. When trained up supports, several plants in a container make an attractive feature. White, yellow or orange flowers, usually with black centres. 4ft/1.2m. Sun or semi-shade. Easily grown from seed sown in spring in a warm greenhouse.

Tropaeolum peregrinum (Canary creeper). A vigorous and self-supporting annual climber with lemon-yellow flowers throughout the summer. 5ft/1.5m. Sun or semi-shade. Seeds should be sown in warmth in the spring.

Thunbergia alata (black-eyed Susan)

Tropaeolum peregrinum (Canary creeper)

Plants for hanging baskets 1

Hanging baskets planted completely with one type of plant can look particularly attractive and are often easier to maintain than a collection of different species. However, there is no reason why a combination of plants should not be used, if preferred.

PLANTS FOR HANGING BASKETS IN CONSERVATORIES

Many of the plants suggested for growing in baskets out of doors (pages 54-61 and 64-5) can also be used under glass, where the extra protection will produce very fine specimens. The list below covers plants that need to be grown under glass in order to survive the winter. All will be found reliable.

Begonia. The pendulous forms of begonia make a splendid show in summer. 18in/45cm across. Semi-shade. Tubers of the Pendula Group are readily available and can be started into growth in frost-free conditions; alternatively, sow seeds in heat (73°F/23°C) and the plants will flower the first summer. Species and cultivars: 'Lloydii' (Pendula Group), 3in/7.5cm across, semi-double and double flowers in white, pink, orange and yellow; *B. sutherlandii*, profusion of small orange blooms borne singly; *B. semperflorens*, usually grown outdoors, but particularly good with protection; its cultivars, 'Frilly Pink', 'Frilly Red' and 'Pink Avalanche' are recommended for hanging baskets.

Chlorophytum comosum 'Vittatum' (spider plant). A popular house plant (page 160), which also makes a fine foliage plant, with creamy-white, green-striped leaves, for a hanging basket under glass. The long stems which trail downwards produce white flowers and also young plantlets on their tips. 24in/60cm across. Semi-shade. Grows well at fairly cool temperatures (45°F/7°C) and is easily propagated from plantlets formed on the stems.

Columnea x banksii and **C. gloriosa.** Tubular, orange-red flowers borne in profusion on slender, trailing stems among the neat, fleshy evergreen leaves. Winter- and spring-flowering. Not difficult to grow and flower. 12in/30cm across and capable of trailing down to 3ft/90cm. Some shade appreciated during late spring and summer when quite high temperatures are tolerated. Lower temperatures in the winter (45-50°F/7-10°C) help

CONSERVATORY BASKET PLANTS

Begonia 'Lloydii'
(Pendula Group)

Chlorophytum comosum 'Vittatum'
(spider plant)

them to flower freely. Keep cold water off the leaves, particularly in winter and spring.

Davallia canariensis (haresfoot fern). A fern particularly suited to hanging baskets. Its common name well describes the creeping, furry rhizomes from which the neat fronds develop. Suitable for quite warm, dry conditions, but should not be watered for about a month during the summer dormant season. A winter temperature of 45°F/7°C is sufficient.

Fuchsia. Trailing forms of half-hardy fuchsias grow well in hanging baskets in cooler, shady conditions and can make quite large plants. 15in/45cm across. Regular watering and feeding are essential for a long season of display. There are many cultivars to choose from, but

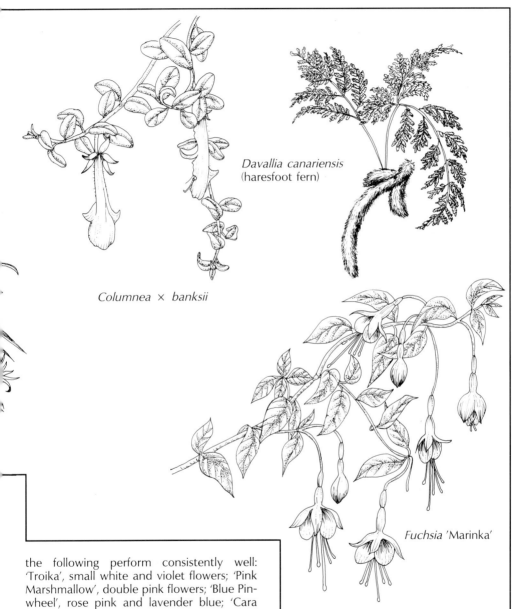

Columnea × banksii

Davallia canariensis
(haresfoot fern)

Fuchsia 'Marinka'

the following perform consistently well: 'Troika', small white and violet flowers; 'Pink Marshmallow', double pink flowers; 'Blue Pinwheel', rose pink and lavender blue; 'Cara Mia', pink and crimson; 'Henri Poincare', red and violet-blue; 'Strawberry Sundae', white and pink. See also pages 55-7.

Hedera helix (common ivy). Hardy outside but grows more rapidly and luxuriously in slight warmth. Trails to 60cm/24in. Semi-shade and shade. Many different cultivars,

some with attractive variegated leaves, as for outdoors (page 57).

Hoya bella. Very heavily scented, waxy, star-shaped, white and magenta flower clusters. 12in/30cm across. Semi-shade. Great care

Plants for hanging baskets 2

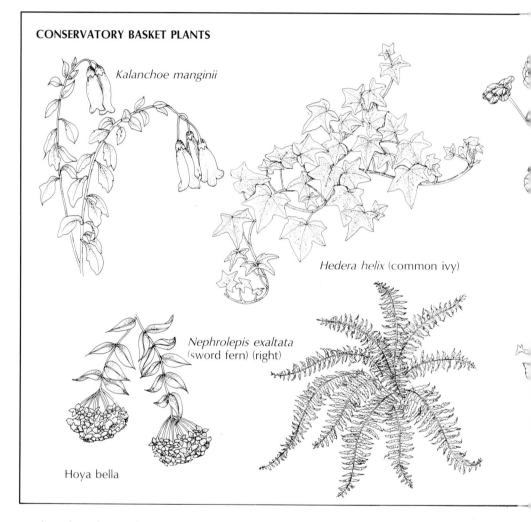

CONSERVATORY BASKET PLANTS

Kalanchoe manginii

Hedera helix (common ivy)

Nephrolepis exaltata
(sword fern) (right)

Hoya bella

needs to be taken with watering, especially during the winter when a temperature of 50°F/10°C is sufficient.

Kalanchoe manginii. An excellent, trailing, succulent-leaved plant ideal for both large and small baskets. Profusion of deep rose pink, tubular flowers in winter and early spring. 15in/45cm. Sun. Does not require high temperatures, but will not stand frosts. A recent selection 'Tessa' has orange flowers and blooms over a long period. Cuttings root easily.

Nephrolepis exaltata (sword fern). Grows happily in cool, semi-shady situations and also succeeds quite well in the home (page 155).

3ft/90cm across. Spray regularly every day with clear water to create good conditions for growth.

Oplismenus hirtellus 'Variegatus' makes long trailing growths with white-variegated foliage and is better suited for conservatories.

Orchids. Although it may seem rather ambitious to grow orchids, many are fairly easy to grow, provided rainwater is used and sufficient humidity maintained. Wooden hanging baskets (pages 14-15), apart from being perfectly adequate for growing all sorts of plants, are especially suitable for certain orchids. An orchid recommended for the

Tradescantia fluminensis

Pelargonium
(geranium)

Plectranthus
oertendahlii
(Swedish ivy)

Tradescantia
zebrina

GROWING ORCHIDS IN WOODEN BASKETS

An orchid grown in a wooden hanging basket makes an excellent feature for a conservatory or greenhouse.

beginner is *Coelogyne cristata*, with leathery leaves and in winter and spring a profusion of white fragrant flowers. A winter temperature of 45-50°F/7-10°C is sufficient.

Pelargonium (often called *Geranium*). (See also pages 58-60 and 146-8.) Ivy-leaved pelargoniums make perfect plants for conservatory display, their trailing stems, up to 12in/30cm, bearing flowers in white, pink, red, lilac or purple over a long period of time. Sun. Although pelargoniums tolerate some drying out at the roots, water regularly for healthy growth. Cultivars: 'Abel Carriere', rosy purple, semi-double; 'Mrs W.A.R. Clifton', scarlet, double; 'Rose Mini Cascade', pink, single; 'Barbe Bleu', deep purple.

Plectranthus oertendahlii (Swedish ivy). Not an ivy, but equally accommodating as a house or greenhouse plant. Produces a mass of glossy leaves and sprays of pale lilac, almost white tubular flowers. It will not, however, tolerate frost. 15in/45cm across.

Swedish ivy. See *Plectranthus oertendahlii*.
Sword fern. See *Nephrolepis exaltata*.
Zebrina pendula. See *Tradescantia zebrina*.
Tradescantia fluminensis. Many selections of this popular plant suitable for conservatory or home are available, some with white or yellow variegation. They do well in sunlight or semi-shade, but the colour of the foliage intensifies in sun. For propagation, see page 164.

Tradescantia zebrina. Very similar in growth to *T. fluminensis* but with larger foliage marked with silver above and purple below. 12in/30cm. Sun or semi-shade. For propagation, see page 165.

109

Fruit 1

Fruits that need warmth can grow very well in containers in conservatories and greenhouses. Citrus and figs are usually best grown in large pots. Permanent containers, especially those constructed from loose bricks which can be extended as required (pages 24-5 and 101), are ideal for growing grapes and peaches. Both grapevines and peach trees will require supporting wires to train them up a wall. Peaches can also be grown as bushes in tubs, but will take up more room than against a wall.

Citrus

Oranges and lemons are easy to grow under glass and make large specimens in pots. Their glossy, evergreen foliage is attractive in itself, and the heavily scented flowers and decorative fruits add to the display. Excessive sunlight should be avoided as this can sometimes damage the foliage. High temperatures are not necessary in winter: 50°F/10°C is quite adequate. The variegated lemon and 'Meyers

Lemon' are both particularly suitable for conservatory cultivation.

Planting Plants raised from pips usually take years to come into fruit and even then the quality can be very indifferent. It is, therefore, much better to obtain plants of known fruiting cultivars from a reputable source, so that regular crops of fruit can be harvested. Use John Innes Potting Compost No. 2.

Pruning The plants will ultimately form small trees which can be quite severely pruned in spring, even cutting into the older wood. They will then produce many new growths which should be thinned out to obtain a more open, balanced shape.

Figs

Because it is necessary to keep fig roots restricted for successful cropping, this fruit is excellent as a container plant. Figs can be grown under glass or on a warm sunny patio, but, if the latter, some winter protection with hessian, straw or bracken (pages 44-5) will be

Citrus: first year

1 During the growing season, to establish a single-stemmed tree, remove low shoots as soon as they appear. Cut back short any over-vigorous shoots that mar the symmetry.

First few years

2 Allow only three or four fruits per plant to set. Feed every 10-14 days from spring to autumn. Do not allow to dry out. Ventilate on sunny days.

necessary. As a further precaution against frost damage, the pot should be buried and the top covered also with straw or bracken. Recommended cultivars: 'Bourjasotte Grise'; 'Rouge de Bordeaux'; 'White Marseilles'.

Planting Potting is best done in March. A 10in/25cm pot is large enough initially, but particular attention will need to be paid to the watering. Although the ultimate size of the plant will increase in a larger pot (say, up to 15in/38cm in diameter), it will be easier to manage as drying out will be less frequent.

Use a loam-based compost such as John Innes Potting Compost No.3. In subsequent years a top-dressing of compost should be given in early spring and any further potting on done at this time.

Pruning The leading shoot should be pruned at planting time to 15in/38cm, unless the aim is to grow the plant on a larger main stem. Subsequent pruning is done during the growing season by removing the tips of the side shoots as illustrations.

Second and subsequent years

3 In early spring, pot on annually into a larger pot until tree is required size. Thereafter, carefully replace about 1 in/2.5 cm of old soil with good potting soil.

Wall-grown figs

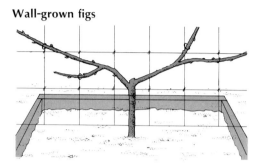

Use wire supports on the wall or hang 6 in/15 cm wire netting 12 in/30 cm away from the glass. When temperature reaches 15°C/59°F, spray plants and damp down floor daily.

Pruning the cropping tree

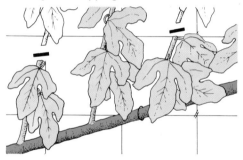

1 In a heated greenhouse, once the first crop of fruits is picked, cut back about one-half of the old fruiting systems to 2 leaves. Repeat after every crop.

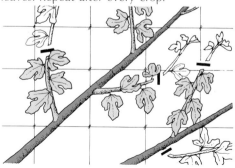

2 In a cold greenhouse, in June pinch out lateral shoots at the fourth leaf. In July thin out unfruitful stems.

111

Fruit 2

Peaches and nectarines

Peaches grown in bush form make good container plants, but are best trained in a fan shape onto a wall. The main branches and new growths should be tied onto wires stretched horizontally along the wall at 6in/15cm apart.

An interesting new cultivar called 'Garden Lady' promises to be an excellent plant for fairly small containers as it is naturally very dwarf. Other cultivars recommended are: 'Hale's Early'; 'Rochester'; 'Bellegarde'; Peregrine'.

The following cultivars of nectarines are treated in exactly the same way: 'Early Rivers'; 'Lord Napier'; 'Humboldt'; 'Pineapple'.

These cultivars of both peaches and nectarines can also be grown successfully out of doors on a sunny patio.

Planting Both bush and fan-trained plants can be obtained from specialist nurserymen or good garden centres. Plant in the dormant season (either autumn or spring). Make sure that the roots are well spread out in a hole sufficiently large and deep to accept the whole root system: for one tree the site should be at least 3ft/90cm square.

Erect supporting wires, starting 12in/30cm above the ground. For trees to be trained under the roof, use long-shanked eye-bolts (vine-eyes) to keep the stems 6-9in/15-23cm clear of the glass.

Pruning wall-trained peaches and nectarines

It is important to encourage new growth each year so that the framework of the tree is maintained and fruiting ensured. If a young, untrained tree is obtained, prune the leading growths to leave two strong lower branches which should be tied out on opposite sides and in turn pruned by about one-third.

The following year, sufficient growths will have been made for four shoots on each side to be selected. Tie these to canes to form an open-centred fan shape and prune each to about 12-18in/30-45cm in length. These shoots will further build up the main frame of the tree.

Regulate the fruiting growth by removing some of the new shoots when they appear in the spring and early summer. The lowest strong-growing shoot on the fruiting branch should be retained, together with another one about halfway up, as well as the leading growth. The shoots surrounding the fruit should be pinched to one or two leaves and not completely removed.

Pruning bush peaches When purchased, the bush should have several side branches so that, when the central growth is pruned away at about 24in/60cm above soil level, two or three of these branches are left to form the framework which in turn should be pruned to an outward-facing bud.

The following year many shoots will form, and should be reduced to nine or ten in number, with the remainder pruned to about 4in/10cm. In future years the aim is to encourage a plentiful supply of fruiting shoots and to keep the centre of the plant open.

Fruit-thinning Whether peaches are grown on walls or as bushes, some fruit-thinning will be necessary, especially in the early years of cropping. As a general guide, once the tree has become well established after four years, fruit should be spaced 3in/7.5cm apart.

Second year

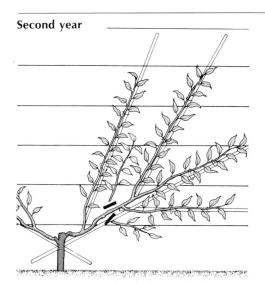

3 In February, cut back the 2 side shoots to 12 in/30 cm. **In summer** (above), prune all but 4 shoots on each arm, one to extend the existing rib, and one on the lower side.

Fan-trained peaches and nectarines: first year

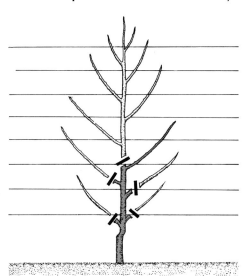

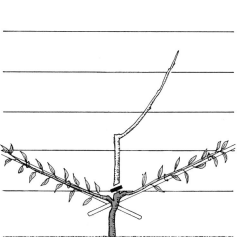

1 In February, cut back a feathered tree to a lateral 24 in/60 cm above the ground, leaving one good bud on each side beneath it. Cut remaining laterals to one bud.

2 In early summer, select 3 shoots, training one vertically. In June or July, tie the two side shoots to canes at 45 degrees. Later that summer, cut out the central shoot.

Third year

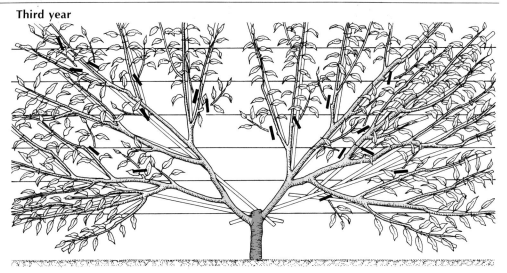

4 In February, shorten leaders by one-third. **In summer**, train outwards 3 leaders on each branch allowing shoots to grow every 4 in/10 cm. **In late summer** (above), pinch out growing points. Tie to canes on the wires. These will fruit next summer. In subsequent years, in May, remove shoots growing towards and away from wall. Leave 1-2 leaves on shoots with flower buds.

Fruit 3

Vines

Traditionally, vines are grown in greenhouse borders, but they are also quite successful in brick-built containers and even, when trained as standards, in pots. The first two methods involve growths trained on wires, ideally stretched horizontally no less than 12in/30cm below the glass and approximately 9in/23cm apart. These wires support the vine's main stem (referred to as a rod) and the fruiting growths that are the result of hard pruning each winter.

Cultivars: 'Black Hamburgh', 'Buckland Sweetwater' and 'Foster's Seedling' are all early-fruiting and reliable.

Planting Plant in the dormant season. A loam-based compost will be found to be very suitable. Care must be taken to ensure there is good drainage, especially in a permanently constructed container. Water and feed regularly during the growing season.

Pruning Vines grown as standards or trained on the inside of the roof must be pruned in November/December when their leaves have fallen. The current year's growth should be pruned back to one or two buds. This hard pruning forms a compact spar system, either as the head of a standard or on either side of the main stem when the vine is trained on wires.

The growths that result the following year should be pinched at two leaves beyond a bunch of grapes, or allowed to go to five or six leaves if no bunch is formed. These growths will need supporting either by tying them securely to a central cane in the case of the standards, or by tying onto horizontally strained wires for roof-trained plants. Throughout the growing season, all tendrils should be removed.

Fruit-thinning A standard vine will usually have only five to six bunches of grapes, but the less confined method of training can result in over-cropping which may affect future fruiting. As a general guide, leave one bunch for every 12in/30cm of rod. In both cases, the berries must be thinned within each bunch, using a pair of sharp pointed scissors. Remove up to half to allow the remaining berries to develop fully and reduce the risk of splitting and rotting.

Vines: pruning

The first and second years

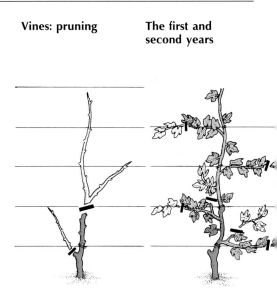

1 At planting, cut back the main stem by two-thirds of the previous summer's growth. Cut remaining laterals to 1 bud.

2 In summer, allow the main stem to reach 10 ft/3m. Cut back laterals to 5 leaves. Pinch out sub-laterals to 1 leaf. Tie loosely to wires.

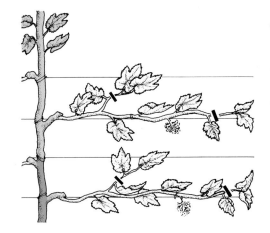

5 When flower trusses appear, pinch out growing tips 2 leaves beyond the bunch, tying each fruiting lateral to a horizontal wire.

Third and subsequent years

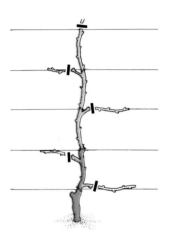

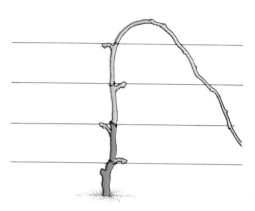

3 In November/December, immediately after leaf-fall, cut back the main stem by two-thirds and the laterals to one good bud.

4 In January, undo all the ties except one about one-third of the way up the rod. Let the rod almost touch the ground. When the buds on the spurs begin to grow, tie the rod back into position.

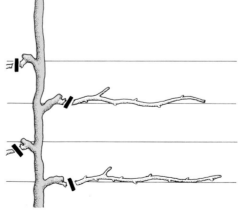

6 In Summer, when the rod reaches the top of the house, pinch out the growing point. Thin the bunches with long-bladed scissors.

7 In December, prune back to 1 bud all the laterals produced the previous summer.

Vegetables and herbs

Vegetables in greenhouses are often grown in borders or raised beds, but many do equally well in containers. One type of container often dedicated to vegetables is the growing bag (page 23 and pages 90-3).

Many herbs such as mint, thyme and small bushes of sage can be overwintered in growing bags and, with the protection of the greenhouse, give early pickings. It is possible to harvest parsley through much of the winter from a summer sowing.

Vegetables to grow under glass

Aubergine (egg plant). Aubergines should be germinated in heat and grown under glass. Three plants can be grown in a growing bag, with fruits limited to three or four to a plant. Cultivars: 'Dusky', 'Moneymaker' and 'Rima'.

Carrot. Good for a cold greenhouse and as a secondary crop in late spring/early summer after, say, tomatoes. Sow seeds thinly in February and March. Cultivars: 'Amsterdam Forcing', 'Early French Frame', 'Rondo'.

Cucumber. Sow seeds singly in small pots from February to May and germinate them at a minimum night temperature of 60°F/15°C. Some of the newer hybrids may need greater warmth. The earliest sowings will need a warm greenhouse to grow on, but an unheated one is perfectly adequate to produce good crops from the later sowings. Grow two plants in a bag. Some support will be needed to hold the fruits clear of the floor.

"All-female" hybrids are strongly recommended when growing cucumbers, as they are very prolific and require little special

Aubergines

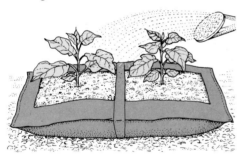

1 In April or May, plant two or three previously watered plants in a growing bag and water. Ideally, keep at 60-65°F/15-18°C.

2 Pinch out the growing points when plants are 9-12 in/23-30 cm high, to encourage 3-4 strong branches. Support with canes.

3 Throughout summer, water sparingly but very regularly, and liquid feed. Spray against aphids and red spider mites.

4 Remove all but 5-6 developing fruits on each plant, keeping even spacing. Pinch out extra flowers. Pick fruits when ripe.

Cucumbers

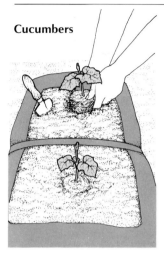

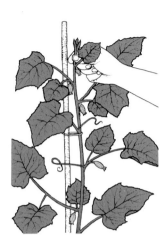

1 In late March, plant 2 plants in a growing bag. Give a little water and liquid feed regularly.

2 In April, tie to canes. Pinch out growing points when main stems reach roof.

3 From April onwards, let cucumbers develop in sequence up main stem. Cut when ready.

training. Cultivars: 'Femspot', 'Landora' and 'Petita'; 'Fembaby'—dwarf with small fruits—will grow in pots on a fairly warm window sill.

Dwarf French bean. Sow directly in March into a growing bag to obtain eight evenly spaced plants. Begin picking in May. Cultivars: 'Kinghorn Wax', 'Masterpiece' and 'Sprite'.

Lettuce. Good for winter and early spring to follow a primary summer crop. Some lettuces require slight heat after being sown in late autumn. Eight or nine plants per bag. Lettuces are also successful in 6in/15cm pots: transplant as individual seedlings into the pots in which they will mature. Cultivars: 'Dandie', for heated greenhouses; 'Fortune', sown in January in slight heat for maturing in unheated conditions in May; 'Kwiek' and 'Marmer', slight heat or cold.

Onion. Another secondary crop for the cold greenhouse, grown to pull young for salads. Sow seeds thinly in September. Cultivar: 'White Lisbon'.

Radish. Sow in February and March as a secondary crop. No heat necessary. Needs a little thinning so that all the roots mature. Cultivars: 'French Breakfast' and 'Saxerre'.

Tomato. Tomatoes are the most commonly grown vegetable planted in growing bags,

under glass and on patios (pages 92-3). Despite the manufacturer's recommendation to grow three plants in a bag, it is best to grow just two, unless particular attention is paid to feeding and watering. Cultivars: 'Alicante'; 'Best of All'; 'Shirley'; 'Sweet 100'. Recent developments have produced dwarf plants which are ideal for small pots or window boxes. The cultivars 'Tiny Tim' and 'Totem' are particularly recommended; the latter can also be used in hanging baskets.

Tomato plants are easily obtained from garden centres, but can readily be raised from seed. For greenhouse crops where heat is available, sow in February in a temperature of 65°F/18°C and grow on at 60°F/15°C. If the structure is unheated, seeds should be sown in heat (possibly, on a window sill) during late March and grown on in the glasshouse from April onward.

Tomatoes should be showing their first flowers before they are planted out. As they develop, overhead spraying with water at midday when the weather is warm will help the fruit to set. Remove any side shoots between the leaf stalk and the main stem.

Once the first fruits begin to swell, feed regularly with a liquid fertilizer formulated for tomatoes. See page 23 for special feeder.

Aquatics

A half-tub can make a very attractive water feature for aquatic plants, both outside and under glass. Given the added protection of a conservatory or greenhouse, especially a heated one, a very interesting range of plants can be grown.

Some light shade is necessary, except in winter. As an added interest, a *very few* fish can be introduced (for every 1in/2.5cm of fish's body length you need 1 gallon/3.8 litres of water).

The depth of water in the tub will depend on the sort of plants to be grown. For really healthy growth, the roots need to be in a 2in/5cm layer of fertile soil. To prevent this soil from clouding the water, place a similar depth of sand on top. Alternatively, grow plants in separate containers placed on the bottom of the tub.

The following are suitable aquatic plants for conservatories:

SETTING UP AN AQUATIC FEATURE

Start with 2 in/5 cm layer of fertile soil and cover with a similar depth of sand to prevent clouding. Alternatively, set the plants in separate containers on the bottom of the tub.

Azolla caroliniana. Very small, dense, overlapping leaflets making moss-like growth which floats freely on the surface. Can make a dense covering but is easily reduced.

Cyperus papyrus. Flowering stems with pendulous stems and graceful tufted flowers. Grows to 6ft/1.8m or more in the warm conditions (65-75°F/18-24°C) in which it is happiest. Best grown in a pot stood within a large tub.

Eichhornia crassipes (water hyacinth). A fairly high temperature (60°F/15°C minimum) and good light are necessary to produce an abundance of lilac-blue flowers on these free-floating plants. At lower temperatures the plant can still be attractive with its inflated stems and broad leaves formed into rosettes. Grows to 12in/30cm.

Nelumbo nucifera (sacred lotus). A beautiful plant requiring warm conditions to grow well and produce a good display of its deep pink flowers. Grows to 3ft/90cm. Very imposing, and best potted into a fairly large container which is then submerged in water.

Nymphaea (water lily). Species and cultivars in a wide colour range are available. Many are strong-growing, but a few can be successfully grown in tubs. Species and cultivars: *N. caerulea*, pale blue flowers opening in the

Aquatic plants

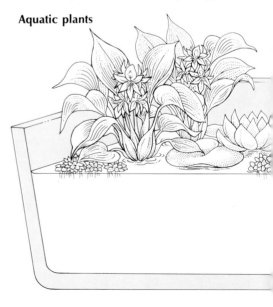

morning, minimum temperature of 60°F/15°C; *N. capensis*, blue flowers staying open all day, 55°F/13°C minimum; *N. pygmaea* 'Helvola', sulphur-yellow flowers opening in the afternoon, will grow in 6-12in/15-30cm of water, 50°F/10°C or even in a little shallow water; *N. stellata*, fragrant blue flowers opening in the morning and early afternoon, 60°F/15°C minimum; *N. tetragona*, white flowers about 2.5in/5cm across, growing in 6in/15cm of water, 50°F/10°C minimum. Suitable for a shallow container in the house.

Nelumbo nucifera
(sacred lotus)

Cyperus papyrus

Terraria and bottle gardens

The cocooned environment of the conservatory can be replicated in miniature in a terrarium. A terrarium is a small glass case in which suitable plants can flourish in a self-contained world, the growing requirements being recycled by the plant life. A popular form of terrarium is a bottle garden, often a carboy, but terraria can take many forms—for example, fish tanks, goldfish bowls, or specially constructed ornamental cases in leaded glass. Indeed, it is possible to use any transparent-sided container that has a narrow neck or can be covered with a sheet of glass or some other clear material.

By keeping the plants in an enclosed container, draughts are excluded and high humidity can be maintained. This means that delicate plants can be grown and appreciated in a miniature landscape. The most usual plants grown in bottle gardens are those also seen as houseplants. With sufficient warmth and careful selection, it is possible to keep small sub-tropical and even tropical plants which are more suited to heated conservatories and would otherwise be difficult to keep successfully in the home. The plants are virtually self-maintaining, because watering is never, or hardly ever, necessary. The greatest danger is waterlogging from overwatering. Terraria should also be kept out of direct sunlight as leaves close to the glass may be scorched by high temperatures drying moisture between the leaves too rapidly.

Preparation When a suitable container has been selected, place a layer of gravel about $\frac{1}{2}-\frac{3}{4}$in/1-2cm deep in the bottom and cover it with a thinner layer of broken charcoal. On top of this place a layer of a peat-based compost about 2-3in/5-7.5cm deep, or less, depending on size of container.

To make it easier to position the layers of gravel and charcoal and subsequently to add the compost, form a cone of stiff paper or thin cardboard, through which to pour the materials.

Firm the compost with a cotton reel fixed on the end of a thin bamboo cane. Miniature landscaping can then be carried out, and pieces of stone or slate strategically placed to make a garden-like effect. Do not use wood as this will quickly rot and be attacked

Terrarium

by fungi.

Plant grouping The grouping of plants will be easier if a dominant plant is positioned to one side and at least one trailing plant selected for the front. It is a mistake to introduce too many plants: about five or six should be quite enough.

Planting Narrow-necked containers such as glass carboys are rather difficult to plant and require some dexterity.

An old teaspoon and fork tied to the ends of canes can be used to hold the plants as they are lowered into position. The teaspoon also makes it easy to scoop out small planting holes, and the fork can be used to neaten the compost surface. Final firming around the roots should be done with the cotton reel.

Watering After planting, carefully just moisten the surface of the compost, without disturbing the plants. A long-spouted can is ideal for directing the water down the inside to clean the glass. The glass may cloud over after a short time, but this can be corrected by removing the stopper. Make sure that it is replaced once the condensation has cleared.

Further watering may not be necessary because the water vapour given off by the plants is recirculated and the garden will become self-maintaining.

Goldfish bowl

PLANTING A BOTTLE GARDEN

Tie an old teaspoon and fork to the ends of canes for scooping out holes and holding plants in position.

Suitable plants

Plant selection for bottle gardens is somewhat limited. Succulent or quick-growing plants are unsuitable. Flowering plants may sometimes be suitable, but it is often difficult to remove the faded flowers which will decay and be a source of disease if left. Only small-rooted cuttings or offshoots should be planted. The following are suitable for bottle gardens and other terraria.

Acorus gramineus **'Variegatus'**. A tufted, grass-like plant with cream-variegated leaves, up to 10in/25cm. It is easy to grow, tolerant of a fair amount of water at the roots.

Begonia rex (see pages 159-60). Only the small-leaved forms are suitable. These make good focal plants for bottle gardens. 6in/15cm.

Chamaedorea elegans (sometimes incorrectly grown as *Neanthe bella*). See page 152. A small palm with slender fronds and narrow foliage. Can grow up to 4ft/1.2m, but only slowly, so it makes an ideal dominant plant for mixed groups in bottle gardens.

Cryptanthus acaulis. Makes a compact rosette of leaves that are mid-green above, with white markings beneath. The central cluster of small white flowers is pleasing but not showy. 3in/8cm.

Dracaena sanderiana. A slender, fairly slow-growing plant with narrow leaves broadly margined with white. 12in/30cm.

Ferns. Several of the small kinds are ideal. Particularly recommended: *Adiantum raddianum*, (page 150); *A. hispidulum*; *Pellaea rotundifolia*; *Pteris ensiformis* 'Victoriae'.

Fittonia verschaffeltii var. *argyroneura*. This small form is best, having bright green leaves netted with white veins. *F. verschaffeltii* has large leaves netted with red veins. They are both low-growing. 3in/7.5cm.

Hedera helix (common ivy). Some of the many cultivars of ivy have quite small leaves, and are suitable for the confined area of the bottle garden. Cultivars: 'Little Diamond'; 'Spetchley'; 'Très Coupé'.

Maranta leuconeura. The several variants (page 163) have very attractively marked foliage. The stems tend to trail. 8in/20cm.

Pellionia pulchra. A creeping plant, dark green leaves with brownish veins, purple beneath. 3in/7.5cm.

Pilea cadierei. Use the dwarf form 'Nana'. Shining silver splashes on the foliage make a very attractive feature plant. 6in/15cm. (See also page 164.)

Selaginella kraussiana. Moss-like growth and branching, prostrate stems are ideal for covering the surface of bottle-garden compost.

Containers indoors 1

Houseplants form a large and ever-increasing part of container gardening, allowing people without access to a garden the opportunity to grow and tend something green and living in their home or workplace.

Situations

Plants can become an integral part of an interior design scheme. A group on a window sill linking the room with the outside world is the most obvious use, but a climber such as *Philodendron* or *Rhoicissus rhomboidea* suitably placed can act as a room divider or screen, especially in an open-plan office or between sitting and dining areas. In a bedsitter such a screen can separate the sleeping quarters from the living area.

A palm, weeping fig or Swiss cheese plant can become the focal point of a room. The luxuriance of a fern will soften the coldness and angularity of a fireplace in summer. The cascading foliage of an ivy, *Tradescantia* or spider plant can soften the hard corners of a bookcase or room divider. A high ceiling can be made to seem lower by means of a hanging basket. A hallway can be made more welcoming with a suitable plant or group of plants. Ferns will flourish in the warmth and humidity of a bathroom. Plants also look well in a kitchen, softening its utilitarian aspects.

Light and shade

The single most important factor determining the choice of plant is the level of light that it will receive. It is difficult to grow healthy plants in very dark areas. A very sunny window facing south can also prove difficult, especially in high summer. The intense heat and direct sunlight can cause scorching or other damage to the foliage. Flowers, too, deteriorate much more rapidly in these conditions. Windows facing east, west and even north (in the northern hemisphere) can provide sufficient light to keep plants growing sturdily.

If it becomes necessary to place a plant temporarily in poor light conditions, leave it there for as short a time as possible.

Growth always stretches towards the light, so it is a good idea to turn plants regularly to maintain an even shape.

Once out of direct sunlight, the amount

Stairwell

Window sill

Situations
Plants may be an important part of the
design of a room, softening hard edges,
providing a focal point, relieving the blank
area of a stairwell, acting as room divider
or firescreen, embellishing and highlighting
an area such as a dining recess in a living
room.

Containers indoors 2

of light an area receives varies enormously. It is difficult to assess merely by eye how bright or dark a spot is. Comparing a few guesses with a photographic light meter will probably show that you have greatly over-estimated the brightness. Certainly, the areas on each side of a window are not among the brighter spots.

The surest method of testing whether a specific position is suitable for a plant is by placing a sheet of white paper in the exact spot planned, and testing with a light meter. With a film setting of ASA 25 and a shutter speed of a quarter of a second, f32 or f64 indicates direct sunlight; f16 indicates bright or filtered sun; f8 shady.

Artificial lighting Daylight can be supple-mented by means of artificial light. Special lamps are obtainable, but must be installed according to the manufacturer's instructions to achieve their full benefit. A single fluores-cent strip light is a simple way of enabling plants to grow in an otherwise dark corner. To grow plants under artificial lights only, the lamps must be kept on for 16-18 hours a day for flowering plants, and 12-14 hours for foliage plants. Most plants are best situated 12-16in/30-40cm away from the light source, except for African violets which should be 8-12in/20-30cm away.

Light levels in a room

The diagram (page 125) demonstrates the different light levels on a cloudless summer day in the northern hemisphere.

Bright light A position in front of any window that does not face north will receive direct sunlight for most of the day, though the strength of light will depend on the latitude. At lower latitudes, the light will be brighter, but will not extend so far into the room. Curtains will reduce the light on either side of the window. Plants such as *Yucca* enjoy such a sunny situation, though few other plants do.

Filtered light A position 3-5 ft/1-1.5 m away from the window receives filtered sunlight. Suitable for plants such as *Dracaena* and palms. When in doubt about the amount of light any plant needs, place in filtered light.

Shady This area is 5-7 ft/1.5-2 m away from the window, or along a side wall, or near a well-lit north-facing window. Ideal for ferns such as *Asplenium nidus* (bird's nest fern).

Poor light No plant will thrive for long in an area more than 7 ft/2 m from a source of light. If you wish to grow something there for aesthetic reasons, investigate some method of artificial lighting or replenish with new plants as necessary.

CREATING ARTIFICIAL LIGHT

Some form of artificial light will lengthen short winter days. An ordinary incan-descent ceiling light is insufficient, and spotlights placed too close can burn. There are special horticultural tubes, but these give a purplish light unpopular with some gardeners.

Probably best and least expensive is a fluorescent fitting with one 40-watt "natu-ral white" tube and one 40-watt "daylight" tube. Fix this 1-2 ft/30-60 cm above the plants. Ideally, such a fitment should have a tray to hold the plants, a support for the lamps and a hood for reflection.

Plants need at least 12 hours of lighting per day, including the daylight hours. A time-switch can prove very useful.

Self-contained light unit

Poor light

Shady

Filtered light

Bright light

Hanging fitment

Spotlight

Growing towards the light

Plants naturally reach towards the light. To prevent straggly growth, turn the pot a little each day.

Containers indoors 3

Temperature

Remember that a typical room does not have a uniform temperature. Opening doors will let in gusts of cold air. In winter a window sill can be a very cold position, particularly when curtains are closed and there is no heating at night. Double-glazed windows will help, but even then very tender plants may suffer. Any plant that is likely to be vulnerable to the cold should be brought into the centre of the room.

However, care must be taken not to site plants too close to a heat source because excessive desiccation can take place. Near a radiator can be too hot a situation unless the plants are protected by a shelf. Even in summer a window sill is not necessarily ideal, because of the risk of strong sunlight scorching some plants.

The safest way to monitor temperatures is with a maximum and minimum thermometer.

Humidity

Dry conditions, such as those of a centrally heated room, are not good for the well-being of most plants. Bathrooms and kitchens have increased humidity, which is beneficial provided that there is sufficient light.

A simple way to create humidity is to spray clear water carefully onto foliage with a fine hand spray. This should be done at least once a day. Alternatively, stand the plant in a container which holds water-laden material or just water. This is not harmful provided that the roots do not become waterlogged.

Plunging a plant in its pot in moist peat (kept damp at all times) works very well, unless the compost is allowed to become excessively dry, in which case the roots will emerge from the drainage holes and seek moisture from the peat.

A layer of small pebbles placed in the bottom of an outer container and kept charged with water will raise the base of the plant pot so that it does not become saturated. Similarly, the pot can be stood on a block of wood submerged in water.

Types of containers

Although plants invariably enhance the appearance of an interior, the containers in which they grow are also important as part of the décor.

Containers should always be in keeping with their situation, bearing in mind also their size in relation to the plants and to the scale

---

INCREASING HUMIDITY

Place a layer of small pebbles in the bottom of an outer container and keep charged with water. Evaporation into the surrounding air will increase humidity.

Alternatively, stand a pot on a block of wood resting on the bottom of the outer container. Submerge the wood, but keep the pot above water level.

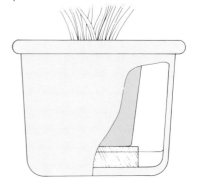

CONTAINERS FOR HOUSEPLANTS

Jardinière

Modern-styled plastic container

Urn

Wooden tub

Terracotta pot

Glazed Chinese pot

Wicker basket

Containers indoors 4

of the area in which they are to be placed. The material from which the containers are made also needs consideration, together with their colour, shape and external decoration.

Outer containers Pot covers, or outer containers, are produced in a variety of sizes and finishes. Many are made in ceramic or glazed terracotta, but those manufactured in plastic or glass fibre can also be attractive. Their size should be dictated by the plant itself and the pot in which it is growing—a small plant will appear pathetically lost in an oversized plant cover, and the rim of a pot should not show

above the level of its pot cover.

Wicker baskets make suitable pot covers, especially if they are either lined with plastic (page 132) or have an inner container to hold excess water. Plastic-lined baskets can also be used to grow plants set directly into compost (pages 132-3), but care is needed with watering because they have no drainage holes.

Jardinières Jardinières are usually made for fairly large indoor displays and can be constructed either as a raised trough or as a bowl on a pedestal. They are often quite ornate.

Grouping containers: contrasting heights and sizes

Macramé Hanging plants look particularly attractive when suspended by macramé work, but need drip trays to protect carpets and furnishings. Stronger-growing plants should be selected, as macramé can be visually rather dominant and detract from the effect of the flowers and foliage.

Self-watering containers Increasing use is now made of self-watering containers, especially in offices and public places (see also page 135). Such containers are produced in various shapes and sizes and are suitable for either groups or single plants.

Grouping pots

How pots are grouped is very much a matter of personal choice, but as a general rule, unless a plant and its container are spectacular, a grouping of several containers will make more impact than the same number dotted about the room. Alternatively, several separate potted plants can be grouped together in one large outer container and then moved individually for maintenance purposes or to change the display.

The diagrams (bottom) show how contrasts of form and texture can be effective.

MACRAMÉ POT HOLDERS

A drip tray fitted under a plant displayed in a macramé pot holder will prevent staining of the carpet. It is best to choose plants with strong features.

Equipment and composts

Equipment
Very few tools are needed for growing and maintaining houseplants. A small trowel and fork, secateurs, scissors and a knife are essential (see pages 28-31). A long, narrow-spouted can is most useful for watering. A mist sprayer is invaluable for creating suitable humidity. Bamboo canes and tying materials (see pages 42-3) are also useful, and a few moss poles (pages 138-9) will help to support some of the taller plants decoratively. An artist's paintbrush is helpful for cleaning leaves and applying small quantities of leaf shine or pesticide.

Composts and fertilizers
The choice of potting compost for houseplants is not critical. The two main mixtures are soil-based and peat-based (see pages 32-3). Large and tall-growing plants will be much more stable in a loam-based compost.

New plants or recently repotted ones will not need feeding for some time. Feed plants in soil-based compost after three months, those in a peat-based one after six weeks.

Equipment for houseplants

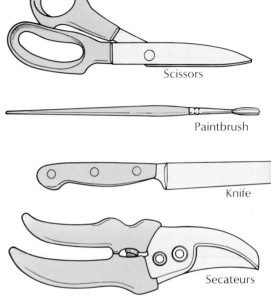

Scissors

Paintbrush

Knife

Secateurs

HYDROPONICS

In place of soil, it is possible to grow plants in containers filled with water and aggregate, to which soluble plant foods are added. The aggregate is bought specially for this purpose: it can be pea gravel, Perlite, grit, or a purpose-made clay granule.

A double container is sometimes used. This consists of a smaller plastic container, pierced with holes or slits, which fits into a watertight outer container. The aggregate and the plant are placed in the inner container, but the roots may grow through the holes into the water in the outer container. In both single and double containers, the water is only in the lower part.

The fertilizer can be either a standard liquid one or a specially formulated hydroculture fertilizer.

A simple example of hydroponics is the use of a hyacinth glass (pages 172-3).

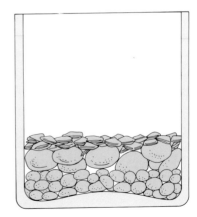

1 Place a 1 in/2.5 cm layer of aggregate previously soaked to remove impurities. Cover with a layer of pebbles, plus a layer of charcoal to keep the water sweet.

Mist sprayer   Trowel   Hand fork

2 Add more aggregate until the container is two-thirds full. Fill the container one-third full with water and let the aggregate absorb the water.

3 Place the plant inside the container and pack aggregate around its roots. If the plant has been growing in compost, care-fully wash off all traces first.

Planting techniques

The basic planting techniques for indoor plants are similar to those for outdoor plants (pages 34-7). However, a few types of container need slightly specialized techniques.

Wicker baskets

Baskets can make charming containers for indoor plants. The best plants for them are those that are already in pots, the basket being used as an outer pot cover.

To prevent water from spoiling the basket and percolating through onto furniture or flooring, the basket must be lined. Insert a sheet of plastic such as a dustbin liner inside the basket and cut it to shape, allowing a small overlap at the rim. Place a 1in/2.5cm layer of porous clay pellets at the bottom of the basket. Fill the basket with 2-2½in/5-6cm of moist peat-based compost and stand the pots on this.

Hanging baskets

Indoor hanging baskets can look very attractive and are functional provided that they are suspended over a non-carpeted floor, are suitably solid, or have a saucer attachment to collect water if they have provision for drainage. Make sure, too, that the fixings are secured to a ceiling joist, and not just set in plaster – the basket will be very heavy when filled.

Line the basket with a 2in/5cm layer of damp moss. Fit a circle of plastic inside: leave an overlap if you wish. Water the plants before taking them out of their pots and planting them in the container.

Indoor window box

With a window that opens outwards or has a wide sill, a trough filled with plants makes an attractive indoor window box. As the box should have holes in the bottom for drainage, it will need a suitable drip tray. A deep box will prevent the compost from drying out too quickly.

Line the bottom of the box with broken terracotta crocks, then place a 2in/5cm layer of potting mixture on top. Set the plants in the box, taller ones at the back and trailing plants at the front. Fill in with more compost. Alternatively, arrange a group of plants already in pots to stand inside the trough.

Planting a wicker basket

1 Line the basket with plastic. It is preferable to have a layer of foil under the plastic to prevent the wickerwork from rotting.

Planting an indoor window box

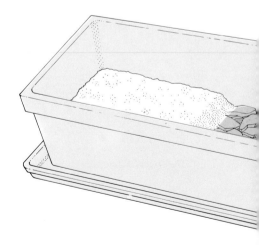

1 Line the box with a layer of crocks, face downwards, so the water will drain off them. Add a 2in/5cm layer of potting compost, a little higher at the back.

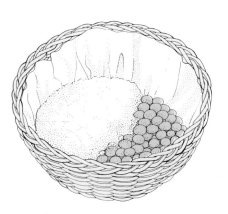

2 Add a layer of porous clay pellets and then fill with peat-based compost. A handful of charcoal will prevent souring. Set plants directly into the compost.

Alternatively, stand pots of plants on the compost, and pack more compost around them. Hang the basket from a universal joint to rotate for even light.

2 Fill the box with compost and set the plants in it, adding a little charcoal to prevent souring. It is most effective to place taller plants at the back.

Alternatively, stand pots already filled with plants inside the trough either on a compost base, or on individual drip saucers. Remove and replace when they deteriorate.

Maintenance 1

Watering

The single most difficult technique to master with indoor plants is watering. Too much or too little can be disastrous, although it is better to keep plants slightly on the dry side.

It is important always to water thoroughly so that the whole of the root ball becomes completely soaked. Small amounts of water dampen the surface, but leave the greater portion of the compost underneath quite dry.

The frequency of watering can never be prescribed, because it will change with the time of year, the age and type of plant, the situation, and the type of compost and container. By feeling just under the surface of the compost you will obtain a very good indication of the state of dryness.

Over-and underwatering Overwatering is probably the worst and most common fault in indoor plant cultivation. Once the root system has begun to die through waterlogging, it is practically impossible to resuscitate

the plant. If compost has become too dry, the root system will be badly affected, but if it is then thoroughly watered there is a chance that it will recover. It is, however, very bad practice to allow a plant to dry out.

Both over- and underwatering will cause foliage and stems to droop, with possibly the loss of some leaves. Usually, where a plant has been overwatered, the foliage will begin to turn yellow before falling.

When a pot plant has been put into an outer container such as a decorative pot cover, great care must be taken that there is no excessive build-up of water in the outer container as it drains through the compost. Tip any excess water away.

Water temperature The temperature of the water is not critical, although some plants do not like really cold water on their leaves. Rainwater is ideal, but tap water is perfectly adequate, unless it is "hard", in which case problems can arise with calcifuge (lime-hating)

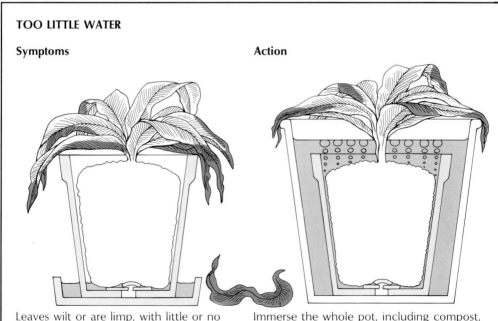

TOO LITTLE WATER

Symptoms

Action

Leaves wilt or are limp, with little or no growth; lower leaves curled and yellow, with edges brown and dry. Oldest leaves fall first. Flowers fall or fade quickly.

Immerse the whole pot, including compost, to compost level in a bucket or bath of water, until air bubbles cease to rise. Drain before replacing in pot cover.

plants. Even then, the occasional use of tap water will do no harm.

Self-watering containers In these, plants are usually grown in a special medium with the water held in a reservoir. An unobtrusive marker moved by a simple float indicates the water level. Another type relies on a reservoir in the base which is fitted with a wick that comes in contact with the growing medium. The wick principle can also be used in a home-made set-up, as shown in the diagram on page 137.

Holiday watering Holiday periods can be difficult if no one is available to maintain plants. However, it is possible to provide for a wide range of plants, even if they are not in self-watering containers, although for periods longer than a week in summer, some deterioration must be expected, especially with flowering plants.

Put the plants in shadier conditions to help prevent them from any drying out. Grouping plants fairly tightly together will also help.

A sink, bowl or other receptacle, even a bath or shower, with no more than 1in/2.5cm of water, also keeps plants from drying out. Place an old towel at the bottom to prevent the containers from damaging the surface. As a short-term device, plants can be stood in deep saucers or shallow bowls of water, which is taken up through the holes in the base of the pot (see page 137).

During the summer, foliage plants can even be plunged out of doors in a shady position. If the soil is well watered, the plant will come to very little harm, even in dry weather.

Feeding
Regular feeding is necessary in the growing season (usually between March and September). There are many proprietary fertilizers on the market which are specially formulated for house plants. They should be used according to the manufacturer's instructions.

TOO MUCH WATER

Symptoms

Action

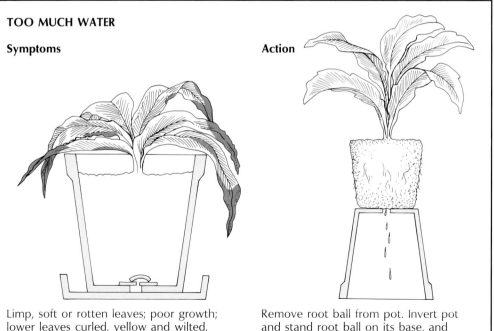

Limp, soft or rotten leaves; poor growth; lower leaves curled, yellow and wilted, brown tips. Both young and old leaves fall simultaneously. Flowers often mouldy.

Remove root ball from pot. Invert pot and stand root ball on its base, and leave for some time to allow excess moisture to drain away.

Maintenance 2

Cleaning

Foliage, especially larger leaves, needs regular cleaning because dust not only looks unsightly but also interrupts the natural functions of the leaves and may lead to some dehydration of the plant. Wipe over leaves with a soft, damp piece of cloth or sponge.

Proprietary leaf-shines also help to clean foliage and give it a high gloss. Such shines need to be applied carefully because they may cause severe damage to young leaves. Also, if used to excess, they can make the plant's overall appearance somewhat artificial.

A simple home-made leaf-shine can be made with a solution of equal parts of milk and water. Apply this with a sponge or soft rag.

Staking and tying

There are various ways to support climbing houseplants. To train them up a wall, wires

Cleaning leaves

Large, smooth leaves are cleaned with a damp sponge or cloth. Use a weak solution of soapy water and rinse afterwards.

Watering methods

Watering from above Pouring water on the surface of the compost controls the amount of water given. Give a good drink each time, rather than frequent dribbling.

Watering from below Stand the pot on a saucer filled with water. The plant will take the water up as required. Flush away mineral salts with occasional top watering.

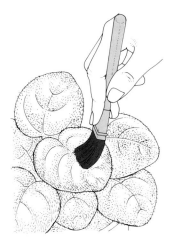

Hairy leaves can be dusted with a soft, dry paintbrush. Anything damp will be trapped in the hairs, encouraging rot.

Total immersion will wash dust off small-leaved or very soiled plants. Use lukewarm soapy water, swirl around and then rinse.

Holiday watering

Stand the pots on an old towel in a sink or bowl filled with 1 in/2.5 cm of water. Group the plants tightly together and keep shaded. Alternatively in summer, plunge out of doors.

A wick and reservoir can be devised, so that the wick transfers water to the compost as and when the plant requires it. This is how self-watering containers work.

Maintenance 3

or strong nylon cord strung between nails or screw eyes will make a good framework. The plant can then be attached with plant ties (page 43).

For shorter plants, there are various forms of support such as a bamboo trellis, rattan canes and rattan hoops. Bamboo stakes can be made into a variety of supports of different shapes.

Making a moss pole To make a moss pole for plants with aerial roots such as *Monstera* and *Philodendron*, wrap chicken netting around a roll of corrugated paper and join the cut edges together. Remove the corrugated paper. Thread two short lengths of bamboo, lashed together crosswise, through the netting about 1in/2.5cm from the bottom. Tie them firmly to the wire column and wedge them into the pot. Fill the pot two-thirds full of compost, and then fill the column of chicken netting with sphagnum moss, ramming it down with a wooden stick. Attach the plant with ties to the pole and water the moss and compost. Spray the pole every day to keep the moss moist.

Another way to make a moss pole is simply to wrap wet moss thickly around a wooden stake and then wrap green, plastic-covered wire around the outside. The plant must be tied on at first, but once the aerial roots start to cling it will be self-supporting.

Making a wire hoop It is quite easy to make a hoop for training plants which cling or twine. Make two lengths of wire the same size, bend them into half-circles and insert in the compost at right angles to each other. Lash them together at the top. Train the plant around the wires. See page 149.

Tidying and pruning

In addition to keeping the general appearance of plants neat and tidy, removing dead foliage and flowerheads is also an important factor in plant hygiene. Sometimes a piece of stem will have to be removed because of die-back, or if it has become too obtrusive and is spoiling the shape of the plant.

Soft growth can easily be cut away with a sharp knife, but secateurs will be needed for woodier material. When making a cut, it is important not to leave any ragged tissue which may be infected by disease.

Similarly, stems should be cut, wherever possible, just above a node (that is, where the leaf joins, or has joined, a main stem). At this point, healing tends to be rapid and the cut looks neater.

After a few years, some plants such as *Ficus elastica* 'Decora' (rubber plant) and *Monstera deliciosa* become leggy, with very little foliage on lengths of the lower stems. Rejuvenate the plant by cutting back the main stem severely in spring or early summer.

Although it seems somewhat brutal, the cut should be made about 6in/15cm from the base of the plant. (Rubber plants will exude a certain amount of latex.) After a few weeks, new shoots will begin to form and in due course a single growth can be selected to form a new main stem if only one is required. All the remaining shoots should be removed as cleanly as possible, making the cuts near to the old main stem.

Potting on

Perennial plants will, at some stage, need to be moved into larger pots; this operation is

Potting on

1 Water the root ball and leave to drain. Choose a pot two sizes larger than the previous pot.

Making a moss pole

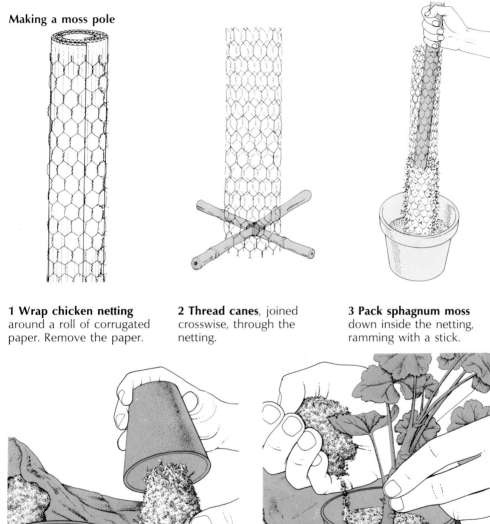

1 Wrap chicken netting around a roll of corrugated paper. Remove the paper.

2 Thread canes, joined crosswise, through the netting.

3 Pack sphagnum moss down inside the netting, ramming with a stick.

2 Hold the plant stem between the fingers and invert the pot, tapping gently so that the root ball slides out.

3 Place the root ball in the new pot and sprinkle moist compost around it. Firm carefully and water again to settle in.

139

Maintenance 4

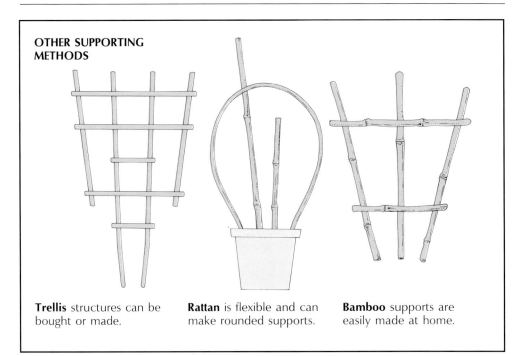

OTHER SUPPORTING METHODS

Trellis structures can be bought or made.

Rattan is flexible and can make rounded supports.

Bamboo supports are easily made at home.

best carried out in spring and early summer, so that the plant can establish itself successfully while there are good natural growing conditions.

As a general guide, choose a pot two sizes larger than the pot in which it is growing. The root ball must be soaked with water and allowed to drain. This will not only make it easier to remove the plant from its pot, but will also ensure that it is thoroughly moistened before the new compost is added and the plant watered again to settle the compost and ensure it is evenly moist throughout.

Repotting

Sometimes it is necessary only to repot a plant. Although this term is often used synonymously with potting on, it really refers to removing the root ball and teasing away some of the old compost (an old kitchen fork is convenient for this), and even some of the roots, before putting the plant back in the same pot, together with fresh compost. The root ball can be reduced by about a quarter. Do this too in spring and early summer.

Repotting

1 Remove the plant from its pot by inverting it and tapping as for potting on. Tease away some of the old compost.

KEEPING PLANTS TIDY

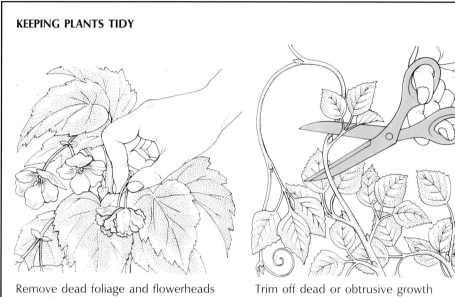

Remove dead foliage and flowerheads regularly to keep plants looking tidy.

Trim off dead or obtrusive growth cleanly and as close to a node as possible.

2 Trim the roots with sharp scissors, a knife or secateurs. With larger plants, prune top growth in proportion.

3 Clean the old pot thoroughly if it is to be reused. Replace the root ball and add fresh compost, firming well.

Flowering houseplants 1

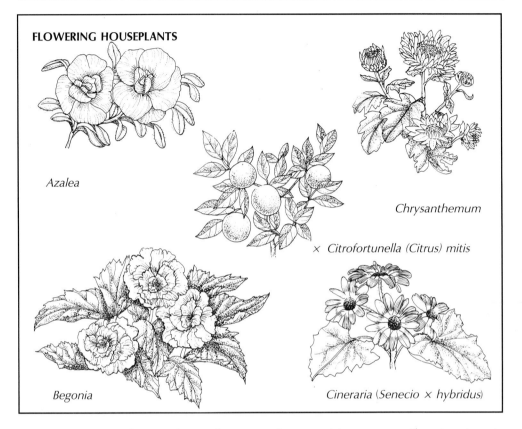

FLOWERING HOUSEPLANTS

Azalea

Chrysanthemum

× Citrofortunella (Citrus) mitis

Begonia

Cineraria (Senecio × hybridus)

Flowering pot plants always make a welcome addition to the home, and last longer than cut flowers. However, some people are intimidated by the prospect of caring for them. Such misgivings are often well founded, since many plants die very rapidly in over-heated rooms or from being overwatered.

Considerable detail has been included in the following descriptions on the care and continued maintenance of these plants. Most tend to flower in the winter months. If treated correctly they can be grown on for a number of years.

The houseplants listed here are some of the most popular. Indoor bulbs, cacti and succulents are described on pages 168-81.

African violet. See *Saintpaulia*.
Azalea. Evergreen shrubs that give a good display of pink, red or white flowers in winter and early spring when forced into flower.

They are sold as compact flowering plants in various sizes, the smallest ones often being included in mixed arrangements in bowls and baskets. From 5in/13cm to 12in/30cm.

Cool conditions suit azaleas best, and light shade and some humidity are essential to maintain a long flowering period. When received from the nursery, the pots are usually full of root, with little space left for watering. If the compost dries out completely, it will be difficult to wet it thoroughly again except by totally immersing the pot in water. Azaleas must never be allowed to dry out at the root, yet must never become waterlogged. Rainwater should be used for watering as they are plants that must have acid soils, and hard water may cause the foliage to yellow. However, any misting of the foliage can be done with ordinary tap water, although in hard water areas this will leave a chalky deposit on the leaves.

After flowering, keep the plants indoors until frosts have finished. Then put them outside again, in a sheltered, semi-shaded spot, and keep them fed and watered regularly throughout the summer and autumn. Bring them back indoors before the onset of the really cold weather.

Potting on into a pot one size larger may be necessary: always use an acid compost with azaleas. Potting on should be done in the spring after flowering.

Begonia. Many kinds of begonias are available as house plants. Most, like *Begonia rex* (page 160), are grown for their attractive foliage. Indoor begonias require some warmth to thrive, but will tolerate quite cool conditions for short periods. Humidity is essential to keep the foliage in good condition, but strong light should be avoided.

Cultivars: the relatively newly introduced Reiger begonias (improvements on the winter-flowering *B.* x *hiernalis*) have become extremely popular. They are very free-flowering over a long period, with white, yellow, pink, red or orange double flowers. 7in/18cm. A dry atmosphere should be avoided, but

indirect sunlight will keep the plant developing steadily. Feed begonias regularly during flowering.

Chrysanthemum. Dwarf plants in pots are available throughout the year and are among the longest-lasting flowering plants, especially when kept reasonably cool. 6in/15cm. They have yellow, pink, red or orange flowerheads and require good light to maintain flower colour. Because of the way they are produced, it is not possible to grow them on to flower satisfactorily from year to year. They should not, therefore, be planted outside, but should be discarded after flowering.

Cineraria (**Senecio** x **hybridus**). Brightly coloured flowerheads in white, pink, red or blue appear in winter and last into spring. Up to 9in/23cm. Cool conditions are necessary and direct sunlight should be avoided at all times because the foliage flags under intense heat, giving the impression that the plant is dry.

Take care not to overwater. A moist atmosphere, and especially the use of a fine hand spray, will help to maintain the plants. Discard after flowering.

Care of *Azalea*

1 Remove withered flowers and pot on, scraping away some of old compost and firming fresh compost around the roots.

2 Immerse pot in rainwater if compost becomes dry. Plunge outside in partial shade from June to September.

3 Feed every 14 days from spring, and every 3-4 weeks from midsummer until August. Bring indoors in September. Water well.

Flowering houseplants 2

Citrus. Oranges, lemons and grapefruits make pleasing evergreen foliage plants when raised from pips, but do not expect them to fruit (for fruiting plants, see pages 110-11). Sow the pips in a little warmth as soon as available.

Several species of citrus have been selected for indoor decorative plants, some having variegated foliage. Unlike those grown from pips, these special cultivars flower and fruit

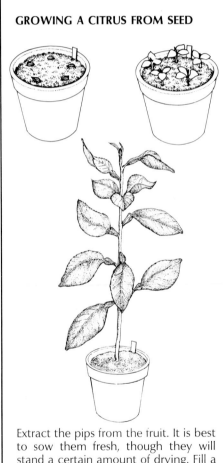

GROWING A CITRUS FROM SEED

Extract the pips from the fruit. It is best to sow them fresh, though they will stand a certain amount of drying. Fill a 5in/12cm pot with seed compost. Space about 5 pips around the surface. Water thoroughly, cover with glass and a piece of paper, keep at 70°F/21°C. Germination should take 3-4 weeks.

regularly, bearing both at the same time. 24in/60cm. Good light is necessary, but avoid intense heat. Spray regularly by hand. Citrus respond well to generous feeding.

Cyclamen. Cyclamen grow well as house plants, with flowers in shades of red, pink or white from autumn to spring, but need some care to be maintained in good condition. Miniatures are 4in/10cm, large-flowered cultivars 9in/23cm.

Purchase plants with plenty of flowers in bud rather than those already in full bloom. Humid conditions are important: a very warm, dry situation causes the leaves and flower stems to wilt and eventually collapse. A cool but draught-free position will prolong the flowering period. Remove old flower stems completely by sharply pulling to detach them from the corm. Any damaged leaves or flowers should be removed regularly.

Regular feeding is necessary, but take care when watering, which is best done early in the day into the side of the pot, away from the centre of the plant, so that water does not lodge at the base of the flower stems.

Cyclamen can be kept from year to year. Continue watering and feeding after flowering until the foliage begins to yellow. Then place the pots on their sides in a cool, shady position and allow the plants to dry off completely. Signs of new growth usually appear in August, and then the pots should be stood upright and the compost thoroughly watered. Either repot into fresh compost or remove some of the top surface and replace it with a top dressing of new compost. When frosts are expected, bring the plant into the house and allow it to develop again.

In subsequent years the plant will need potting on.

Cymbidium. There are many hybrids of this easily grown orchid in yellow, pink, bronze or combinations of these colours. The shorter-growing ones are particularly suitable for window sill culture. Dwarf plants are from 12in/30cm; others can reach 4ft/1.2m. High temperatures are not required: 50°F/10°C, or even lower on occasion, is adequate.

Use rainwater for watering and for misting the plants over regularly. Feed at intervals during the growing season, which starts in the winter.

FLOWERING HOUSEPLANTS

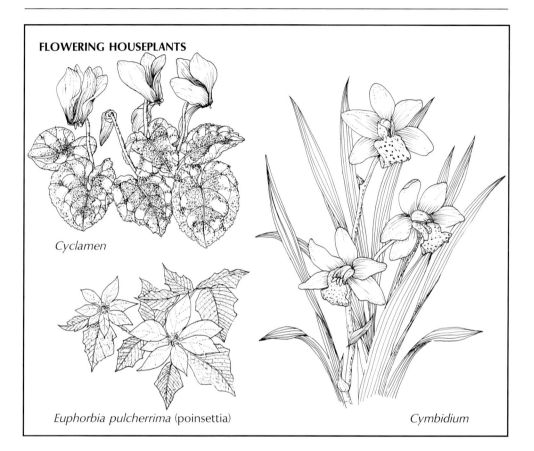

Cyclamen

Euphorbia pulcherrima (poinsettia)

Cymbidium

After flowering and once all fear of frost has gone, place the plant out of doors in a semi-shaded position. Cymbidiums can, if preferred, remain indoors all the time.

Potting on does not need to be done regularly, but, when it is, special orchid compost must be used (obtained from good garden centres).

Euphorbia pulcherrima (commonly known as Christmas poinsettia). These flamboyant plants give a long period of colour and are popular at Christmas and throughout the winter. The flowers are small and insignificant, and it is the surrounding leafy growths (bracts) that are decorative. These are usually in shades of red, but pink and cream cultivars are also available. 18in/45cm, although both smaller (6in/15cm) and much larger (24in/60cm) specimens can be purchased.

RECOLOURING *EUPHORBIA* (POINSETTIA)

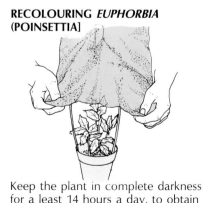

Keep the plant in complete darkness for a least 14 hours a day, to obtain red bracts in second and subsequent years (see page 146).

Flowering houseplants 3

These plants need good light, and a temperature not below 55-60°F/13-15°C. Regular misting will create the ideal humid conditions. After flowering, gradually decrease watering and keep the plant dry throughout the summer.

When frosts have finished, remove the tips of the old flowering stems and place the pot on its side in a sheltered situation outdoors. In the latter part of summer, new growths will be produced from the old stems. It will be necessary to thin out some of the new growths, leaving only a few to develop. This keeps the plant more compact and helps to increase bract size. Start watering again, and do any potting on required at this stage.

Before the onset of frosts, the plant must be given indoor protection, but to ensure a second colourful display, it is essential that the plant receives at least 14 hours of complete darkness each day for several weeks so that flowers are initiated and the bracts formed: if the plant is usually positioned in a room that is lit during the evening, move it during this period to a totally dark situation such as a cupboard.

At all times take care to avoid overwatering. Regular feeding is necessary during full growth.

Geranium. See *Pelargonium*.

Gloxinia. See *Sinningia speciosa*.

Hoya. *Hoya carnosa* and its variegated forms are strong-growing climbers with heavily scented, waxy flowers (white ageing to pink, with pink centres) in spring and summer. The plant will need support but can be confined to about 3ft/90cm by tying the stems on to a framework held in a container (see also pages 102-4).

A temperature of 50°F/10°C is necessary in winter, but more warmth is beneficial in summer. Good light is required in the winter, but semi-shade at other times will maintain leaf colour. The thick, leathery foliage can soon wither, so regular watering during full growth is necessary. Avoid too much water in the winter months. Feed with a tomato fertilizer to encourage flowering. The flower stems must not be removed, as they will produce more flowerheads the following year.

Hydrangea. This hardy shrub can be forced

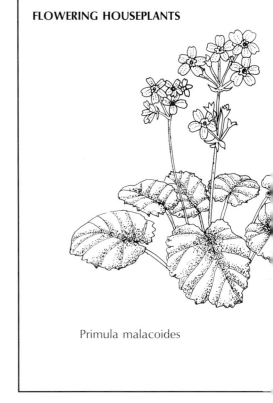

FLOWERING HOUSEPLANTS

Primula malacoides

into flower and makes a long-lasting pot plant with a bold display of white, pink, red or blue flowerheads. In subsequent years a special proprietary colorant is required to keep the flowers blue. 12-15in/30-43cm.

Low temperatures and humidity are necessary, as well as copious watering during the growing season. Water sparingly in winter. If possible, use rainwater at all times.

When the plant has finished flowering, remove the old flowerheads and pot on in an acid compost. In the spring, prune again to keep the plant compact and to remove any shoots that are too weak to develop flowerheads.

Pelargonium (also called *Geranium*). There are many cultivars available, some with very colourful or aromatic foliage (see also pages 58-60 and 109). Regal and zonal pelargoniums are the most popular, the latter flowering

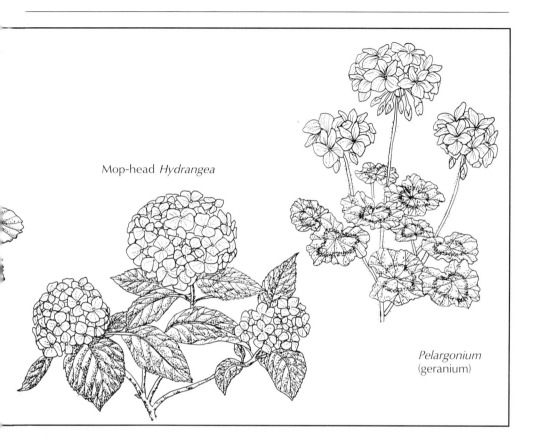

Mop-head *Hydrangea*

Pelargonium
(geranium)

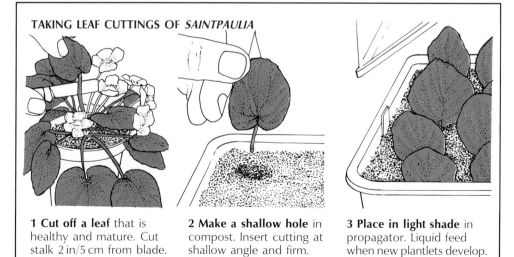

TAKING LEAF CUTTINGS OF *SAINTPAULIA*

1 Cut off a leaf that is healthy and mature. Cut stalk 2 in/5 cm from blade.

2 Make a shallow hole in compost. Insert cutting at shallow angle and firm.

3 Place in light shade in propagator. Liquid feed when new plantlets develop.

147

Flowering houseplants 4

over a long period. Both require very good light and can tolerate hot conditions. Avoid waterlogging. Although pelargoniums will tolerate dryness at the roots, it is best to keep them just moist from spring to autumn.

The regals have a marvellous colour range: white, pink, salmon, orange, red, crimson or purple. The flowers are quite large (up to 3in/7.5cm) across. The main flowering period is late spring through to early summer. The zonals also have a good colour range—white, pink or red, with the addition of attractive foliage, usually marked with a distinct dark zone. There are also forms with variegated leaves. Zonals flower from spring to autumn.

Regal pelargoniums should be pruned after flowering, but zonals are best pruned in the spring. Both can be potted on or top-dressed in March.

Poinsettia. See *Euphorbia pulcherrima*.

Primula. Coloured primroses and polyanthus, and hybrids between the two, have become extremely popular for winter- and spring-flowering. They come in a very wide range of colours: white, yellow, pink, red or blue. 4in/10cm. Primulas require cool, semi-shaded conditions, respond to regular watering and feeding, and are easy to maintain. *Primula malacoides* (fairy primula) is a dainty plant and produces flowers (white, pink or lilac) in winter and spring. Up to 9in/23cm. It requires the same conditions as primroses and polyanthus, but more care must be taken with watering, as the fine root system can soon become waterlogged.

Saintpaulia (African violet). A very popular plant with velvety flowers in white, pink, mauve, red, blue or purple. 4in/10cm. In recent years hybrids have been produced that are very small-growing, with small flowers (2in/5cm). Care must be taken when watering, as saintpaulias are very susceptible to cold water damage, which shows up as irregular scarring and blotching on the foliage. Tepid water is necessary during the winter and preferable at all times.

Bright, direct sunlight should always be avoided. Because these plants require a humid atmosphere, kitchens and bathrooms make good situations. To maintain humidity, the pot should be plunged in peat or stood on a layer of pebbles in a shallow depth of water,

but care must be taken that the compost does not become waterlogged. Saintpaulias also require a fairly high temperature (60-70°F/15-21°C) to thrive, but some of the newer hybrids can perform well at somewhat lower temperatures. Feed regularly from spring to autumn and pot on every second year, using a peat-based compost.

Sinningia speciosa (often known as *Gloxinia*). The white, pink, red, blue or purple trumpet-shaped flowers are borne in the spring and summer. 6in/15cm. The tubers (swollen storage organs) are often sold in gift packs.

Semi-shade and a temperature of at least 60°F/15°C are required for starting the tubers into growth. Humid conditions should be provided by standing the pot in moist peat or a container of shallow water, but overhead misting should not be given.

As soon as the plant has died back in the autumn, keep the tuber in its pot without water until growth restarts in the spring.

Solanum capsicastrum. A small, compact, shrub grown for its orange, ball-like fruits which form in autumn and winter. 7in/13cm. Humidity helps to keep the foliage and fruits fresh. During growth, water and feed regularly. Good light is necessary, and cool but draught-free conditions suit these plants best. They can be grown on to flower and fruit the following year if required. After fruiting the more straggly and weaker growths should be removed and the main stems pruned back by one-third to encourage branching and the production of a compact, well-furnished plant. Feeding during the growing season with a tomato fertilizer will encourage the production of the decorative fruits. Misting is advisable during hot, dry weather.

Stephanotis. The growth of this fairly rampant climber with white flowers can be confined by pot culture, as this restricts the root action and subsequent top growth. The growths should be tied to a circular wire frame. This training helps to encourage flowering, as does feeding with a fertilizer that has a higher potash element than usual during spring and summer. After flowering, cut out weak and surplus shoots but maintain the main framework shoots which will produce the following year's growth and flowers. Needs a temperature of 60-65°F/15-18°C. 18in/45cm.

FLOWERING HOUSEPLANTS

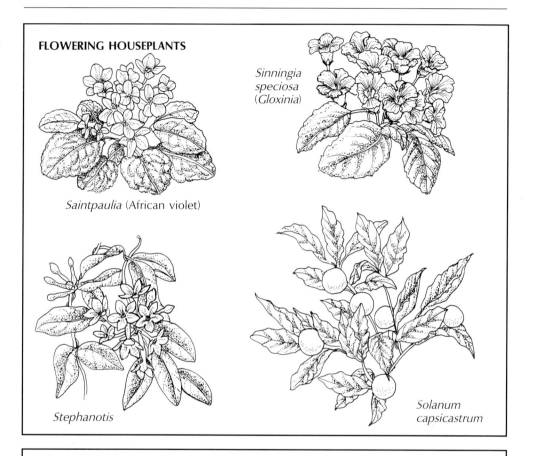

Sinningia speciosa (*Gloxinia*)

Saintpaulia (African violet)

Stephanotis

Solanum capsicastrum

TRAINING *STEPHANOTIS* AROUND A HOOP

1 Bend wire into a half-circle. Insert ends into compost.

2 Tie the growths carefully on to the wire frame with plant ties.

Containing in a pot restricts root action and subsequent top growth.

Green houseplants 1

Although flowering houseplants are very attractive, most plants in the home or workplace will be non-flowering. Such foliage plants are, however, extremely pleasing in their own right.

Some types of houseplant have cultivars that are mostly green-leaved, but with variegated or coloured variants also available. To avoid unnecessary duplication, such plants are described among the green houseplants list below, but with a cross-reference to them in the list of coloured and variegated plants (pages 158-65).

Adiantum raddianum (maidenhair fern). There are several cultivars of this plant with feathery arching fronds. About 18in/45cm. Tolerates winter temperatures as low as 50°F/10°C, but direct strong sunlight should be avoided.

Regular misting during spring and summer, liberal watering when in active growth, and regular dilute feeding are necessary. Any potting on should be done in the spring, at which time the old fronds can be completely cut away to allow new growth to rejuvenate the plant.

Araucaria heterophylla (Norfolk Island pine). This erect-growing small tree has tiered branches bearing bright green needles. It is at its best when fairly young; later on, it loses its lower branches and looks somewhat ungainly. 4ft/1.2m. Semi-shade is necessary in summer, but good light is needed in winter, when the plant tolerates a low temperature of 40°F/5°C. Water and feed regularly in spring and summer.

Asparagus. Several species and cultivars are available, all with fern-like growth. The long, trailing stems bear fine foliage which turns yellowish in full sun. Tolerates quite cool conditions in winter and needs semi-shade. Water regularly during the growing season, but keep drier in winter. Feed every fortnight during summer and pot on in spring to maintain the production of vigorous young basal shoots. Species and cultivars: *A. densiflorus* (*A. sprengeri*), 18in/45cm, has masses of very narrow leaflets held on arching and trailing stems which become prickly with age. *A. setaceus* (better known as *A. plumosus*), 24in/60cm, has even finer foliage, giving the impression of a fern; growth has a tendency to climb.

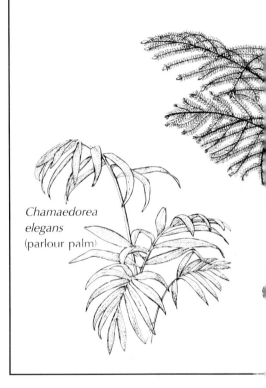

GREEN-FOLIAGED HOUSEPLANTS

Chamaedorea elegans (parlour palm)

Aspidistra elatior. This plant has several common names, but "cast-iron plant" is very apt, because the plant seems almost indestructible. Tolerant of all kinds of situations and indifferent attention, although it can be overwatered, and it loses its dark green colour in strong sunlight. Up to 3ft/90cm.

There is no need to pot on regularly. Feed only once a month in spring and summer. Minimum winter temperature of 45°F/7°C. There is a variegated form, but it has a tendency to lose this characteristic; it is not a strong grower, and requires careful watering.

Asplenium nidus (bird's nest fern). A fern with broad, glossy leaves growing up to 4ft/1.2m in length. A winter temperature of at least 55°F/13°C should be maintained. Needs plenty of water and a humid atmosphere, except in winter. Feed regularly in spring and summer.

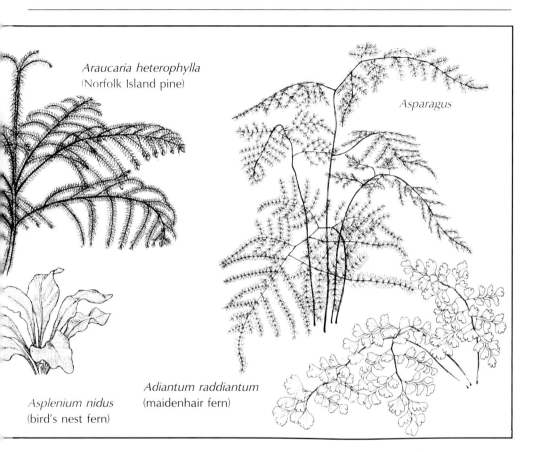

Araucaria heterophylla
(Norfolk Island pine)

Asparagus

Asplenium nidus
(bird's nest fern)

Adiantum raddiantum
(maidenhair fern)

Root division of *Aspidistra*

1 Invert the pot, supporting the root ball with your other hand, and remove the plant from its pot.

2 Pull the root ball apart, making two or more pieces. It does not matter if a few small rootlets break off.

3 Replant each new rooting section into a separate pot with drainage crocks and fresh compost.

151

Green houseplants 2

Begonia. See page 159.

Chamaedorea elegans (often grown as *Neanthe bella*) (parlour palm). One of the most suitable small palms for indoor culture. 4ft/1.2m. Needs a minimum winter temperature of 55°F/13°C, with semi-shade to keep the foliage fresh and bright. Mist, water and feed regularly from spring to autumn.

Cissus antarctica (kangaroo vine). A vigorous climber with leathery green leaves, having toothed margins. The plant can be kept within bounds by pruning and growing in a smaller pot. Winter temperature of 50°F/10°C. Semi-shade suits it best. Water and feed moderately throughout the growing season, reducing quantities in winter.

Cyperus alternifolius (umbrella grass). The leaves are held on top of stiffish stems and form a head rather like the spokes of an umbrella. Easy to grow and a plant that cannot be overwatered. It is best grown standing in a saucer of water. 18in/45cm. Light shade and a minimum winter temperature of about 50°F/10°C. Feed regularly at all times, as growth is more or less continuous. Pot on in spring.

x **Fatshedera lizei**. A semi-climbing plant that needs tying to a support. It is grown mainly for the glossy green, large, ivy-like foliage. There are also variegated forms. Both have greenish flowerheads in late autumn. Up to 6ft/1.8m. Tolerates temperatures just above freezing, but care must be taken not to overwater. At other times water and feed regularly. Pinch out the tips of the main growths to encourage bushiness.

Fatsia japonica (false castor-oil plant, sometimes called fig-leaf palm). An impressive shrub, with large, glossy, palmate leaves. 3ft/90cm. Easy to grow and hardy, though semi-shade is necessary, particularly when it is grown as a houseplant, to keep the foliage in a fresh green condition. Feed only once every two weeks, but keep the compost moist at all times. Cut the top shoots back quite hard in March.

Ficus benjamina (weeping fig). An easily grown shrub with arching branches bearing glossy, evergreen leaves. There is a variegated form. 6ft/1.8m. Needs a humid atmosphere in semi-shade, but can tolerate periods of drier conditions. Water and feed regularly in spring and summer. In winter keep the compost moist and the temperature at no less then 50°F/10°C. Very large pots are not necessary; any potting on should be done in March.

F. elastica 'Decora' (rubber plant). One of the most popular foliage plants. Apply a leaf-shine and sponge its large, glossy, dark green leaves at intervals. A dark-leaved form, 'Black Prince', and the variegated types, are equally decorative variants. 8ft/2.4m or more. A winter temperature of 60°F/15°C is ideal. Water more in summer than winter but, as growth is fairly continuous, feed throughout the year. Rubber plants respond to very hard pruning in spring and summer if the main stem becomes bare at the base (see also page 138). Pot on every two years in spring.

F. pumila. A very small-leaved evergreen with trailing stems up to 24in/60cm long. Ideal in a mixed group. Variegated forms are also available which have slightly indented leaves. The plant will withstand fairly cool conditions (45°F/7°C) and semi-shade, but will then need to be kept drier at the roots. Any pruning necessary should be done in spring or summer.

Grevillea robusta. The evergreen, fern-like foliage of this shrub or small tree makes it an ideal feature specimen or a foil for other subjects. Reaches about 6ft/1.5m after three years, when hard pruning in spring will produce new growth at the base of the main stem. Easy to maintain, thriving in cool conditions and semi-shade. Keep the compost moist at all times and feed throughout the year. Extremes of temperature and moisture will cause leaf-fall. Pot on in spring, using a loam-based compost to give more stability if the plant is free-standing.

Hedera (ivy). Ivies are very adaptable and are happy at quite low temperatures, although care will then be needed not to overwater. Very cool conditions are best for all ivies. Shady situations also suit them, but the variegated types will produce better leaf colour in more sunlight. *Hedera helix* (common ivy) and its variants (pages 57 and 121) are easy to grow; they need to be kept moist at all times and to be fed regularly throughout the year. 12in/30cm. There are several variegated varieties. Pot on in the spring.

GREEN-FOLIAGED HOUSEPLANTS

× *Fatshedera lizei*

Ficus elastica 'Decora' (rubber plant)

Grevillea robusta

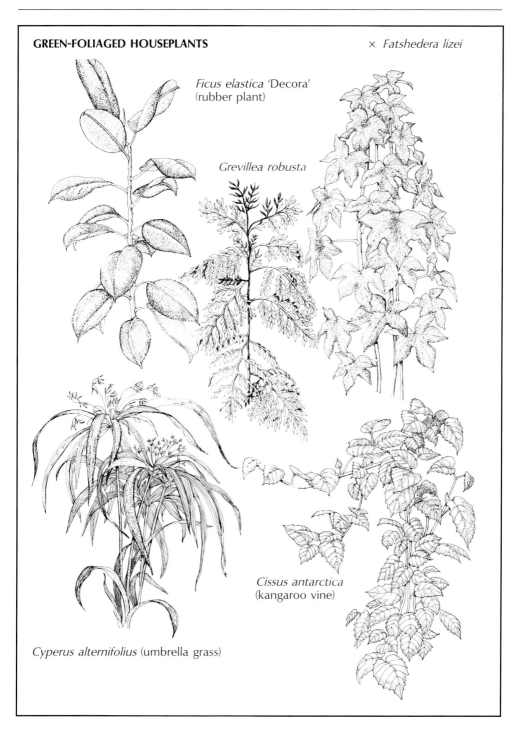

Cissus antarctica (kangaroo vine)

Cyperus alternifolius (umbrella grass)

Green houseplants 3

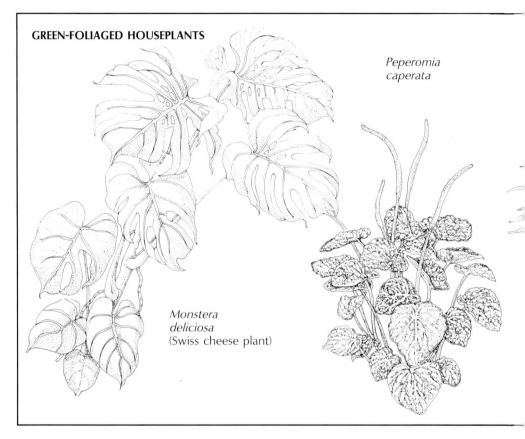

GREEN-FOLIAGED HOUSEPLANTS

Peperomia caperata

Monstera deliciosa (Swiss cheese plant)

Propagating *Monstera* in water

1 With a sharp knife, trim the stalk of a healthy leaf to 1½-2 in/4-5 cm. Ideally, use several leaves.

2 Cover a jar of water with polythene. Insert the stalk through a hole in the polythene.

3 Cover the whole growth with a polythene bag secured to the container until new roots form.

*Howea
forsteriana
(Kentia)*

H. canariensis (Canary Island ivy) is a strong-growing plant with the same watering and feeding requirements as *H. helix*. It makes a good climbing plant, although it needs some support. Pinch out the tips of the stems at any time to keep it shapely. Variable height, but usually kept to about 4ft/1.2m by training onto a support. A most attractive variegated form is available; it is a little more demanding, but even so it is not difficult to grow.

Howea forsteriana (previously known as *Kentia*). A very popular indoor palm, thriving as long as a winter temperature of 55°F/13°C can be maintained. In a large container a height of 10ft/3m can be attained. The roots must be kept moist at all times and, although the plant can stand a dry atmosphere, it is best to give it regular mistings. Sponge the foliage at regular intervals and apply a leaf-shine. Feed regularly and pot on, if required,

in the spring.

Monstera deliciosa (Swiss cheese plant). Large holes that occur naturally in the deeply slashed, large, glossy leaves give this climber its common name. It makes an imposing plant for a semi-shaded situation. 10ft/3m or more. Easy to grow, provided a winter temperature of 55°F/13°C can be maintained. A variegated form is also available. Keep the compost moist all the time and feed regularly throughout the year. Some support from a moss pole or similar structure is necessary. If it grows too tall, cut back very hard in the spring to force new growth from the base of the main stem (see also page 138). At times the plant forms long aerial roots: cut these off close to the stem if they make the plant look ungainly. Spray the leaves regularly, sponge over periodically with clean water, and apply a leaf-shine. Any potting on required can be done every two years in spring or summer.

Nephrolepis exaltata (sword fern). This long-lived fern, ideal for conservatory hanging baskets (page 108), also makes an excellent pot plant, especially when grown as a single specimen. When small, it is often included in mixed arrangements, but is quite capable of making fronds 24in/60cm long. Easy to grow in semi-shade, with regular misting and a minimum temperature of 50°F/10°C. There are several cultivars with different foliage forms, including: 'Bostoniensis', the most commonly grown with long, drooping fronds; 'Elegantissima', very frothy effect; 'Rooseveltii', dark green fronds with wavy leaflets. Keep the compost moist throughout the year, giving more water in the summer. Feed regularly in spring and summer.

Peperomia. There are several species and cultivars of this easily grown group of plants, some green, some variegated, and varying considerably in growth characteristics. Some have heart-shaped leaves on slender stems. Others have broad, oval leaves that are succulent in texture. 6in/15cm. Peperomias are best in a winter temperature of 55°F/13°C. Water sparingly in winter, and with care at other times, allowing the compost to dry out between each application. Feed only at monthly intervals. Species and cultivars: *P. caperata* is a tufted plant with many slender

Green houseplants 4

but stiff stems bearing broad, oval, somewhat wrinkled leaves. A white-variegated and a bronze-leaved form are available. All have slender flowerheads formed like long tails and held 4in/10cm above the foliage, giving an overall height of 7in/18cm. *P. griseoargentea* (*P. hederifolia*) is small with heart-shaped leaves borne on pinkish stems; the leaves have a silvery grey sheen, dark veins and a quilted surface. *P. magnoliifolia* is especially popular in its variegated forms. The leaves are succulent in texture but quite firm. Prefers slightly drier conditions than other peperomias. Most peperomias prefer some humidity, so should stand on a tray of wet pebbles or alternatively be plunged in moist peat.

Philodendron scandens (sweetheart plant). An easily grown climber with heart-shaped leaves, tolerant of fairly shady conditions and some pollution. A minimum winter temperature of 55-60°F/13-15°C is required. Variable height but can be kept to 3ft/90cm when trained on canes or a moss pole. Keep the roots moist at all times and water liberally during the summer. Mist and feed regularly and stand the plant on a tray of wet pebbles or plunge in moist peat if possible. Pinch out the new shoots to encourage bushiness, and allow the whole plant to twine up a central moss pole. Pot on in spring.

Pilea peperomioides. This distinctive plant with rounded leaves centrally poised on fairly stiff stems has become popular recently, and seems tolerant of a wide range of conditions. 9in/23cm. Best in semi-shade and a minimum temperature of 55°F/10°C. Keep the compost moist all year, but give more water in spring and summer. Occasional feeding and light misting are required to keep the plant fresh. Cut back the main stems if required in spring to allow new growths to come from the base and encourage bushiness.

Platycerium bifurcatum (stags-horn fern). The antler-like fronds give this fern its common name. In the wild it grows on trees, but indoors it can be grown either in a pot (when the sterile growths can completely envelop the container), on bark, or in a hanging basket. Given semi-shade, regular misting and a minimum winter temperature of 55°F/13°C, it is easy to grow. Water and feed

GREEN-FOLIAGED HOUSEPLANTS

Philodendron scandens (sweetheart plant)

throughout the year, although more regularly in spring and summer. Use a peaty compost for potting on every second or third spring.

Rhoicissus rhomboidea (grape ivy). Another easily grown climbing plant with shiny evergreen leaves. Up to 6ft/1.8m. Needs semi-shade and a minimum winter temperature of 55°F/13°C. Moderate watering throughout the year and regular feeding and misting will keep the plant in good condition. Pinch out the young growths to keep a neat shape. The stems intertwine and cling by tendrils to supports, such as a central moss pole, but occasionally it will be necessary to tie them in. Pot on in spring.

Schefflera actinophylla. Easily grown, with glossy foliage divided into fingered leaflets. 8ft/1.2m. There are also yellow-variegated forms. High, but not direct, sunlight is required. A minimum temperature of

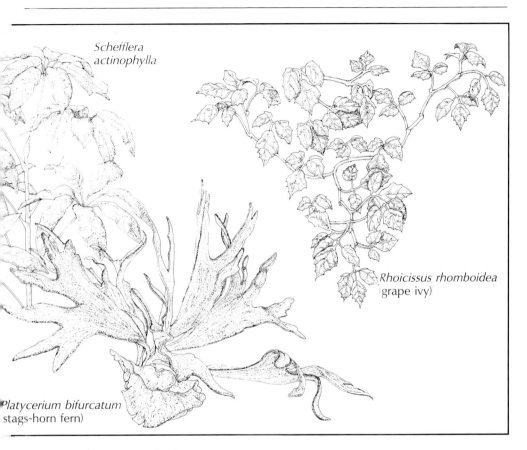

Schefflera actinophylla

Rhoicissus rhomboidea (grape ivy)

Platycerium bifurcatum (stags-horn fern)

Growing *Platycerium* on bark

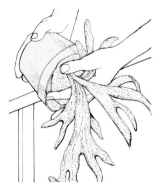

1 Invert the pot, to remove the plant, supporting the root ball with your other hand.

2 Firmly wrap the root ball with wet sphagnum moss. Place it in a natural-looking position on bark.

3 Attach the root ball to the bark with green plastic-coated wire. Spray moss regularly with tepid water.

157

Coloured and variegated 1

COLOURED AND VARIEGATED HOUSEPLANTS

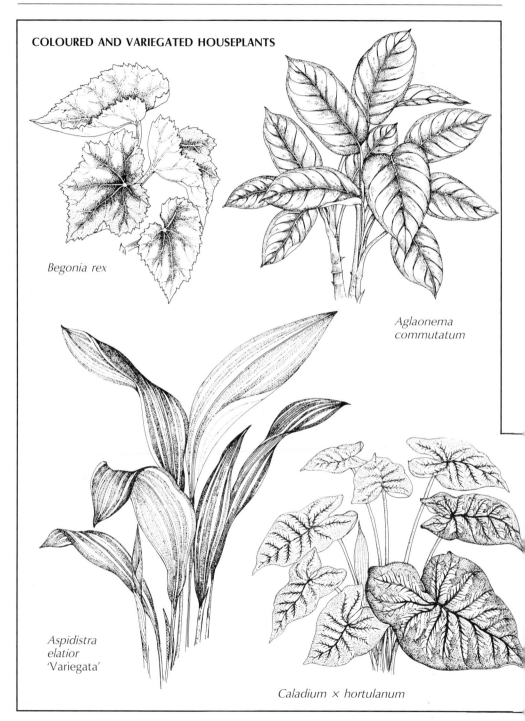

Begonia rex

Aglaonema
commutatum

Aspidistra
elatior
'Variegata'

Caladium × hortulanum

55°F/13°C is ideal, although it will tolerate cooler conditions. Keep the compost moist at all times and mist regularly. Fortnightly feeds are desirable. Pot on every second spring.

Syngonium podophyllum (goosefoot plant). Broad, arrowhead-shaped leaves are produced on a fairly compact plant, but the maturing foliage becomes lobed, resembling the goose's foot from which the plant derives its common name. The stems also climb, so some support will be needed. Alternatively, it can be grown in a hanging basket. Grow in semi-shade, with a fairly high minimum winter temperature of 60°F/15°C. Keep the compost moist at all times; water liberally and feed regularly in spring and summer.

Tolmiea menziesii (pick-a-back plant). A good, easily grown plant. The common name comes from the small plantlets formed on the upper surface of the leaves where the blade joins the leaf stem. The flowers, which are brown, are not particularly attractive so the flower spikes should be removed at an early stage of development. 6in/15cm at most. The plant will stand cold conditions and shade, although the more attractive variegated form will colour better in lighter situations. Water regularly throughout the year and feed during spring and summer.

Calathea makoyana

COLOURED AND VARIEGATED PLANTS

Houseplants with coloured and variegated foliage are interesting in themselves and can also be used to add emphasis to a mixed arrangement. They may have red or yellow leaves, or delicately muted silvery ones. Variegation may be in gold or cream, or blotched with brown or silver.

Listed below is a selection of some of the most popular foliage houseplants that have coloured leaves, or variegation, or both. It should be noted that to prevent unnecessary duplication, descriptions of some plants are to be found in the green foliage section (pages 150-8).

Aglaonema commutatum. The silvery foliage and compact growth of this popular *Aglaonema* makes it a useful plant for grouping with others in an arrangement. The small pale green, waxy spathes (flower sheaths) appear in summer. 10in/25cm. Easily grown, provided that it is given semi-shade, a moist atmosphere, and regular watering and feeding in spring and summer.

Aphelandra squarrosa 'Louisiae' (zebra plant, tiger plant). This plant's two common names aptly describe its dark green leaves striped with silver. The cultivar 'Silver Queen' has very silvery foliage. All cultivars are further enhanced by cone-shaped inflorescences of red-edged, yellow bracts (leaf growths) and yellow flowers which appear between April and August. 18in/45cm.

Needs a minimum winter temperature of 55°F/15°C and semi-shade, along with regular misting, watering and feeding in spring and summer. The compost must never be waterlogged. When the plants become defoliated and leggy at the base, cut them hard back to an old leaf joint, from which they will sprout again.

Aspidistra elatior 'Variegata'. See page 150.

Begonia. Many begonias have very attractive foliage, as well as in many cases decorative flowers (page 143). They require a humid atmosphere, especially in the summer, when regular watering and feeding are also necessary. Keep the compost moist in winter. Pot on in spring, using a peat-based compost. Species and cultivars: *B. bowerae* is spotted brown on the edges of the leaves. It has produced several good, small-leaved hybrids,

Coloured and variegated 2

including the very popular 'Tiger Paws' (4-6in/10-15cm), with small, yellow-green leaves heavily veined in brown. *B. masoniana* (the Iron Cross begonia) has fairly large, grey-green leaves with a puckered, somewhat hairy surface. A prominent brown cross shape as a bold central mark on each leaf gives the plant its common name. 10in/25cm. *Begonia metallica* has olive-green leaves with a metallic sheen and crimson veins underneath. 3ft/90cm. *Begonia rex* and its many hybrids have the most decorative leaves of all, marked in combinations of silver, pink, red, purple and brown. 12in/30cm.

Caladium x hortulanum cultivars. Some of the most beautiful of all foliage plants, with heart-shaped leaves ranging in colour from white, through pink, to red, usually on a background of green. Not, however, the easiest plants to maintain in good condition. Up to 15in/38cm. Avoid direct strong sunlight. When the plant is in full growth, water and feed freely, and provide regular misting and a night temperature of 65-70°F/18-21°C. Keep plants somewhat cooler and reduce watering until the leaves die off and the tubers go dormant. During dormancy the compost must not be allowed to dry out completely.

Calathea makoyana. The light green leaves are marked in a regular pattern with greenish-brown blotches repeated in purple on the underside. 12in/30cm. Plenty of water and humidity will maintain the plant in good condition. Feed regularly in spring and summer; maintain a shady position at all times.

Carex oshimensis 'Evergold' (grown incorrectly as *C. morrowii* 'Variegata'). A grass-like plant with yellow-striped narrow leaves. It is tough and easy to grow, but to succeed well, its compost must always be kept moist and the plant fed in spring and summer. 12in/30cm. Pot on only every second year, in spring.

Chlorophytum comosum 'Vittatum' (variegated spider plant). 12in/30cm. Extremely easy to grow and tolerant of a wide range of conditions, but better in light shade. Minimum temperature of 40°F/5°C. It is fast-growing and requires plenty of water and regular feeding in spring and summer. Reduce watering during winter. Pot on in spring, when the small plantlets, formed as tufts on the ends

COLOURED AND VARIEGATED HOUSEPLANTS

Chlorophytum comosum 'Vittatum' (spider plant)

of the flower stems, can be separated and potted individually into small pots (see also page 106).

Codiaeum variegatum (croton). An evergreen whose glossy, highly coloured foliage is very showy. Up to 24in/60cm. The plant is not easy to keep in good condition, requiring plenty of light (an east- or west-facing window is suitable) and winter temperatures that do not go below 60°F/15°C. Water and feed plentifully from April to September, but water carefully at other times. Regular misting is necessary and the foliage will be further enhanced by using a leaf-shine.

Coleus blumei. An easily grown, brightly coloured foliage plant requiring plenty of light at all times. Water and feed during the growing season but greatly reduce quantities in winter. Pinch out the tips of the shoots to promote bushiness. Up to 12in/30cm.

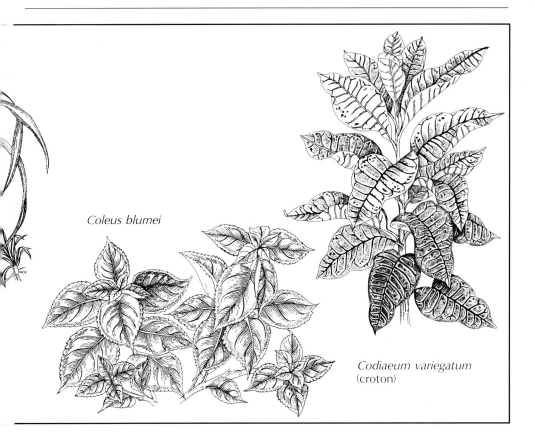

Coleus blumei

Codiaeum variegatum
(croton)

Propagating *Begonia* from leaf cuttings (slashing)

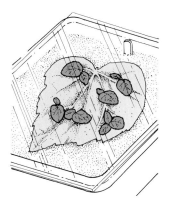

1 Make a 1 in/2.5 cm cut
across a major vein. Repeat
every square inch.

2 Place the leaf topside up
on the compost surface.
Pin with a wire staple.

3 Cover with glass. Put in a
warm, shaded place. Leave
there when plantlets emerge.

161

Coloured and variegated 3

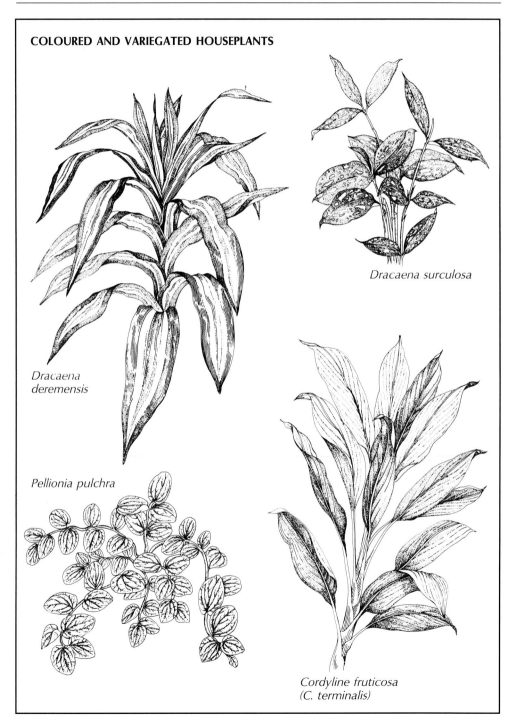

COLOURED AND VARIEGATED HOUSEPLANTS

Dracaena surculosa

Dracaena deremensis

Pellionia pulchra

Cordyline fruticosa (C. terminalis)

Cordyline fruticosa (*C. terminalis*). A valuable, palm-like plant with long, green leaves flushed cream, red or purple. 18in/45cm. Needs good light and a winter temperature of 60°F/15°C. Misting regularly will keep the plant in good condition. Give plenty of water in summer, but reduce in winter.

Dieffenbachia seguine (*D. picta*). Although this plant has poisonous leaves and stems, it is popular because of its attractive leaf markings and because culture is easy. Up to 3ft/90cm. A winter temperature of 60°F/15°C is best. Keep the compost moist at all times, mist regularly, and feed during spring and summer. Pot on in spring.

Dizygotheca elegantissima. Best as a young plant, when its narrow, tooth-edged leaflets assume a coppery tint. The older leaflets are dark green and coarse-toothed. Can grow quite tall (up to 5ft/1.5m), and is usually single-stemmed; can become bare at the base. Hard pruning in the spring will encourage new growth. Water and feed regularly from April to September, but reduce quantities in winter, when a minimum temperature of 50°F/10°C is necessary.

Dracaena deremensis. The glossy, green leaves have two silver markings running their full length. Up to 5ft/1.5m, depending on pot size. Easy to grow, needing regular watering and feeding in summer; water sparingly in winter. Semi-shade and a temperature not lower than 50°F/10°C are suitable. Pot on in spring. *D. surculosa* (*D. godseffiana*) is more shrubby in appearance and has rounded leaves, which are dark green and variably marked with creamy-yellow spots. 24in/60cm. It is also more difficult to maintain in good condition than. *D. deremensis*. Water sparingly in winter but quite frequently in summer. Regular feeding is also required in the growing season.

Epipremnum aureum (*Scindapsus aureus*). A climbing plant with yellow-splashed leaves. It is largely self-supporting when trained up a central moss pole, but will need to be tied in if allowed to scramble on canes or a trellis. Can attain a height of 6ft/1.8m, but is not a rampant grower and is therefore a good central plant in a mixed grouping. Over-watering can be a danger in the winter when a minimum temperature of 55°F/13°C is

required. The tips of the stems should be pinched to promote branching in spring.

x *Fatshedera lizei* 'Variegata'. See page 152.
Ficus benjamina. See page 152.
Ficus elastica 'Decora'. See page 152.
Ficus pumila. See page 152.
Grevillea robusta. See page 152.
Hedera canariensis. See page 155.
Hedera helix. See pages 152-5.

Hypoestes phyllostachya (formerly *H.sanguinolenta*) (polka dot plant). A slightly tender plant, excellent as a specimen or in a mixed group. The small, hairy leaves spotted pink aptly explain its common name; there is a white-spotted variant. The mauve flowers are fairly insignificant and borne on thin wiry stems; they do very little to enhance the plant and, if necessary, can be removed as the flower spikes appear. 18in/45cm. It is moderately strong-growing, and the young shoots may need to be pinched back so that it remains compact in habit. Indirect but fairly strong light is required to keep the foliage in good condition. Take care with watering, especially in winter, when the temperature should be no lower than 55°F/13°C. Feed at weekly intervals throughout the growing season and pot on in the spring.

Maranta leuconeura var. *kerchoveana* (prayer plant). A very popular plant, even though it requires a fairly high winter temperature (55-60°F/13°-15°C). Although not difficult to grow, it needs careful watering and misting. Broad, flat leaves marked with greenish-brown blotches. 8in/20cm. *M. leuconeura* 'Erythroneura' is a particularly attractive variant, having dark green leaves with yellowish-green margins and crimson veins. It is more difficult than the var. *kerchoveana* to cultivate well. Both are ideal low-spreading plants, making good single specimens or dominant subjects in mixed groups. No pruning is required. Pot on in spring or summer.

Monstera deliciosa. See page 155.

Pellionia pulchra. This plant forms hummocks of silvery-green leaves with dark green vein markings. 3in/7.5cm. It works particularly well at the front of a mixed arrangement. Requires a minimum winter temperature of 55°F/13°C, and ample light to ensure good leaf colour. The compost should never dry out, although watering will need to be done carefully in

Coloured and variegated 4

winter. A feed every two weeks will be sufficient in spring and summer.

Peperomia. See pages 155-6.

Pilea cadierei (aluminium plant). Has shining silver patches on its dark green leaves, an ideal plant for grouping in a mixed arrangement. Needs a minimum temperature of 50°F/10°C and good light conditions. 12in/30cm. Although it becomes leggy in time, it can be cut back in spring and will sprout again. A dwarfer, more compact form is also available (see page 121). Water liberally in the growing season but sparingly in winter. Occasional misting will be beneficial. Pot on in spring.

Sansevieria trifasciata '**Laurentii**' (mother-in-law's tongue). Easy to grow, as it is tolerant of sun, shade and a dry atmosphere. The ideal plant to site near a heat source. A minimum winter temperature of 50°F/13°C is required. The stiff, upright, sword-shaped leaves have yellow margins. 24in/60cm. Water moderately in the summer, but take care in winter not to overwater, especially with smaller plants. An occasional feed is necessary, but potting on is seldom required.

Tolmiea menziesii. The pick-a-back plant, or mother of thousands. See page 159.

Tradescantia fluminensis. The variegated

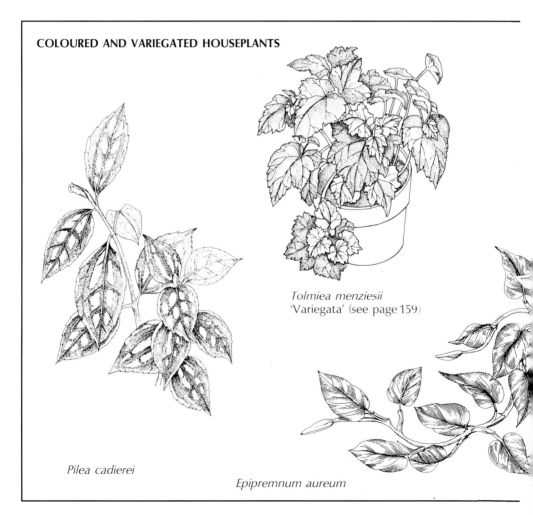

COLOURED AND VARIEGATED HOUSEPLANTS

Tolmiea menziesii
'Variegata' (see page 159)

Pilea cadierei

Epipremnum aureum

forms of this very popular trailing plant are easily grown, preferring indirect but good sunlight to enhance leaf colour. A good subject for mixed groups (see also page 109). The overall height is about 4in/10cm, but the pendulous growths can reach a length of 24in/60cm. Regular watering and feeding should be given throughout the year, although less of both will be required in winter when a minimum temperature of 50°F/10°C is adequate. Each of the stems, if pinched from the parent plant at a length of about 2-3in/5-7.5cm, will root very readily. Pot on in spring.

Tradescantia zebrina (*Zebrina pendula*). An easily grown trailing plant. The leaves have silver stripes, and purple and green undersides. Good indirect sunlight is required to maintain strong colour. It is excellent in hanging baskets (see also page 109), but also mixes well with other plants. Height 4in/10cm, trailing to 18in/45cm. A minimum winter temperature of 45°F/7°C is needed, together with regular watering and feeding throughout the year (reduced during the winter). Easily propagated in the same way as *Tradescantia fluminensis*.

Zebrina pendula. See *Trandescantia zebrina*.

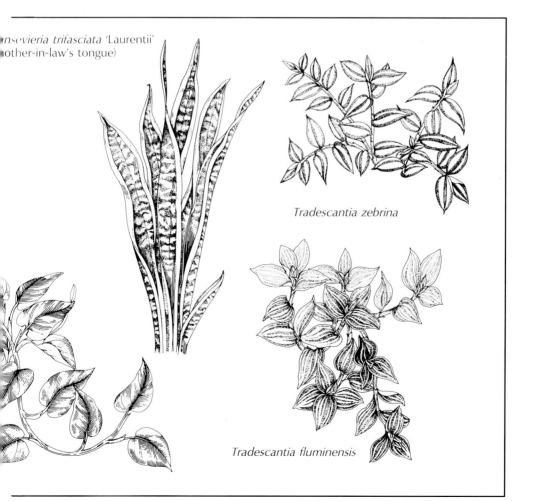

nsevieria trifasciata 'Laurentii' (other-in-law's tongue)

Tradescantia zebrina

Tradescantia fluminensis

Choosing and grouping

The choice of plants for a particular situation is governed by a number of factors (see pages 122-9) although their grouping will be very much a matter of personal taste. Strong-growing plants should not usually be mixed with slower-growing ones, which will soon become swamped. Any selection should be confined to those plants requiring the same conditions for healthy growth. This is especially important in planted bowls.

Plants should be in scale with their container, bearing in mind that they will grow and sometimes change shape as they mature. Generally speaking, there needs to be one dominant plant with two or more lower-growing plants, either of the same or different species. Trailing plants are particularly suitable to furnish containers raised on pedestals.

When choosing for a particular situation, or when grouping plants together, it is important to consider plant form and shape. The impact a plant makes will depend on whether it is arching, bushy, trailing, upright, climbing, rosette-shaped or weeping.

Another factor is the shape of the leaves, which may be oval, heart-shaped, wavy-edged, lance-shaped, perforated (like *Monstera*), and so on. Contrasting or harmonizing leaf shapes provide special interest. Other points to consider are the colour of the leaves, and whether or not they are variegated.

In the box on this page are some suggested ways to group plants together effectively.

Pot et fleur

A good way to introduce instant colour into an arrangement of green houseplants planted in a bowl or basket is to make a *pot et fleur*, by adding a small flower vase, sunk into the potting mixture almost to its rim. Insert a few seasonal flowers into a flower arranger's pinholder or a block of specially manufactured absorbent material.

Alternatively, a small pot containing a flowering houseplant can be plunged into a space left in an arrangement of foliage plants.

COMPOSITION

Houseplants offer a wide range of foliage types that can be combined in effective groupings.

A contrast of leaf sizes and shapes makes an eyecatching feature

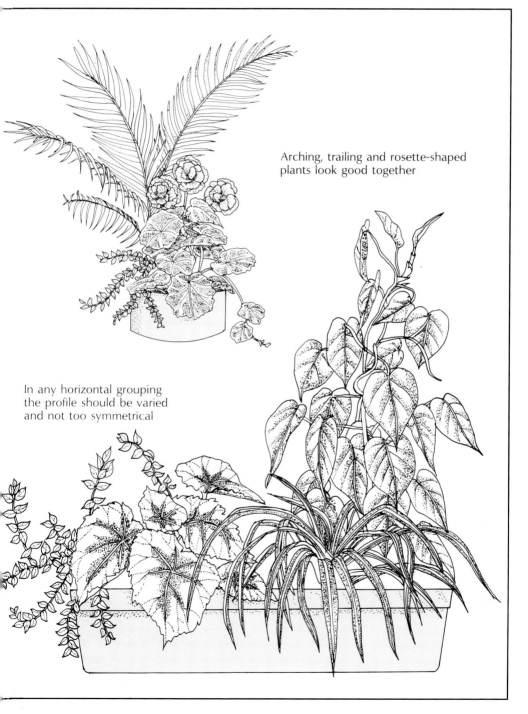

Arching, trailing and rosette-shaped plants look good together

In any horizontal grouping the profile should be varied and not too symmetrical

Growing bulbs and corms 1

Bulbs indoors make a wonderful splash of colour, and the spring-flowering ones are especially valuable. It is perfectly possible to force bulbs for Christmas display.

Most of the bulbs recommended below are for late winter- and spring-flowering and will require planting in the autumn. Although they can be grown on from year to year, there can be a marked deterioration, so it usually pays to buy new bulbs for indoor cultivation each season.

Planting

Select and buy sound bulbs as early in the autumn as possible. The smaller kinds should be planted buried in pots filled with bulb fibre (see below) about 1in/2.5cm deep. Larger bulbs can have their necks protruding well above the surface of the compost. Most bulb bowls have no drainage holes, so it is important that a very open growing medium is used, such as specially prepared bulb fibre, which often has added pieces of charcoal.

Hardy bulbs Hardy bulbs such as hyacinths, daffodils and tulips need to be planted in pots or bowls, then watered and placed in a dark cool place. Alternatively, they can be plunged outdoors, or in a cold frame, the containers buried 3in/7.5cm deep in moist peat or sand.

Alternatively, place the containers in an opaque polythene bag and keep in an unheated cupboard or shady room. This initial dark, cool period is important to build up a strong root system which will lead to healthy growth and proper flowering.

As soon as growth has developed to about 2in/5cm, bring the containers into a lighter situation, but screen them from the direct rays of the sun. Temperatures above 70°F/21°C can be damaging and may cause flower buds to abort. Mist daily.

Correct watering is important to prevent the compost from becoming too dry or too wet, both of which will affect proper flowering.

Tender bulbs Tender bulbs are potted in much the same way, but some, such as freesias, are planted in the autumn. There is generally no need to plunge the pots outdoors or to keep them in a dark place.

Plunging bulbs in an unheated frame

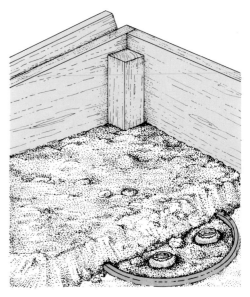

1 In October, fill frame with a 12 in/30 cm layer of sand, peat or a mixture of gravel and weathered ashes. Water. Allow to settle.

2 Plant bulbs, such as hyacinths, in pots. Plunge the pots up to the rim in the frame. Exclude light with 3 in/7.5 cm layer of peat.

PLANTING BULBS IN A BOWL

***Scilla* or Crocus bulbs** can be planted close together in a bowl with a drainage hole.

Some bulbs, such as *Narcissus*, must be kept dark and cool so that a good root system is produced prior to forcing in warmer conditions. Here, a bowl is covered with opaque paper.

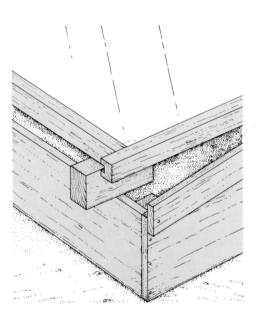

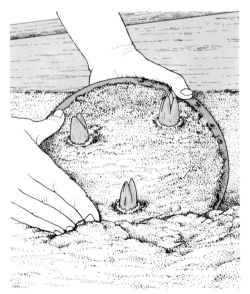

3 Place lights over frame to protect pots from heavy winter rainfall. Keep the frame well ventilated.

4 After 8 weeks, remove pots from frame and take indoors for flowering.

Indoor bulbs and corms 1

The following are bulbs and corms, both hardy and tender, that can be grown successfully indoors.

Amaryllis. See *Hippeastrum*.

Crocus. These cheerful, early-flowering plants should be planted in the autumn. They need not be plunged in order to form roots, but initially still require a cool position outside: too high a temperature early on can prevent them from flowering. Protect them with fine-meshed chicken netting, as mice are particularly fond of their corms. It is best to bring the bowls inside when the crocuses are about to flower. Cultivars: 'Jeanne d'Arc', white; 'Remembrance', purple; 'Dutch Yellow'.

Special crocus bowls in plastic or terracotta are available. These squat containers have several holes in the sides, in which the corms are placed, with their noses protruding outside. Fill the containers with potting compost to keep the corms in position. The resulting flowers will create an overall mass of colour, covering the bowl.

Freesia. These half-hardy corms produce delicate flowers in white, yellow, mauve and red, some being heavily scented. 18in/45cm.

Plant the corms as soon as available in the autumn, in a standard John Innes No. 2 compost or an equivalent peat-based compost: twelve corms at a depth of 2in/5cm in a 9in/23cm pot, or six in a 6in/15cm pot.

Cool, frost-free conditions are important throughout the growing period to produce sturdy plants. Support with four or five thin canes round the container. As the leaves and stems elongate, secure them to the canes with several lengths of garden twine. Flowers can be expected in March and April.

Gloriosa. This attractive climber produces red and yellow lily-like flowers in summer. 5-6ft/1.5-1.8m. It forms swollen tubers which are rather brittle and therefore need careful handling when planting.

Plant in the spring by laying the long tubers horizontally and covering them to a depth of about 3in/7.5cm. Fairly large containers are required, and the growing plants will need some support so that their self-clinging leaves can scramble upwards. When the foliage begins to yellow after flowering, gradually dry

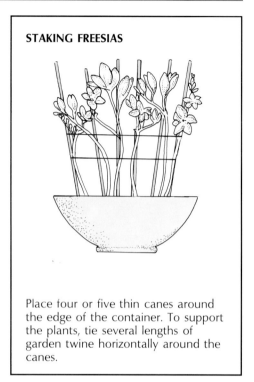

STAKING FREESIAS

Place four or five thin canes around the edge of the container. To support the plants, tie several lengths of garden twine horizontally around the canes.

the tuber off, store in dry frost-free conditions and replant the following spring.

Hippeastrum (usually sold as *Amaryllis*). Huge, trumpet-shaped flowers in white, pink or red. Up to 3ft/90cm. The bulbs are obtainable in early winter, and are often packaged as gifts. Plant as soon as available. As the bulb is so large, it need not be deeply buried but should be positioned so that about half of it is above the surface of the compost. After a thorough watering, place it in a warm spot: an airing cupboard is ideal.

As soon as roots have formed and some top growth is showing, place the pot in a light, warm position for the flower stem to develop. Once the stem has fully grown, put the plants in cooler but still frost-free conditions to flower. At all times, water with care and feed regularly, especially when the leaves start to develop (usually after the flower stem has emerged).

After flowering, cut the stem off to allow the bulb to build up its resources for the following year. A position in full sun, together

BULBS AND CORMS

Crocus

Freesia

Gloriosa

Hippeastrum (Amaryllis)

Indoor bulbs and corms 2

with regular feeding with a fertilizer high in potash (such as used for tomatoes), helps to ensure flowering the next season.

When the foliage begins to yellow and die, gradually discontinue watering and feeding. The compost can then be kept dry until it is top-dressed in the late autumn for new growth to start again.

Hyacinthus (hyacinth). The spikes of heavily scented flowers in red, pink, white or blue can be obtained from winter to early spring; the warmer the conditions in which the bulbs are kept, the earlier the flowers appear. Cultivars: 'Lady Derby', pink; 'Delft Blue'; 'L'Innocence', white. 'Roman hyacinths', which have fewer-flowered, slender stems, are particularly suitable for early flowering, if they have been specially prepared for forcing.

There are several methods of growing:

Method 1: Bowls with no drainage holes can be filled with bulb fibre or a mixture of equal parts of coarse peat and sand. Several bulbs should then be evenly spaced and planted with their necks protruding slightly above the surface. One difficulty that often arises when several bulbs are planted in this way is that one or more do not always flower successfully, and an unbalanced display results. To over-come this problem, see Method 2 below.

Method 2: Plant the bulbs individually in 3.5in/9cm pots, using an ordinary potting compost. Once the flowering stems have developed properly, knock the bulbs out of their pots and plant into bowls or other containers to make up an even display.

Method 3: Hyacinths will grow and flower in water (see hydroponics, pages 130-1). Speci-ally made hyacinth glasses can be used. The bulbs sit in the small bowl-shaped top and the roots grow downwards into the water below. Add a small piece of charcoal to prevent the water becoming stagnant.

Whichever of these three methods is chosen, it is important to give hyacinth bulbs cool, dark conditions initially for root formation, or growth and flowering will be affected.

Hyacinth flower stems can soon become top-heavy. Stake with a thin cane as shown (right). If the top of the cane is allowed to reach up into the flowerhead, added support is given there.

GROWING HYACINTHS IN WATER

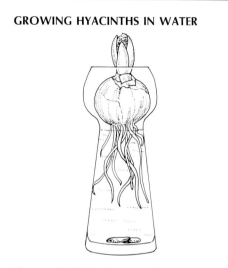

Place a bulb in the top of a narrow-necked container such as a hyacinth glass. The water in the glass should not touch the bulb. Add a piece of charcoal.

Staking hyacinths

Push a thin cane into the middle of the bulb and close to the stem, with its top reaching into the flowerhead. Tie the stem to the cane neatly at the top and bottom.

Growing hyacinths

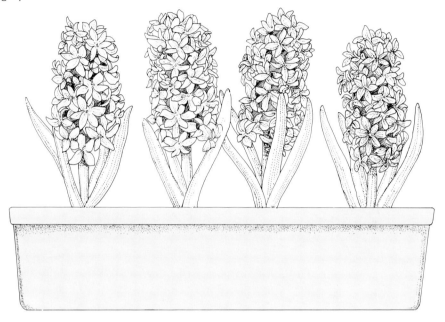

Hyacinths for an indoor window box are best planted by Method 2 (described below)

Method 1 Fill a bowl with bulb fibre or equal parts of coarse peat and sand. Space bulbs evenly in this, their necks protruding slightly above the surface.

Method 2 Plant each bulb in potting compost in a separate $3\frac{1}{2}$ in/9 cm pot. Once they start to flower, knock out and plant together without disturbing root balls.

Indoor bulbs and corms 3

BULBS AND CORMS

Lachenalia aloides
(Cape cowslip)

Large-cupped
Narcissus

Lachenalia aloides (Cape cowslip). A tender South African bulb that deserves to be much more popular. Its tubular flowers, yellow with orange and green markings, hang down from slender stems. The leaves are strap-shaped and often spotted chocolate-purple. 12in/30cm. The plant is easy to grow and requires cool conditions.

In August, plant several bulbs in pots or in bowls with drainage holes, using an ordinary potting compost. There is no need for plunging. Take care that waterlogging does not occur. A light position is essential at all times after flowering begins in March. *Lachenalia* bulbs respond to regular feeding so that their reserves are built up for the following year.

Narcissus (daffodil). Daffodils can be grown in various ways. As they are hardy, they are best flowered in cool conditions so that they last as long as possible. Plant as soon as the bulbs are available, especially the cultivars prepared for early forcing to flower at Christmas, such as 'Paper White' and 'Soleil d'Or'. There are three methods of planting. *Method 1*: In a 6in/15cm pot, plant two layers,

Planting *Narcissus*

Method 1 Plant 6 bulbs in two layers in a 6 in/15 cm pot filled with bulb fibre. The top layer of bulbs should have their necks protruding above the surface.

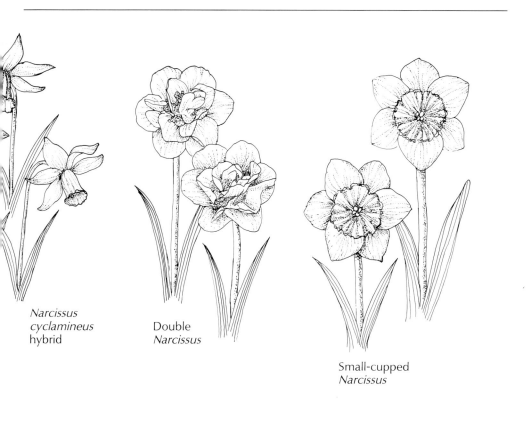

Narcissus
cyclamineus
hybrid

Double
Narcissus

Small-cupped
Narcissus

Method 2 Place a 2 in/5 cm layer of gravel into a shallow bowl. Nestle the bulbs into the gravel. This method is specially good for shorter cultivars.

Method 3 Plant each bulb in a small pot, even if they are not buried to any extent. When flowering, insert into a larger container with other plants.

Indoor bulbs and corms 4

each of three bulbs, the top ones with their necks above compost level. Despite the difference in planting depths, there will be no variation in their flowering times.

Method 2: Nestle the bulbs into a layer of gravel placed in a shallow bowl. This is a particularly attractive way to grow shorter varieties such as 'Hawera' and 'Tête à Tête'.

Method 3: Plant bulbs individually in quite small pots, even if they are not buried to any great depth. When they flower, they can be grouped together with other plants in a much larger container.

It is important with all three methods that the bulbs are kept in a cool, dark situation to allow for proper root development and successful flowering.

Specially prepared bulbs will grow away rapidly once the root system has established, and need to be brought from cool into warmer conditions earlier than non-treated bulbs.

Scilla. These bulbs produce brilliant blue flowers in the spring. 6in/15cm. Plant during autumn in pots or "crocus" bowls (page 170). Nine or ten bulbs will fit into a 5in/12.5cm pot. Plunging in peat or sand will help to establish a good root system but is not essential.

Scilla

Cool growing conditions are needed to keep the foliage from becoming too long and soft, and scillas are best grown completely cold, either out of doors or in a cold greenhouse, and brought indoors at flowering time.
Tulipa (tulip). *Tulipa greigii* and its hybrids have attractive leaves mottled with purple; they are therefore interesting over a longer period. Cultivars: 'Bokhara', orange-red petals with black base, edged with yellow; 'Margaret Herbst', scarlet with yellow base; 'Oriental Splendour', petals carmine on the outside, edged with lemon yellow, lemon yellow on the inside, with black base.

Although tulips can be planted in bulb fibre, a good potting compost is more suitable. Plant five or six bulbs in a 5in/13cm pot with their necks just below the surface. They need not be plunged, although this would help to keep them cool and allow the roots to develop strongly. Avoid excessive heat at all times, especially when in flower.

If grown in a potting compost and fed and watered regularly, especially after flowering, bulbs of *T. greigii* and its hybrids can be retained to flower for a second year.

Tulipa *greigii* hybrids, showing different variegations in the foliage

Cacti and succulents 1

For light, dry conditions indoors, many cacti and succulent plants cannot be bettered; indeed, several have become very popular as houseplants. The smaller-growing types can be grouped together in miniature gardens, but it is important to select those that are compatible in their growth requirements. For example, species or cultivars of *Epiphyllum*, *Rhipsalidopsis* and *Schlumbergera* must always have the compost on the moist side, whereas other cacti and succulents generally require dryness at the roots, especially during the winter.

Those plants requiring constant moisture should have their pots stood in an outer container filled with peat that is kept constantly damp. During spring and summer the compost can be watered regularly. In warm conditions the plants will benefit from a fine spray with clear water. In fact, the three genera mentioned above benefit by being placed out of doors in light shade during the summer, but they must never be allowed to dry out.

Regular feeding with a fertilizer that has a higher than usual potash content (as used for tomatoes) will help promote good flowering.

Cacti and most succulents require a drier period in the winter, but plenty of water and feed can be given throughout the growing season. It will also be necessary to pot them on into larger containers as they increase in size. This should be done in spring or summer, using a specially prepared cactus compost, usually obtainable from a garden centre.

Cacti and succulents
True cacti are, strictly speaking, members of one plant family (*Cactaceae*). With the exception of *Mammillaria*, the plants listed below are succulents, not true cacti. However, it is worth trying to cultivate a wide range of cacti in a well-lit window. Many of the small and medium-sized species and hybrids can be grown successfully as houseplants, provided that care is taken with watering in the winter: the roots must never become waterlogged.

The following plants are reasonably easy to grow in the home, rather than in greenhouses.
Agave americana. A rosetted succulent with

Making a desert garden

1 Place 1 in/2.5 cm of gravel in a shallow container. Cover it with 1 in/2.5 cm layer of a mixture of one part coarse sand to two parts soil-based potting compost.

2 Try out arrangements. Leave the plants in their pots to avoid damaging them.

CACTI FROM CUTTINGS

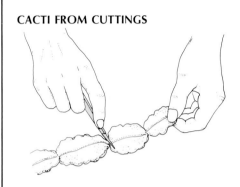

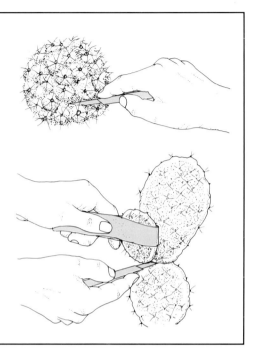

Take cuttings with a sharp knife, holding with a loop of folded brown paper to protect your hands from any spines. Allow to dry for a day or so. Plant about $\frac{1}{2}$in/1.25 cm deep in a small pot filled with moist (not wet) compost of equal parts of peat and coarse sand. Keep in propagator at 70°F/21°C. Do not water for ten days.

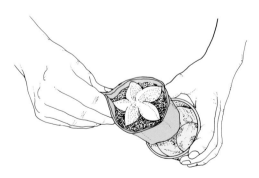

3 Fold a piece of brown paper and wrap it round the cactus to protect your hands from the spines. Lift the plant out, pulling the pot away with the other hand.

4 Plant up the desert garden, trickling potting compost gently around plant roots. Add a scattering of coloured marble chippings (from a stonemason or aquarist).

Cacti and succulents 2

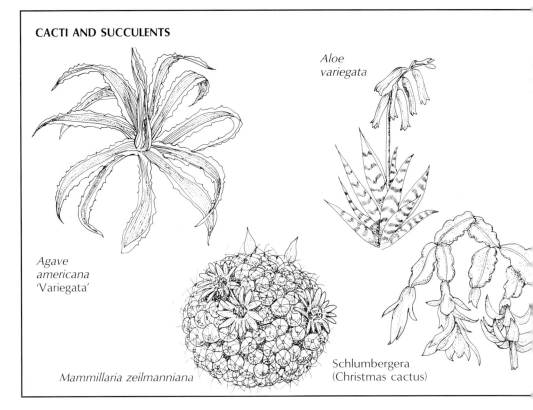

CACTI AND SUCCULENTS

Agave americana 'Variegata'

Aloe variegata

Mammillaria zeilmanniana

Schlumbergera (Christmas cactus)

sword-shaped, sharply toothed, grey-green leaves, growing to quite a large size (up to 3ft/90cm or more). Offset rosettes can readily be removed and potted, when the main rosette becomes too large to accommodate in the house. There are several attractive variegated forms. May be kept dry for long periods without harm.

Aloe aristata. Makes a small rosette of dark green leaves covered in soft spines. The inflorescence is usually branched and has orange-red flowers. 4in/10cm. Water well in summer.

A. variegata (partridge-breasted aloe) Deservedly popular, with its rosettes of dark green leaves with white markings growing in a fairly dense clump. 5in/13cm. Can be kept on the dry side for long periods.

Crassula ovata (*C. argentea*) (jade plant). A small tree-like succulent that is very easy to grow. The stubby branches bear thick, fleshy, glossy green leaves, sometimes red-edged

and oval in shape. In good light, the plant may produce clusters of starry white flowers. In large pots can attain a height of 24in/60cm or more. Water well in summer.

Euphorbia milii (var. **splendens**), (crown of thorns). Easy to grow, this spiny succulent bears clusters of small red bracts enclosing tiny greenish-yellow flowers. 18in/45cm. Keep dry in winter.

Kalanchoe blossfeldiana. An attractive succulent with dark green toothed leaves and clusters of long-lasting tubular scarlet flowers. Many hybrids have been produced with a wide range of colour from yellow, orange and shades of pink through to bright red. Up to 6in/15cm. Water freely in summer.

K. manginii. A species that has also received fairly recent attention from the hybridist, makes a good late winter- and spring-flowering pot plant or hanging basket plant. The tubular flowers of the hybrids are pink, orange and red, and hang from wiry stems. 6in/15cm.

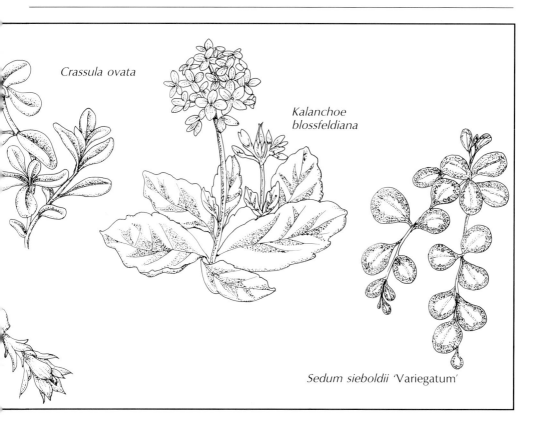

Crassula ovata

Kalanchoe
blossfeldiana

Sedum sieboldii 'Variegatum'

K. tubiflora. Fairly tall-growing (24in/60cm), with upright stems from which arise narrow, cylindrical leaves. At the tips of the leaves, tiny plantlets form which can be removed and used for propagation. The tubular flowers are orange-red. Water freely in summer.

Mammillaria zeilmanniana. Has masses of purplish-red flowers borne on spiny, spherical or oblong stems. 3-6in/7.5-15cm.

Schlumbergera (Christmas cactus). These are succulent plants that flower in winter and early spring. Most have naturally pendent growths and flowers, white, pink or red depending on the cultivar. It is important not to change their growing conditions when they are in flower as draughts or overwatering can cause the blossoms to drop.

Schlumbergeras prefer semi-shaded conditions and should be kept well watered during the summer. During the autumn and winter growing seasons, misting is beneficial. Watering needs to be less frequent. The compost, however, should not be allowed to become too dry. A temperature of 50°F/10°C is sufficient. Good light is required. Feed regularly when the flower buds have formed.

Sedum sieboldii. A graceful plant bearing fleshy leaves in groups of three along the lengths of slender, pendent stems. Starry pink flowers are formed at the end of these stems in late summer. A particularly beautiful yellow-variegated form is also available. 4in/10cm. Keep dry during the dormant season in winter. Water fairly frequently during summer. The whole plant sometimes loses its leaves and dies back in the winter, but in spring new growth appears from the base again to give a display from spring through to late autumn.

Synadenium grantii. A semi-succulent shrub eventually reaching 10ft/3m with lance-shaped or oval leaves and small red flowers in autumn. A red-leaved form is available. 24in/60cm. Water well in summer.

Houseplant ailments

Yellowing foliage

Yellowing foliage is the major cause for concern with houseplants, but this condition can occur for various reasons and does not necessarily mean the plant is going to die.

If the odd lower leaf shows signs of discoloration, it is more often a sign of old age and its loss is a natural process.

Yellowing can be caused by excessive direct sunlight in some plants, or by watering lime-hating plants with "hard" water. More frequently, yellowing foliage is due to insufficient feeding or changes in temperature which may affect foliage adversely and cause leaf discoloration.

Leaf-fall

Where leaf discoloration is followed by leaf-fall, it can be the result of over- or under-watering. Rapid temperature change may have a similar effect, particularly in winter.

Sometimes there can be a fairly rapid leaf-fall, together with the loss of flowerheads, but with leaves and flowers looking quite healthy: this usually comes about when conditions are too dry. It can easily be prevented by spraying plants that are growing in too dry an atmosphere regularly with clear water through a fine hand spray.

Red spider mites

Regular spraying with clear water will also help to discourage an infestation of red spider mites. These are very small, but when present in large numbers cause leaf yellowing and create a mottled appearance often accompanied by fine webs. Red spider mites are not easy to control by chemical means.

Greenfly (aphids)

Deformed leaves, particularly young ones, are often the result of an attack by greenfly (aphids). Despite their name, these insects can sometimes be black, strawy or even pinkish in colour. Infestations can be controlled by spraying leaves and shoots with pirimicarb, pyrethrum, insecticidal soaps or derris.

Whitefly

Tiny, white, moth-like flies are sometimes present on the undersides of leaves. They tend to favour lighter-coloured or aromatic foliage. Whitefly can be difficult to control, in all stages of their development, but adults can be killed with permethrin, pyrethrum or pirimiphos-methyl. Spraying will need to be regular, according to the instructions on the bottle.

Scale insects and mealybugs

A sticky substance on leaves or even furniture, sometimes with black velvety-looking growth, indicates that there may be an infestation of either scale insects or mealybugs.

The former appear as small, oval or rounded organisms. They may be brown, yellowish or a dirty white, and like the whitish, woolly masses of mealybugs, excrete honey-dew. The sooty mould that forms on this sugary secretion is unsightly and in severe cases can inhibit the natural functions of foliage, and have a debilitating effect on the whole plant.

Soft leaves and stems can be sprayed with dimethoate, malathion, pirimiphos-methyl or insecticidal soaps. Scale and mealybugs present in only small quantities can be carefully removed with a pointed stick or the tip of a knife.

A form of mealybug attacks roots and causes wilting if the attack is particularly severe. The root ball should be thoroughly soaked with malathion at spray strength.

Vine weevil

Another pest that attacks the root system is the vine weevil. It seems to be particularly fond of plants with fleshier roots and cyclamen, begonias and primulas are prone to attack. The small, whitish grubs with light brown heads can be controlled by watering with gamma-HCH.

Mildew

The main disease encountered on houseplants is mildew. This appears as a white, powdery covering on foliage. Control by spraying with a fungicide containing benomyl, bupirimate with triforine, carbendazim, thiophanate-methyl or propiconazole.

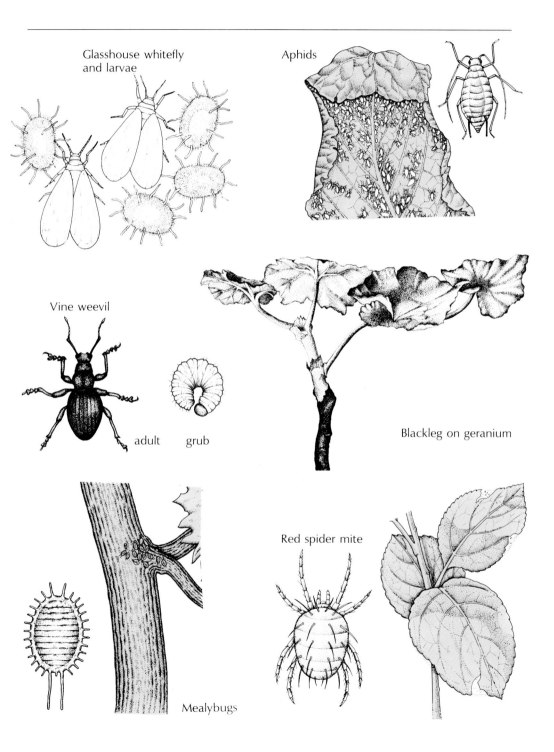

Glasshouse whitefly and larvae

Aphids

Vine weevil

adult   grub

Blackleg on geranium

Mealybugs

Red spider mite

Common houseplant ailments

Flowering plants

Plant	Symptom	Cause
Azalea	Leaves shrivel	Too dry at the root and in the atmosphere
	Yellow foliage	High alkalinity in water and potting compost
	Flowers deteriorate quickly	Atmosphere too hot and dry (keep away from full sun and artifical heat sources)
Begonia	Buds drop	Dry atmosphere or under-watering
	Leaves drop	Too little light if growth is spindly; dry atmosphere if foliage has puckered appearance; overwatering if foliage is limp
	Foliage covered in felting of white	Powdery mildew (spray with a suitable fungicide)
Cineraria	Wilting foliage	Over- or under-watering; or exposure to direct, intense sunlight (plant will right itself in shade)
	Flowers deteriorate quickly	Atmosphere too hot and dry
	Pests	Aphids, leaf mites
Cyclamen	Yellowing foliage but centre of plant firm	Atmosphere too hot and dry
	Plant collapse	Over-watering; or atmosphere too hot and dry
Fuchsia	Leaves drop	Atmosphere too hot and dry
	Buds drop	Over- or under-watering; or atmosphere too hot and dry
	Pests	Whitefly, red spider mite
	Orange blisters on foliage	Rust
Gloxinia	Brown tips on foliage	Atmosphere too hot and dry
	Buds shrivel	Atmosphere too hot and dry; or cold draughts
	Plant collapse	Over-watering; or watering with cold water
Impatiens	Leaves drop	Too cold for too long a period
	Flowers and buds drop	Atmosphere too hot and dry; or light too weak; or over-feeding; or too cold

Plant	Symptom	Pests
Pelargonium	Stem blackened at base	
	Elongated growth	
	Poor flowering	
	Small swellings on foliage	
	Pests	
Poinsettia	Flower heads droop and drop	
	Foliage wilts and drops	
	Pests	
Primula	Flowers deteriorate quickly	
Saintpaulia	Leaf discoloration	
	Scarring on foliage	
	Foliage limp with rotten plant centre	
	No flowers	
Foliage plants		
Aglaonema	Foliage shrivelled	
	Foliage contorted	
	Pests	
Asparagus	Foliage yellow	
Chlorophytum	Brown tips on leaves	
	Pale, limp foliage	
Coleus	Leggy stems	
	Leaves drop	
Dieffenbachia	Yellowing lower foliage	
	Leaves drop (but note that mature leaves fall naturally)	

Aphids, red spider mite, whitefly

'Black leg' disease (destroy plant and watch for over-watering in future)

Light too weak

Light too weak

Oedema, caused by too much water uptake

Whitefly, vine weevil

Atmosphere too hot and dry, especially if foliage is yellowing

Light too weak

Red spider mite, whitefly

Atmosphere too hot and dry

Too much direct sunlight

Cold water damage

Over-watering; or too cold; or fluctuating temperatures

Weak light; or failure to use high potash feed (tomato fertilizer)

Atmosphere too dry

Cold air

Red spider mite, mealybug

Light too strong; or compost too dry

Atmosphere too dry; or inadequate feeding

Too hot; light too weak

Light too weak

Under-watering

Too cold

Too cold

Plant	Symptom	Cause
Ferns	Yellow fronds	Atmosphere too hot and dry; or incorrect watering
	Scorching on foliage	Too much direct sunlight
	Fronds die off	Atmosphere too hot and dry; or under-watering
Ficus	Leaves drop (but note that lowest mature leaf will fall naturally)	Over-watering or too cold in winter
	Yellowing foliage	Possibly faulty root action (treat as for under-feeding)
Hedera	Spindly growth	Light too weak
	Brown tips on leaves	Dry atmosphere; or possibly red spider mite
	Green foliage on variegated forms	Light too weak
Maranta	Brown tips on leaves	Dry atmosphere
	Limp, rotting stems	Too cold; or compost too wet
	Discoloured foliage	Too much sunlight
Monstera	Spindly growth	Light too weak
	Yellowing foliage	Over-watering
	Foliage browning, especially at edges	Atmosphere too dry
	Foliage produces globules of moisture	Compost too wet
Palms	Brown tips on foliage	Atmosphere too dry; or too cold; or under-watering
	Yellow foliage (note that browning of lower leaves is caused by natural ageing)	Under-watering; or too much direct sunlight
Peperomia	Brown leaf edges	Rapid temperature fluctuation
	Sudden leaf drop	Too cold
Sansevieria	Basal rot	Over-watering in winter; or too cold
	Leaf blotches	Unknown, but appears to be a cultural disorder
Tradescantia	Spindly growth, sparse foliage	Light too weak
	Green leaves on variegated forms	Light too weak

Index 1

Index 2

Index 3/Acknowledgments

Acknowledgments

The author wishes to thank Allan Robinson of the RHS's Garden, Wisley, for
suggestions on plants for sink gardens.

Artists: Isobel Balakristnan, Rick Blakely, Steve Cross, Vana Haggerty, Coral Mula,
Stan North, Val Sassoon.

The Royal Horticultural Society and the Publishers can accept no liability for
failure to achieve satisfactory results by the methods recommended, or for any
consequences of these methods. We specifically draw the reader's attention to
the necessity of carefully reading and following the manufacturer's instructions
on any product.

Typesetting by Lasertext Ltd, Stretford, Manchester
Origination by M&E Reproductions,
North Fambridge, Essex
Produced by Mandarin Offset
Printed and bound in Hong Kong

THE R.H.S. ENCYCLOPEDIA OF PRACTICAL GARDENING

EDITOR-IN-CHIEF: CHRISTOPHER BRICKELL

Mitchell Beazley and the Royal Horticultural Society have joined forces to produce this practical, clear and fully comprehensive library of gardening.

"hard to fault" *Stephen Lacey*

Also available: **GARDENING TECHNIQUES** by Alan Titchmarsh

Forthcoming titles include:

ORGANIC GARDENING by Roy Lacey, **WATER GARDENING** by Philip Swindells

MITCHELL BEAZLEY